A SCIENTIST RESEARCHES
MARY

MOTHER AND
COREDEMPTRIX

by Professor Courtenay Bartholomew, M.D.

The 101 Foundation
P.O. Box 151
Asbury, NJ 08804-0151

Phone: (908) 689-8792
Fax: (908) 689-1957

IMPRIMATUR:
Bishop John Mendes
Port of Spain
Trinidad, West Indies
March 2, 1998

First Printing: 15,000 copies – 4/98
Printed in the USA by:
The 101 Foundation
P.O. Box 151
Asbury, NJ 08804-0151

Phone: (908) 689-8792
Fax: (908) 689-1957

Front cover:
A photograph of the bleeding statue of Our Lady of Lourdes in
the Corpus Christi Carmelite convent in Trinidad

ISBN: 1–890137–10–3

Acknowledgment

I wish to express my thanks to Sharon Baynes,
Karen Raphael, Tracy Edwards, Terry Richards,
and Roger Moe for assisting in the typing and
formatting of this manuscript, and to Sir Ellis Clarke
and Mary Pinder for reviewing the text.

Dedication

This book is dedicated to the many priests and nuns,
those consecrated sons and daughters of God,
who venerate Mary and have remained faithful to her.

Table of Contents

20th Century

Introduction

This book began with researching the life of and the prophecies given to a holy Franciscan Tertiary, Berthe Petit (1870–1943), in Belgium, just prior to and during World War I and World War II. I was requested to do so by Dr. Rosalie Turton of the 101 Foundation, New Jersey, U.S.A., who wanted me to rewrite the life story of Berthe. The emphasis was to be placed on the devotion to the *Sorrowful and Immaculate Heart of Mary*, a mission which was said to be given to Berthe by Our Lord in 1909.

Berthe Petit received great support from Cardinal Francis Bourne, Archbishop of Westminster, England, and the equally renowned Cardinal Desiré Mercier of Belgium. However, as my research on her progressed, I began to appreciate that the call for this devotion to the *Sorrowful and Immaculate Heart of Mary* was intimately linked to Mary's cooperation with her Son, the Redeemer of mankind, and what is termed her "cooperative salvific role" in this redemptive act.

I also discovered that the messages given to Mademoiselle Petit were frequently of a political nature, and so, I decided to research in great detail the political prophecies of the Blessed Virgin over the years, prophecies which I consider to have been poorly researched. While there on a visit, I spent a day in the book shops of Dublin, where I was able to find most of the books which I needed to research the history of European politics from the 15th century onwards.

I believe that during the course of this book I have emphasized, hopefully with sufficient clarity, that the term "Coredemptrix" as applied to Mary does not make her a fourth person of the Blessed Trinity, which, in any event, would be mathematical anathema. It certainly does not put her on an equal footing with the Redeemer. This would be theological anathema. Hers was a subordinate and cooperative role as helpmate to the Redeemer, the only one who could effect the act of redemption of mankind. This, of course, is not a new doctrine.

According to Edouard Cardinal Gagnon, years ago a number of cardinals and bishops presented a petition for the definition of Mary as Coredemptrix, and the response given at that time was that it was not necessary, since it

i

was already clearly a doctrine in the Church. Indeed, it dates back to the early days of the Church, but the actual term Coredemptrix was first used by Pope St. Pius X in 1908, and then by Pope Pius XI in 1933. As Rev. Francis P. Filice said in *Inside the Vatican*, January, 1988: "The proclamation of the Marian Dogma as Coredemptrix would not *make* Mary Coredemptrix, but would only express a reality that already exists."

She is the daughter of the Father, the bride of the Holy Spirit (Luke 1:35), and the mother of the Son, and so, to Christians, she is the mother of God. God, therefore, created His own mother, and the second Person of the Blessed Trinity, the Word, became flesh. Now, the question has been asked whether there would have been this mother if sin had not entered the world, necessitating a Redeemer. There are those who hold that God predestined her to be the mother of His Son and for that reason decreed that she should receive the fullest share of His grace irrespective of whether the rest of the human race would fall or be redeemed.

Fr. Martindale, S. J., in the *Canadian Messenger*, May, 1941, has expressed this viewpoint: "I hold (and, though this is not a Catholic dogma, yet it is in harmony with it and is held by many) that, even had sin not been sinned, the Incarnation would have taken place, so that in every possible way communion between man and God might be established. Imagine saying that because there had been no sin, *therefore* there would be no Jesus, no Blessed Sacrament, no Mary! But given that the Incarnation—the birth of the Son of God from a human mother—was eternally decreed, then in God's mind that mother was immaculate, that is, filled with grace, the supernatural life, from the first moment of her existence. The Immaculate Conception, then, is no disconcerting, edge-ways-on privilege. It simply means that Mary was exactly what God always intended that she should be."

She is the mother of God, and, therefore, she is the mother of all mankind, the mother of all nations. Indeed, she officially became so when her Son made his last will and testament on Calvary, and bequeathed His mother to be our mother: "Woman, behold your son!" Then He said to the disciple: "Behold your mother" (John 19:25-27).

The Redeemer accomplished His work on a Friday at three o'clock in the afternoon, and man was brought back into friendship with God. But Love is still not loved, and sin continues to be sinned; in fact, we are 'in love' with our sins. And so, the mother continues to wage battle against the ancient serpent, particularly in this 20th century. This is the century when, literally, all hell has broken loose. It is the century of wars as have never been experienced in known human history. It is the century of World War I and World War II, with the threat of World War III looming like a sword of Damocles over our heads.

In fact, there are those who believe that the Second Coming is close at hand, whatever "close" means. However, we were warned by Jesus: "But when the Son of Man comes, will He find any faith on earth?" (Luke 18:8). Indeed, there is a great loss of faith in the world today, but there are "pockets of resistance." For example, many Marian shrines have sprung up in this century, and they have been particularly effective in bringing many back to the worship of God and the veneration of His mother. As the December 30, 1991 issue of *Time* Magazine said: "Among all the wonders who have ever lived, the mother of Jesus Christ is the most celebrated, most venerated, the most portrayed, the most honoured... Mary may also be history's most controversial woman... Yet in an era when scientists debate the causes of the birth of the universe, both the adoration and the conflict attending Mary have risen to extraordinary levels. A grass-roots revival of faith in the Virgin is taking place worldwide. Millions of worshippers are flocking to her shrines, many of them young people." History's most controversial woman! But so was her Son controversial. And so, like mother, like Son: "This child is destined to be the downfall and the rise of many in Israel, a sign that will be contradicted" (Luke 2:34).

There are numerous reports that Mary is appearing all over the globe with messages for us. If this is truly so, then it would be a fatuous and foolhardy man who would neither take them seriously nor enquire of them. As for the scientists, St. Augustine criticized us as far back as the fifth century AD: "They neglect to investigate the source of the intelligence by which they conduct their research... They show no interest in a devout search for the Truth who put the universe together" (The Confessions of St. Augustine, Book Five).

Thousands have claimed to have seen her in recent times, particularly in Medjugorje, Yugoslavia, and in Betania, Venezuela. Indeed, I have been among the fortunate ones to have seen her in Medjugorje, albeit very briefly and at night. The Gospel of Jesus Christ says: "Blessed are they who have not seen and yet have believed"

(John 20:29). I have seen, and so, in a sense, I am not 'blessed'—but very grateful!

"Honour thy father and thy mother," the fourth commandment tells us, and Catholics are taught to honour this mother, to venerate her, but never to worship her. Worship belongs to God alone. Timothy Ware, an Orthodox priest, speaks of the similarities of the Roman Catholic Church and the Orthodox Church with respect to this aspect of Mary when he said in his book *The Orthodox Church:* "Among the saints a special position belongs to the Blessed Virgin Mary whom Orthodox reverence as the most exalted amongst God's creatures, more honourable than the cherubim and incomparably more glorious than the seraphim. Orthodox, like Roman Catholics, *venerate* the mother of God but in no sense do the members of either Church regard her as a fourth person of the Trinity, nor do they assign to her the *worship* due to God alone... We honour Mary because she is the Mother of God. We do not venerate her in isolation, but because of her relation to Christ. Thus, the reverence shown to Mary, far from eclipsing the worship of God, has exactly the opposite effect. The more we esteem Mary, the more vivid is our awareness of the majesty of her Son, for it is precisely on account of the Son that we venerate the mother."

This is the teaching of the Magesterium of the Roman Catholic Church. It has been voiced *over and over again*, and yet the Church is continuously being accused of worshipping the Virgin, and boringly so by unread and unintelligent critics. When, however, in addition, some of those who claim to love Jesus consider it their divine right to break the fourth commandment and *dishonour* and criticize His mother, I am confronted with an illogicality which defies all intelligent comprehension. I encounter an imprudence which apparently does not fear God's judgment on this. And so, as someone once said, God has put a limit to man's intelligence, but apparently no limit to his folly.

Now, God has given us His word through the Holy Scriptures, through the teaching of the Church, and also, in His wisdom and discretion, through private revelations. The latter, however, are never approved by the prudent Church without painstaking and thorough investigations. Even when approved, the Church does not make an infallible pronouncement. She merely declares that the private revelation contains nothing contrary to Sacred Scripture and to Catholic teaching.

I have quoted in this book some of the private revelations of a few well-known visionaries and mystics, who have led exemplary lives and have received inexplicable privileges from God, as manifested, for example, by receiving the stigmata, and their bodily incorruption after death—manifestations which science has investigated and for which there can be no other answer but that these are "divine interventions." However, once the scientist believes in God, he must then appreciate that with God all things are possible. Therefore, when a supernatural phenomenon occurs, we scientists can only attest to the historical occurrence of the event and then declare, and, indeed, confess with humility that the nature of the event is beyond the boundaries of ordinary scientific knowledge. And there science stops! Indeed, the link between science and religion is Faith.

I have attempted to link world history, politics, religion, science, and the end times—in chronological sequence. In so doing, I have paid particular attention to the political aspects of the prophecies of the Blessed Virgin over the years. In the course of this research I have realized that one can dispel any notion that God does not interfere in the politics of men, especially when requested to do so. I have also devoted several chapters to matters concerning science and the rapid advancement of the scientific discoveries in this 20th century, which threaten the survival of the human race. It is an advancement in warfare, which has progressed from the propeller-driven airplane in the 1914–18 war to the onset of the nuclear age in 1945, and then to the pilotless intercontinental missile which can span thousands of miles and, with the push of a button, annihilate nations.

In this enquiry, I soon realized that the apparitions of the Blessed Virgin, which occurred in 1531, in Guadalupe, Mexico, in many ways, are perhaps the most important of all. They were the firstborn of her apparitions in the New World, and signalled the great battle between mankind and the principalities and powers of the spirit world (Ephesians 6:12). And so, I have spent much time in researching Aztec history in an attempt to understand the mind of God with respect to His choice of the kingdom of the Aztecs to send His mother there on December 9, 1531.

This particular research took me to the libraries and museums of Mexico City, and other libraries, and became so fascinating and instructive to me that, whereas I had originally expected to express my findings in four or five chapters, it was not until after eight chapters that I thought that I had sufficiently covered the ground. Indeed, I have covered new ground in my attempt to link the ancient history of the Aztecs with Old and New Testament parallels. I have also proffered different and new insights into the interpretation of the image of the Virgin on the tilma of Juan Diego.

It is a thesis which also incorporates Aztec beliefs and their legends about the end of the world, or more accurately, the end of an era or cycle, which they believed will occur around the year 2000 *y poco* (and a little). Of course, I record this history knowing full well "that as far as the exact day or hour, no one knows it, neither the angels in heaven nor the Son, but the Father only" (Matthew 24:36). Nonetheless, there are many "prophets" of all religions, who do believe that we are indeed in such an end-time period. Maybe they are right. In fact, many Christians are convinced that this is why the "Blessed Mother" is appearing all over the world, pleading with her children to convert before it is too late. She is busy, as never before, in her quest to save us from the clutches of Satan, who is like "a roaring lion, seeking to devour whom he may" (1 Peter 5:8).

She has come to us not only because of her love as the greatest mother of all, but as a mother who also wants to ensure that her Son has not died in vain, and that His heart will not be rent again and again by man's ingratitude.

March 18, 1997

— I will put enmity between you and the woman, and between your seed and her seed; she will crush your head and you will lie in wait for her heel (Genesis 3:15). —

The Holy Bible—Douay Rheims Version
First Published by the English College
at Rheims, AD.

Chapter 1

Scientists and Religion

The French astronomer Camille Flamarion once remarked in 1880 during the troubled times in Europe: "If mankind knew what profound inner pleasures await those who gaze at the heavens, then France, nay, the whole of Europe, would be covered with telescopes instead of bayonets, thereby promoting universal happiness and peace." Indeed, I truly believe that too little science of the universe is taught in the schools and in the media, and so, we know more about microbes than the stars. We peer down our microscopes but hardly look up at the skies. We therefore tend to have an over-proportioned dimension and opinion of ourselves.

An amateur telescope with a twelve-inch lens can spot billions of stars, nebulae and comets. With such an instrument, in July 1995, two astronomers discovered the Hale-Bopp comet, 570 million miles away from earth, just beyond the orbit of Jupiter. The Hubble Space Telescope, named after Edwin Hubble, the astronomer who discovered in the 1920s that the universe is expanding, was launched in 1990, floating out of the cargo bay of the space shuttle Discovery. Orbiting above earth's light-distorting atmosphere, however, Hubble can create images that are five to ten times clearer than those of the most powerful ground observatories in the world. It has unlocked many secrets of the universe.

A theologian in the 1650s confidently dated Genesis to 4004 B.C., but Hubble was not around in those days. The universe is now thought to be 15 billion years old. That is the supposed age of the so-called Big Bang. In fact, the images in the Hubble Deep Field appear as they were roughly 11.7 billion to 10.4 billion years ago! As *Time* magazine asked: "What do these objects look like today? Only an astronomer living 10 billions years in the future would know... The Hubble has extended humankind's eyes to the farthest reaches of time and space. Even more, it has extended our imagination."

The universe is composed of some 100 billion galaxies, all fleeing one from another as if they are remnants of an enormous explosion. Our Milky Way is comprised of gas and dust and about 400 billion suns, one of which is our sun. It is our nearest star, and has a diameter close to 1 million miles (the diameter of the earth is only 8,000 miles). Accompanying the sun is a retinue of small worlds; some are planets, some are moons, some asteroids, and some comets. Eta Carinae, in the southern constellation Carina, is one of the most massive and luminous stars known to astronomy, 150 times as big and 4 million times as bright as our sun! In other words, we are less than a grain of sand in the immensity of God's creation. Certainly, this calls for great humility.

Another great and wise French scientist, Louis Pasteur, once justly commented: "A little acquaintance with science distances us from God; greater acquaintance with science brings us even closer." And as Pope John Paul II recently said: "Science can purify religion from error and superstition; religion can purify science of idolatry and false absolutes. Each can draw the other into a wider world, a world in which both can flourish... Such bridging ministries must be nurtured and encouraged."

In the *Telegraph*, one of Britain's leading daily news-papers, an article by Clifford Longley on September 15, 1995, under the caption *Science cannot make a monkey out of Religion*, began: "A certain man of letters likes to drop in his public speeches the information that he is an atheist. He sometimes adds, with pained and innocent bafflement, that the evidence for the nonexistence of God being so clear and obvious, those who refuse to see it must be wrong in the head. A more mischievous version of this would be the claim of the biologist Dr. Richard Dawkins that religious belief may be caused by a defective gene. Yet both of them and the large constituency which shares their mind-set must be aware that several coaches could be filled with Nobel Prize scientists who definitely believe in God."

While we were recently in Rome together, Roy Barghese gave me a copy of his book *Cosmos, Bios, Theos*. In it he records his interviews with over twenty Nobel Prize winners and distinguished scientists of different disciplines, concerning their views on science, God, and the origins of the universe. It was heartening to discover that many of these great scientists do believe in God.

On the question of the origin of the universe, there is a large cadre of scientists who believe in the Big Bang theory. Professor Vera Kistiekowsky, Professor of Physics at the Massachusetts Institute of Technology, remarked: "There remains the question of how the Big Bang was initiated, but it seems unlikely that science would be able to elucidate this... The exquisite order displayed by our scientific understanding of the physical world calls for the divine."

Professor Arthur Schawlow, Nobel Prize winner for Physics in 1981, made this comment: "It seems to me that when confronted with the marvels of life and the universe, one must ask why and not just how. The only possible answers are religious... I find a need for God in the universe and in my own life... Current research in astrophysics seems to indicate that the ultimate origin of the universe may not be only unknown but unknowable. That is, if we assume the Big Bang occured, which present evidence strongly supports, there is no real way to find out what came before the Big Bang. it is surely right to pursue as far as possible the scientific understanding of the origins of the universe, but it is probably wrong to think that we have final answers and that there are no further surprises to come. From a religious point of view, we assume that God did it and hope to find out something about how He did it."

Professor Vladimir Preloge of Prague, Czechoslovakia, a Nobel Prize winner for Chemistry in 1975, professed that "winners of Nobel Prizes are not more competent about God, religion, and life after death than other people; some of them like myself are agnostics. They just don't know... Indeed, my agnosticism goes so far that I am not even certain whether I am an agnostic. I am pleased, for instance, by Faust's answer to Gretchen's question. I often cite Max Planck: 'God is at the beginning of every religion and at the end of the natural sciences... I follow with interest the discussions concerning the origin of the universe, of life, and of man, especially in the molecular area. I marvel at the courage of the scientists who deal with questions of the origin and seek answers for them.'"

Professor Ragnar Granit, a Nobel Prize winner for Physiology/Medicine in 1967, when asked about his view on how should science and the scientist approach origin questions, specifically the origins of the universe and the origin of life, he simply replied: "Humbly."

Professor Robert Naumann, Professor of Chemistry and Physics at Princeton University, holds that "God is the totality of the universe; this includes all scientific principles, all matter and energy, and all life-forms. The existence of the universe requires me to conclude that God exists."

Professor John Russell, distinguished Emeritus Professor of Astronomy at the University of Southern California, mused: "Although we have made great strides with science in pushing back the boundaries of the unknown, I am not convinced that science would take us to the threshold of complete understanding... For me, the true nature of God is beyond my comprehension. However, I find some solace in the thought that He understands me better than I understand Him..."

Professor D.H.R. Barton of the University of London, the 1969 Nobel Prize winner for Chemistry, was quite precise: "God is Truth. There is no incompatibility between science and religion. Both are seeking the same truth. Science shows that God exists. Our universe is infinitely large and infinitely small... We can never understand infinity. It is the ultimate truth, which is God... The observations and experiments of science are so wonderful that the truth that they establish can surely be established as another manifestation of God. God shows himself by allowing man to establish truth."

Indeed, Albert Einstein himself once said: "The most beautiful and the most profound emotions we can experience is the sensation of the mystical. It is the sower of all true science. That deeply emotional conviction of the presence of a superior reasoning power, which is revealed in the incomprehensible universe, forms my idea of God."

But, Professor Steven Bernasek, Professor of Chemistry at Princeton University, had what I may call the *last word*: "There was some presence or being existing prior to the moment of the Big Bang. It is hard to assign any description to this being. Perhaps the closest is in John 1:1. 'In the beginning was the Word...'"

My favourite commentary, however, occurred during a Jewish theological seminar. There was an hours-long discussion about proofs of the existence of God. After some hours of debate, one Rabbi got up and said: "Look, God is so great, he does not even need to exist!" The meeting ended abruptly.

And so, the origin of the universe stupefies human intelligence and has made many great scientists of the world humble, but the perplexity of perplexities humbles humility itself. I am referring to the origin of God Himself.

Chapter 2

On Love

But how little the empirical sciences have to offer on the subject of love! The textbooks of psychology hardly recognize the subject and to a great extent it has been left to poets, philosophers, and holy men and women. And so, there appears to be too much love of science and too little science of love. As St. Therese of Lisieux once wrote: "The science of love! How sweet is the echo of that word in the ear of my soul! I desire no other science than that. For the sake of love, having given all my riches, like the spouse in the Canticle, I feel as though I had given nothing. There is nothing except *love* which could render us agreeable to God."

Indeed, the crucifixion and the death of Jesus Christ was the greatest act of love in world history. "God so loved the world that he gave his only son so that everyone who believes in him may not be lost but may have eternal life" (John 3:10). The beloved apostle continued his Gospel, saying: "Anyone who fails to love could never have known love, because God is love" (John 4:8).

Paul was obviously as romantic as he was courageous. See how he speaks of love!: "Though I command languages, both human and angelic, if I speak without love, I am no more than a gong booming or a cymbal clashing. And though I have the power of prophecy to penetrate all mysteries and knowledge, and though I have all the faith necessary to move mountains, if I am without love, I am nothing... Love is patient and kind; love is not jealous or boastful; it is not arrogant or rude. Love does not insist on its own way; it is not irritable or resentful; it does not rejoice at wrong but rejoices with the truth. It bears all things, believes all things, hopes all things, endures all things. Love never fails... There are in the end three things that last: faith, hope, and love, and the greatest of these is love" (1 Corinthians 13:1-13).

But lest we forget, in His farewell discourse at the Last Supper, Jesus said to the apostle Philip: "He who obeys the commandments he has from me is the man who loves me" (John 14:21). And so, Paul omitted at least one requirement of love. Love is obedient! John, the great apostle of love, also adds: "There is no fear in love, but perfect love casteth out all fear" (1 John 4:18). Yet, whereas fear without love can be likened to cowardice, love without fear (of losing that love) is presumption, and so, we should fear. Of course, I am not speaking of servile fear, but the "filial" fear of God, which we all should have.

But why do I even try to describe God's love? It is the inadequacy of inadequacies. It is the vanity of vanities for there is no human description, no author's pen, which can qualify and quantify the incomprehensible and immeasurable love of God. It is "love unlimited." It is all that Paul says, but much more. It is the perfect love. Perfect love, on the other hand, is rare among creatures and, indeed, it is to be wondered if any man has ever achieved it. This is not to say that it should not be a goal devoutly to be striven for.

Among other things, the perfect lover is described as one who gives all and expects nothing. However, there are few, if any, who are so loving as to give without expectation, and although no man can insist that someone he loves, loves him in return, he can only hope that his love will be requited. But there can never be any assurance, never any guarantee. Only God's love guarantees that.

Neither can love be bartered for, nor can it be forced upon anyone. It can only be given voluntarily and so, God, who is Love, had to give His creatures a *free will*. He had no choice. As Ghandi once said: "There is no love where there is no will." The great French poet Lamartine was, therefore, absolutely wrong when he said: "*L'argent ne fait pas le bonheur, mais l'achète.*" (Money does not make happiness, but it buys it). Indeed, how limited are the powers of money. It may be able to buy a bed, but not sleep; a house, but not a home; medicine, but not health; amusement, but not happiness. A man may buy another's earthly possession but can never buy love. It is not for sale.

Moreover, if a man expects equal love in return, eventually he surely will be disappointed, for it is not likely that all people can love with an equal intensity and devotion, and to expect others to love us as we do them is often unrealistic. Nature abhors sameness, and whereas each man has an endless capacity to love, each love is also different just as each person, each flower in the field, each blade of grass, each fingerprint, each DNA is unique. And so, the capacity to love is frequently realized differently, as each person grows at his own rate, in his own manner, at his own time. Indeed, life is an experience through which we are expected to grow, but it is this very difference in rate of growth which sometimes creates disharmony in a previous bond of love.

Augustine of Hippo went in search of love and confessed that for years he was *in love with love*. "To love and be loved was sweet to me," he wrote. But his was a creature-love with all its lusts and imperfections, and soon after his conversion he felt compelled to exclaim in regret: "Too late have I loved You, O Lord." Of this creature love, Fr. J. Boudreau, S.J. wrote in 1872: "Think of this, you mortals, who crave after human love. You desire to love and to be loved. Love is the sunshine of your lives. But do what you will, it can never give you perfect happiness here below; for when you have at last succeeded in possessing the object after which you so ardently sighed, you discover its imperfections which you had not suspected before, and these lessen your happiness."

And so, Augustine eventually realized that he could not love the creature more than the Creator of the creature. It is the law of God, and in answer to the question: "Master, which is the greatest commandment of the Law?," Jesus told the Pharisee lawyer: "You must love the Lord your God with all your heart, with all your soul, and with all your mind. This is the greatest and *first* commandment. The *second* is like it: You must love your neighbour as yourself" (Matthew 22:36-39). Indeed, placing the second commandment before the first is a reversal which always leads to disharmony.

Now, this ordained sequence, the first before the second, frequently calls for sacrifice since love and sacrifice go hand in hand, and there can be no great love without sacrifice, without suffering. Therese of Lisieux knew this and in a letter to her sister Celine, she wrote: "Let us not imagine we can love without suffering, and bitter suffering, too." In fact, sacrifice and not satisfaction is one of the supreme expressions of love, and the willingness to deny the satisfaction of expressing affection is the highest and hardest form the sacrifice can take.

The sacrifice of the Lamb of God on a hill one Friday in April in 33 AD, was the greatest expression of love the world has ever known. This was not the *undying* love which many creatures have. It was a love that chose to *die* through suffering and sacrifice. It was the "April Fool" on the Cross.

One may, therefore, well say that it is foolish to love and in fact, Francis of Assisi, who had a great love of God, was once called "God's fool" by his biographer Julien Green, novelist and diarist. The English poet Samuel Johnson (1709–84) also scoffed at love: "Love is the wisdom of the fool and the folly of the wise." And so, God who is Love, is, in a sense, foolish. It is the folly of Wisdom. It is the folly of the Cross and His heart loves beyond the comprehension of the wisdom of the wisest of men. This foolish heart loves us even when His love is not returned, and suffers in silence the magnitude of our *ingratitude.*

Once upon a time there was a love which stood at the foot of the Cross, her heart pierced by a sword. The writer of that great 13th century hymn *Stabat Mater*, believed by some to be the Franciscan St. Bonaventure, began his woeful refrain, chanting: "At the Cross her station keeping, stood the mournful mother weeping, close to Jesus to the last." Then, midway through the hymn he adds: "Make my soul to glow and melt, make me feel as you have felt..." It was well-meant, but in reality it is an impossible dream and an unrealistic request, for no one, but no one, could feel the sorrow she felt. Which heart of a mother has felt a greater sorrow?

The Bible simply states: "...there stood by the cross of Jesus his mother, and the disciple standing by..." (John 19:25). It was the greatest understatement in history and underplayed the unspeakable anguish of Jesus on the Cross and of His mother beneath the Cross. True, it was Jesus who was nailed to the Cross, but being forced to simply stand by helplessly and watch a loved one suffer can be the most excruciating pain of all. It can be so devastating that one would rather suffer the crucifixion oneself if the loved one could go free. So it was with the *Mother of Sorrows* on that Friday on a hill called Calvary.

Chapter 3

Mother and Coredemptrix

Time magazine's front cover of December 30, 1991, featured the Virgin Mary with the caption: *The Search for Mary*. The inside article read: "When her womb was touched by Eternity 2,000 years ago, the Virgin Mary uttered a prediction: 'All generations will call me blessed.'" Five years later, the December, 1996 issue of *Life* magazine also devoted its front cover to Mary with the caption *The Mystery of Mary*, and the words: "Two thousand years after the Nativity, the mother of Jesus is more beloved, powerful and controversial than ever." *Newsweek* then gave her front coverage on August 25, 1997, with the headline: *The Meaning of Mary*. The cover story inside began: "A growing movement in the Roman Catholic Church wants the Pope to proclaim a new, controversial dogma: that Mary is Co-Redeemer. Will he do it, maybe in time for the millennium? Should he?"

Deploying the headlines of these three famous magazines, namely, *The Search for Mary*, *The Mystery of Mary*, and *The Meaning of Mary*, may I say that in my own personal search for Mary, I began to discover the meaning of Mary, and I am now awed more than ever by the mystery of Mary.

Preaching on the *Mother of God* in his series *Reflections*, Fr. Leo Clifford O.F.M., quoted Canon Sheehan, once a parish priest in County Cork, Ireland, who said: "It was decreed by God at the fall of our first parents, that as their children would have inherited graces and glory if his commands had been obeyed, so, because of their disobedience, their children were to inherit only sin and shame. This law is universal. Not even the greatest saints were exempt from it. Once, and once only, did God create a soul as pure and beautiful, at the moment of its conception, as it is now in heaven; a soul to which the Almighty could turn when weary of the deformity which sin had stamped upon mankind. It was the time when the fullness of years had come and it was decreed that the Son should leave the bosom of the Father and take flesh among men.

"For centuries, God had not created a soul in grace. Yes, he had fashioned and sent them into the world, but they were in the power of the enemy before they left his Almighty hand. But now, for an instant, the old time was to come back again when God could look upon his work and say that it was 'good,' and that it did not repent him that he made it. And so, the Blessed Trinity fashioned and formed and sent into the world, the soul of Mary. And God admired his handy work, and the angels bowed down and paid homage to their Queen, and hell trembled at the conception of a woman who was destined to break the power of its prince.

"When the Angel Gabriel left the throne of God and came to Nazareth to ask Mary to be the mother of God's Son, he bowed down before her, so dazzlingly beautiful was she. Remember she was God's masterpiece. This is the girl chosen from all women to give God the colour of his eyes and his hair. She was to teach the Word to speak in her own accent. She was to help the Almighty to walk his first baby steps. She was to give him the body and blood in which he would live and suffer and die to redeem us all. The body and blood that you and I receive in Holy Communion comes from Our Lady.

"What can we say about her? Words cannot magnify her, whom our thoughts can hardly reach. Our praise of Mary, like our praise of God, is best embodied in our wonder and in our love. She was called Mary, a famous name in Jewish history, Miriam. Miriam was the sister of Moses and in God's inscrutable providential plan, Miriam helped Moses, the lawgiver, grow." Sheehan ended his sermon by remarking that "in the New Testament, the new Miriam, Mary, is going to help the Redeemer of the world grow, to help to save us all." It was Irish eloquence at its best.

12

Now, our first mother, the first Eve (Eve means
"Mother of the living"), brought death to the world and to
her children by her sin of disobedience and by wanting to
be like God. She and the first Adam fell prey to "the
father of lies," the ancient serpent, who deceived them and
contradicted God's command to them: "You surely will not
die. No, God knows well that the moment you eat of it
your eyes will be opened, and you will be like God knowing
good and evil" (Genesis 3:4-5). They believed Satan and set
a pattern which many of their children throughout
the ages have followed.

It was then that God made His first promise to
mankind, when He said to Satan: "Because you have done
this... I will put enmity between you and the woman;
between your seed and her seed; (s)he will crush your
head..." (Genesis 3:15). God was talking about the new Eve
and the new Adam, Mary and Jesus. Eventually, the new
Eve, in the fullness of time, was born. She was to be the
companion and mother of the man, the new Adam,
who was to restore life and the friendship of God with
man. She was to be the new *Mother of the living, Mother
of Mankind.*

The first Adam was immaculate at birth. The second
Adam was the sinless One. He was the Son of God. He
could not have been any mortal man. This is because, as
St. Thomas Aquinas in his *Summa* theologized, when man
rebelled against God, God's justice required that adequate
reparation be made; justice meaning, "giving to everyone
his due." But since God is infinite, an infinite insult was
made to Him when man rebelled against Him, and if the
reparation was to be adequate, that is, if justice were to
be satisfied, such an insult required infinite reparation.

Justice also required that the reparation be offered by
man, but man is a finite being and incapable of making
infinite reparation. Left to himself, therefore, man would
forever be separated from God. The only solution to the
impasse was that the infinite God should become man, and
as man, offer reparation to God. Since the person offering
the reparation would Himself be infinite, the reparation
would equal the crime and man would once more be united
in the friendship with God. So in His loving mercy, God
sent His Son to make reparation for the sin of man: "God
so loved the world that he sent his only begotten son..."
(John 3:16).

The first Eve was also immaculate at birth. Sin had not
entered the world as yet. After the fall, there was to be a
new beginning and so, the second Eve, too, by a special

privilege of God, was immaculate at birth. She was *the Immaculate Conception*. She was to be the helpmate of the Redeemer.

And so, we insult God when we fail to recognize this woman as being His most special creation. We insult Him when we fail to appreciate that God, who is Purity itself, would not choose any ordinary woman to be His mother, to be His tabernacle, and to be His companion during His sojourn in time. That God, who is without sin and who lives in the empyrean heavens with the angels who are also sinless, would choose to dwell in a womb which was, *even for a moment*, under the dominion of Satan, is an insult to the integrity and reputation of the Godhead.

And when, in the fullness of time, she said "yes" to the gilt-edged invitation delivered to her by the Ambassador of the heavenly court, the Archangel Gabriel, she immediately conceived the God-man, "and the Word was made flesh" (John 1:14). Redemption was begun. Of course, He could have chosen to appear first on earth as a full grown adult, but in His wisdom and humility He chose otherwise. He chose to confine Himself in her womb for a full gestation period. The Uncontainable was contained in the womb of a mere mortal woman, and from her breast she gave milk to the "Bread of Life." Just as the ancient Ark of the Covenant contained some of the miraculous manna which fell from heaven to feed the Israelites, Mary contained in her womb the true Bread come down from heaven (John 6:48-51). She then became the living Ark of the Covenant.

At the moment of the conception, two wondrous things happened: a virgin while remaining virgin became a mother, and more wondrous yet, a woman became the mother of her own Creator. It was the marriage between God and His creation, man. It was the union between heaven and earth. It was the expression of God's love, His humility, His charity, and His magnificence. Indeed, it surpasses the comprehension of many that true greatness is always humble, and that God, who is the greatest, is at the same time the most humble of all. As Francis of Assisi once said: "O sublime humility. O humble sublimity!"

The Coredemptrix

Now, the first Adam gave birth to the first Eve. She was born out of the rib of the first Adam ("...the man said: 'This one at last, is bone of my bones and flesh of my flesh; this one shall be called *woman*, for out of man this

14

one has been taken'" —Genesis 2:23). On the other hand,
the second Eve gave birth to the second Adam. The tables
were turned. Indeed, she gave Him the very instrument of
Redemption—His human body ("Sacrifices and offerings
you have not desired, but a body you have prepared
for me..." —Heb. 10:5-7). No human father was involved.
Scientifically speaking, therefore, His DNA was totally
Marian!

The first Eve believed Satan ("You surely will not
die..." —Genesis 3:4). The second Eve believed Gabriel
("Thou shall conceive in thy womb, and bring forth a
son, and shall call his name Jesus" —Luke 13:1). Following
the seduction of the serpent, the first Eve cooperated with
Satan. Following the invitation of Gabriel, the second Eve
cooperated with God. The first Eve was disobedient and
said "no" to God's command. The second Eve was obedient
and said "yes" to God's invitation. It was a new beginning.

The first Eve ate the fruit and then gave it to Adam.
She was the *Peccatrix* ("It was the woman you gave me as
helpmate who offered me the fruit of the tree" —Genesis
3:13). The first Adam was the *Co-peccator* (the Co-sinner).
And so, the second Adam was the *Redeemer* and the
second Eve the *Coredemptrix*.

It was the fruit which hung from a tree which was the
instrument Satan used to bring death to the world. It was
the "fruit of her womb" (Luke 1:42), who died and hung
from a tree on Calvary which the Godhead used to restore
life to mankind. The first Eve brought death to the world.
The second Eve gave birth to the Reedemer and restored
life to mankind. The situation was reversed.

In short, it was a man *and* a woman who had sinned
and, therefore, it had to be a man *and* a woman to restore
what was lost by sin. It is as logical as that! In fact, in my
opinion, it does not call for any theological sense, simply
common sense. But apparently common sense, even among
some theologians, is not so common after all!

As Rev. Cyril Papali, O.D.C., in his book *Mother of
God, Mary in Scripture and Tradition,* said: "Her's is the
most spiritual, and the most pure, the most selfless, the
most intense, incomprehensible suffering ever known. One
solitary creature suffering *with* God and *for* God, suffering
for all mankind and *from* them—that is the price of
becoming *Coredemptrix*. That is the meaning of being
the second Eve."

Saint Bernard of Clairvaux also recognized the
appropriateness of God's redress to the Eden situation

when he said: "One man and one woman harmed us grievously. Thanks to God, all things are restored by one man and one woman, and that with interest. It is true that Christ would have been adequate, since all our sufficiency is from Him, but it was not good for us that it should be a man alone. It was more appropriate that both sexes should take part in our reparation, since both had wrought our ruin. But her cooperation means much more than this. It implies the true dependence of the whole work of redemption on her free will, because God Himself willed it to be conditioned by her consent. In that sense redemption in its entirety is her *cooperative* work also, and for that reason alone she deserves to be called *Coredemptrix*."

Undoubtedly, God could have redeemed us *on His own*, but He willed otherwise. It would not have been perfect. The important point is that Mary could never have redeemed us *on her own*. Her role was secondary and subordinate. She was the *Coredemptrix*, and "**Co**" certainly does not mean **co**-equal, but **co**-operating with. I wish to make this abundantly clear, because it is of major theological importance. The **co**-pilot is certainly subordinate to the pilot. Indeed, she always knew her role. Who would dare say otherwise?: "I am the handmaid of the Lord. Let it be done to me according to your word" (Luke 1:38). But it was her *Immaculate Conception* which properly prepared her for and made her worthy of the intimate and unique cooperation she was to have with the Redeemer in the work of salvation.

Now, when Jesus saw His mother and the disciple whom He loved standing under the Cross, He said to His mother: "Woman, behold your Son!" Then He said to the disciple: "Behold your mother!" (John 19:25-27). The term "woman," therefore, unites the mother of the Saviour at the foot of the Cross with the "woman" of the *seed* of Redemption in Genesis 3:15, who was destined to work with the Redeemer in the triumph over Satan and his *seed*. And so, we were redeemed on Calvary with the blood of the Son and the tears of the mother. Redemption came from this suffering. Indeed, the mother of the Redeemer was predestined to suffer with her Son. She was predestined to be the *Coredemptrix*. Simeon only confirmed what she already understood *before* she gave her *fiat* to Gabriel: "And a sword shall pierce thine own soul" (Luke 2:35). It was a suffering which stemmed from love.

She lies hidden in the Old Testament but many of the great women of the Bible foreshadow her. Sarah, Rebecca, Rachel, Judith, Esther, and many more, are preeminently types of Mary, prefiguring different sides of her all-embracing majesty. In the New Testament, Mary's presence is more evident. The story of the conception, birth, and infancy of Jesus is in fact the story of His mother. He is almost lost in her shadow for a full thirty years. And when at last He did manifest Himself to the world, it was her maternal authority which brought about His first public miracle, even though His "time had not yet come" (John 2:4).

Mary then recedes into the background. For example, she is nowhere to be seen during the glorious procession of Palm Sunday. Neither is her place on Tabor. But she is with her Son on His sorrowful "Way of the Cross" to Mount Calvary. That was her place. It was near the spot where Abraham was ordered to immolate his son Isaac, but was spared the agony at the last moment. His wife Sarah was also spared the anguish. But God did not spare the sorrowful agony of His own mother. No angel held back the hand as in the case of Isaac. A lance pierced her Son's heart and a sword pierced hers. It was the ultimate sacrifice—a Man on the Cross and beneath it, the mother stood. *Stabat mater dolorosa*. And if there were a thousand mothers standing at the feet of a thousand crosses bearing their thousand crucified sons, the sum total of their anguish could not measure the sorrow of that woman on that hill on that Friday that some men call "Good." That was the price of being *Coredemptrix*.

Neither Matthew, Mark, Luke, nor John recorded the great anguish of the mother during the Friday evening, Saturday, and early Sunday morning following the crucifixion. It was meant to be the Gospel of Jesus and not of Mary! Undoubtedly, this must also have been her wish and instruction to the apostles. However, a few favoured mystics have been privileged to receive detailed visions of her life. One such mystic, Maria Valtorta (1897–1961) of Italy, in her book *The Poem Of The Man-God*, wrote about her longing for the company of her earthly spouse, St. Joseph, to console her during those long three days: "Let me lean on a Joseph!... O, happy Joseph, who has not seen this day," she moaned.

Valtorta then recorded her visions of the first meeting of Jesus and His mother after the Resurrection: "Mary is prostrated with her face on the floor. She looks like a poor wretch. Suddenly the closed window is opened with a violent banging of the heavy shutters, and with the first ray of the sun, Jesus enters. Mary, who has been shaken by the noise and has raised her head to see which wind has opened the shutters, sees her radiant Son, handsome, infinitely more handsome than He was before suffering, smiling, dressed in a white garment and He advances towards her... He calls her, stretching out His hands: 'Mother!' And He bends over His mother and places His hands under her bent elbows and lifts her up. He presses her to His heart and kisses her...

"With a cry, she flings her arms around His neck and she embraces and kisses Him, laughing in her weeping. She kisses His forehead, where there are no longer any wounds; His head no longer unkempt and bloody; His shining eyes, His healed cheeks, His mouth no longer swollen. She then takes His hands and kisses their backs and palms, their radiant wounds, and she suddenly bends down to His feet and uncovers them from under His bright garment and kisses them. Then she stands up and looks at Him... She kisses and kisses Him and Jesus caresses her. She never tires kissing..."

Valtorta continued: "Jesus speaks now: *'It is all over, mother. You no longer have to weep over your Son. The trial is over. Redemption has taken place. Mother, thanks for conceiving me. Thanks for looking after me, for helping me in life and in death... I heard your prayers come to me. They have been my strength in my grief. They came to me on the Cross... They have been seen and heard by the Father and by the Spirit who smiled at them as if they were the most beautiful flowers and the sweetest song born in Paradise.*

*'I will now go to the Father in my human appearance. Paradise must see the victor in his appearance of man, by means of which he defeated the sin of man. But I will come again. I must confirm in the faith those who do not yet believe... Then I will ascend to heaven. But I will not leave you alone, mother. You will never be alone. These past days you have been alone, **but that sorrow of yours was required for the Redemption.** Much is continuously to be added to redemption because much will be continuously created to it in the way of sin. I will call all my servants to this redeeming participation, but you are the one who, by yourself, will do more than all the others together... Then I will come to fetch you and no longer shall I be in you, but you will be in me, in my kingdom, to make Paradise more beautiful. I am going now, mother. I am going to make the other Mary (Magdalene) happy. Then I will ascend to the Father. Thence I will come to those who do not believe. Mother, your kisses as a blessing, and my peace to you*

as a companion. Goodbye.' And Jesus disappeared in the sunshine that streams down from the early morning clear sky."

This was one of the most moving sections in Valtorta's book. Indeed, I always felt certain that Jesus must have appeared to His mother before appearing to Mary Magdalene. After all, He is the Author of protocol and she is the *Coredemptrix*. It was a tribute and a privilege to man that "one of us" was chosen to be God's copilot on man's return journey to Him. Who then would deny her that title?

The Search   The Mystery   The Meaning

Stabat Mater Dolorosa

The Pieta

The Sorrowful Mother

Statue of the Mother of Sorrows in the
Church of the Immaculate Conception in Caracas
(Courtesy of Michael Milne)

Chapter 4

Mediatrix and Advocate

Mediatrix

Saint Paul says that "there is one God, and there is one mediator between God and man, the man Christ Jesus, who gave himself as a ransom for all" (1 Tim. 2:5-6). This, of course, is a teaching that the Catholic Church fully acknowledges. However, the text of Paul's *Letter to Timothy*, while excluding any other *parallel* mediation, does not exclude *subordinate* mediation.

At the wedding in Cana, Jesus performed the "first of his signs," which "manifested his glory" (John 2:11) and thereby commenced His public ministry. But this first public manifestation of His divinity was in turn *mediated* by His mother. He responded to the *intercessory* plea of His mother by miraculously changing the water not only into wine, but into the *best* wine (John 2:10). It was as though God's protocol demanded that it was the mother who would authorize the beginning of His ministry.

It is at Cana, therefore, that we see the first public manifestation of both the divinity of Christ, the one Mediator, and the motherly *intercession* of Mary for the needs of her children. Mary, then, is *Mediatrix with the Mediator*. And so, in his encyclical *Redemptoris Mater*, Pope John Paul II professed Mary as the "*Mediatrix*," who in her position as mother has the right to intercede for mankind.

Speaking at the General Audience of Wednesday, October 1, 1997, the Pope said: "Mary's maternal mediation does not obscure the unique and perfect mediation of Christ. Indeed, after calling Mary '*Mediatrix*,' the Council (Vatican Council II) is careful to explain that this 'neither takes away anything from, nor adds anything to the dignity and efficacy of Christ, the one Mediator'" (Lumen Gentium, n. 62).

Previous to this, in the General Audience of Wednesday, September 24, 1997, he had said: "Having entered the Father's eternal kingdom (referring to her bodily Assumption) she can more effectively exercise in the Spirit the role of maternal intercession entrusted to her by divine Providence... As maternal *Mediatrix*, Mary presents our desires and petitions to Christ, and transmits the divine gifts to us, interceding continually on our behalf."

With respect to this mediating role, as claimed by Fr. Stefano Gobbi, Mary herself once said to him on July 16, 1980: "I am the safest and shortest way to Jesus." Fr. Gobbi is the founder of the Marian Movement of Priests, and claims to have received inner locutions from the Blessed Virgin Mary since 1973. These ceased on December 31, 1997.

Advocate

The Church also teaches that Mary intercedes to God the Father through the Son and by the Holy Spirit on behalf of humanity as our *Advocate*, especially in times of danger and difficulty. As Dr. Mark Miravalle, Professor of Theology and Mariology at Steubenville University, wrote in his book *Mary—Coredemptrix, Mediatrix, Advocate*, we can see an authentic foreshadowing of the role of the mother of Jesus as *Advocate* in the Old Testament role of the queen mother, the role and office held by the mothers of the great Davidic kings of Israel.

In the kingdom of Israel, the mother of the king held the exalted office of the queen mother. At times, she even sat enthroned at the right side of the king (1 Kings 2:19-20). This office and authority of the queen mother made her the strongest advocate *to* the king *for* the people of the kingdom, as exemplified in 1 Kings 2:19-20: "And the king rose to meet her, and bowed down to her; then he sat on his throne, and had a seat brought for the king's mother; and she sat on his right. Then she said: 'I have one small request to make of you; do not refuse me.' And the king said to her, 'Make your request, my mother; for I will not refuse you.'"

This Old Testament role of the queen mother as *advocate* prophetically foreshadows the role of the great queen mother of the New Testament, for as the mother of Christ, King of all Nations, she is automatically queen and mother in the kingdom of God. Thus the Church teaches that Mary not only mediates the graces of God to humanity as Mediatrix, but she also mediates the petitions of the human family back to God as our Advocate. And so, she is not only *Coredemptrix*, but because she is *Coredemptrix*, she is also *Mediatrix* and *Advocate.* These three concepts are one.

The Marian Dogmas

Now, the Council of Ephesus in 431 AD defined the *first* Marian doctrine *Mother of God* (*Theotokos*), proclaiming that Mary is truly the Mother of God the Son made man: "The Holy Virgin is the *Mother of God* since according to the flesh she brought forth the Word, God made flesh."

A few centuries later, the Church defined the *second* Marian doctrine, *the Perpetual Virginity of Mary*, at the Lateran Council in 649 AD: "She conceived without seed, of the Holy Spirit...and without injury brought him forth...and after his birth preserved her virginity inviolate."

The *third* Marian doctrine was declared by Pope Pius IX in 1854, more than 1,000 years later: "The Most Holy Virgin Mary was in the first moment of her conception, by the unique gift of grace and privilege of Almighty God, in view of the merits of Jesus Christ, the Redeemer of mankind, preserved free from all stain of original sin." This statement by Pope Pius IX in 1854 defined *the Immaculate Conception* of Mary.

Then in 1950, Pope Pius XII proclaimed *the Assumption of Mary* as the *fourth* Marian doctrine: "Mary, the immaculate perpetually Virgin *Mother of God*, after the completion of her earthly life, was assumed body and soul into the glory of heaven." In short, he was saying that the woman who intimately shared the victory of Christ over the serpent (Genesis 3:15) could not have suffered corruption in the grave; the death which came from the evil one and his seed, and with whom she was given complete enmity by Almighty God.

But the precedent was already set. I thought about it. Was not the great prophet of Israel, Elijah, taken up by a whirlwind into heaven (2 Kings 2:11)? If God did this for the prophet of Carmel, would He not do the same for the "Woman of Carmel," the "Woman of Israel," His mother?

All these dogmas encountered much opposition before the Popes eventually proclaimed them. The question of ecumenical discord was always cited as one of the causes for concern. Indeed, the ecumenical obsessions of some theologians have always made it difficult to speak of traditional Catholic doctrines concerning Mary. At the same time while they are wary of offending Protestant sensitivities, their Anglican brothers did not hesitate to ordain women to the priesthood, a decision which has certainly impaired any complete reunion of the Protestants with the Catholic Church in the near term.

However, what is prophesied and is being requested and promoted as the *fifth* and *final* Marian dogma is still to be proclaimed in the fullness of time by the Holy Father. The other four had to come first. Undoubtedly, more than ever before, there will also be much opposition. And so, there is nothing new under the sun. Yes, there will also be that great concern about ecumenical friction, but I ask you, must truth be sacrificed at the altar of ecumenism? As Dr. Mark Miravalle, head of *Vox Populi Mariae Mediatrici*, a group which has gathered more than 4 million signatures on behalf of this dogma, wrote: "When Mary is *officially* declared *Coredemptrix, Mediatrix,* and *Advocate,* then, and only then, will the Church have courageously and definitively proclaimed *the whole truth about Mary,* Mother of Christ and Mother of the Church."

Indeed, for those of us who are in *search* of Mary, it will then give full *meaning* to the *mystery* of Mary. The full *meaning* of Mary! In my interpretation, **M** stands for **M**ediatrix, **A** for **A**dvocate, **R** for **R**edemptrix (**Co-**), and **Y** is for the "**Y**es" she said to God, after which she conceived the Redeemer of the world. Put them all together, they spell **MARY**.

Then the day will soon come when all the children of God will in one voice invoke Mary as our common mother, so that in addition to calling God *Abba* (Father), we will all call Mary *Imma* (Mother). And after the tumult and the clamour is over, all generations will be grateful to her and will call her "blessed" (Luke 1:48), for this is the hour when Genesis 3:15 will be fully understood and appreciated.

Mediatrix of Graces

Chapter 5

The Protestant Reformation
1517–1650

In 1054, the Church was rent asunder by a division that still has serious repercussions today. It marked the beginning of the schism of the Roman Catholic and the Orthodox Churches. Disunity was introduced into the Church of Christ. This disunity was the culmination of differences in the cultural, linguistic, spiritual, and political traditions that had grown between the western and eastern halves of Christendom.

However, this breach between west and east was more political than theological. Orthodox Churches are churches of Byzantine rites and share many essential matters with Catholicism: matters of faith and morals, sacraments, sacerdotal orders, Marian devotion, and much of the liturgy. The issue eventually focused mainly on the supremacy of Rome and whether the Pope, the Patriarch of Rome, was preeminent or one among equals.

Since the 9th century, the eastern patriarchs had favoured rule by the five patriarchs of Rome, Alexandria, Antioch, Constantinople, and Jerusalem, with the implication that all were equal. Rome, however, was less than happy with this formulation, pointing out, for example, that Constantinople, unlike the others, did not have a direct connection with the holy Apostles.

The two Churches then went their separate ways, and their mutual excommunication officially ended only in 1965. But the schism is still technically in effect. Indeed, the religious and cultural differences between the two Churches resurfaced in the early 1990s during the civil war in former Yugoslavia, which was primarily between Catholic Croatia and Orthodox Serbia. However, several separated Churches eventually resumed communion with Rome while still retaining their Oriental-rite liturgies. These Churches (often called Uniate, referring to union with Rome) do recognize the primacy of the Pope.

The Church in the Middle Ages was often upset by scandals and internal struggles, and endured the scandal of the three Popes from 1378 to 1417. As if that was not enough, Alexander VI Borgia (1492–1503) became one of the worst Popes in history. Made Cardinal at the age of twenty-five by his uncle, Pope Calixtus III, he amassed enormous wealth and was constantly involved in political intrigues. He had four children with a Roman noblewoman Vanizza de Cataneis. Once elected Pope in 1492, amidst allegations of massive simony, he, nonetheless, persisted in a corrupt, worldly, and scandalous life. Indeed, it was a way of life common to many world rulers of that era.

Eventually, during the 16th century, Europe was rocked by a number of reforming movements that challenged the Catholic Church, which had become somewhat worldly and lost much of its authority. These movements, collectively known as the Reformation, altered the face of Christianity. They gave birth to new Churches known as Protestant, because of their "protest" against the Roman Catholic Church. More and more splinter groups or Churches were formed, each claiming to be more pure and faithful to the Gospel of Jesus Christ than the other groups, and the Reformation split the Roman Church into many fragments and divided bodies.

Martin Luther (1480–1546)

The most important reforming movement was begun by Martin Luther (1480–1546), a German Augustinian monk, who was a professor of biblical theology at Wittenberg University in Germany. Luther was the founder of the Protestant Church in 1520. He was scandalized by the corrupt life of some of the clergy at the time, and was outraged by the practice of selling indulgences, which gave the impression that divine forgiveness could be bought or sold. He was not against indulgences per se, which is the remission of the temporal punishment to be expiated because of our sins, but, correctly so, against the abuse of selling and buying them. He was particularly upset by the Dominican Johann Tetzel, who preached that as soon as the people's money was cast into the chest, the souls of their departed could fly out of purgatory!

On October 31, 1517, Luther posted his famous ninety five theses on the door of Wittenberg church. The theses were forwarded to Rome. Luther's doctrines were thoroughly examined, and a Papal Bull condemned forty-one of his propositions, indicted his writings, and threatened him with excommunication unless he retracted within sixty days.

On December 10, 1520, Luther burnt the Bull and also declared that the priesthood and the episcopal office must be done away with. He denounced the authority of the Catholic Church and the Popes, and rejected the sacraments of the Church, except Baptism, the Eucharist, and Penance. He appealed to the cupidity of the princes in Europe by offering to make them heads of the Church in their own states if only they threw off the Pope. The German princes were among the first to ally themselves with Luther.

Luther was formally excommunicated from the Catholic Church at the Diet of Worms in 1521. However, much to the disgust of his friends, he eventually laid aside his religious habit and married the ex-Cistercian nun, Catherine Bora. After his marriage, Luther urged all monks, nuns, priests, and even the Archbishop of Mainz, to follow his example. Having thus definitely set himself against the whole Roman position, he began to organize his followers into a new Church.

Catherine eventually bore him six children. Indeed, some contemporaries thought that Luther's first son would be the Antichrist. This was because a popular legend had said that the Antichrist would be born of a monk and a nun, to which Erasmus of Rotterdan (1465–1536), well known for his humorous satires poking fun at the distortions of Catholic life and the spiritual confusion at the time, sarcastically commented: "Were this true, there would have been too many antichrists in the world already."

Luther died of a stroke on February 18, 1546, in his sixty-third year. But as Alan Schreck wrote in *The Compact History of the Catholic Church*: "It is enough to say that

Lutheranism was the most Catholic form of Protestantism, because Luther retained many aspects of Catholic belief and traditions, except those things that he felt were not in the Bible." The other streams of the Reformation were to depart even more radically from Catholicism.

Huldreich Zwingli

Huldreich Zwingli (1484–1531), parish priest of Zurich, was for Switzerland what Luther was for Germany. In 1516, he began to preach against the Blessed Virgin and against pilgrimages. He also taught that the Lord's Supper was simply a commemorative meal and that there is no real reception of Christ in the Eucharist. In 1522, he requested the Bishop of Constance to suppress clerical celibacy, citing his own case as proof that it was impossible for anyone to observe it.

Shortly afterwards, he married a widow with whom he had been living in sin for some years. After thus providing for his own reformation, he had recourse to violence in order to reform others. Supported by the town council of Zurich, he broke into churches, destroyed their altars, statues, and pictures, and set up in place of the altars plain tables for the celebration of the Lord's Supper.

Eventually, in 1529, the practice of the Catholic religion was interdicted by the city council. Switzerland was being rapidly "reformed" by men who disagreed with the reform of Wittenberg in many important points of doctrine and practice. Luther was in a rage. He denounced Zwingli as a liar and as possessed by the devil, and as a man for whose salvation it was useless to pray because he denied the Real Presence of Christ in the Eucharist. Previously Luther himself was anxious to reject this doctrine in order to spite the Pope, but, on his own admission, the words of Scripture were "too strong" for him.

Before his death in 1531, Zwingli ordered the drowning of a group of men in Zurich who insisted on rebaptizing adults and who taught that only an adult baptism, or a believer's baptism, could be valid. These Anabaptists (rebaptizers) had gone too far for Zwingli!

Jean Calvin

Jean Calvin (1509–1564) was of French origin and after studying theology and law in Paris, he was suddenly converted to the principles of the Reformation begun by Luther. Calvin had departed more radically from the Catholic faith than Martin Luther. In fact, it was through Calvin that Protestantism became a world powerful religion. Calvinism spread to Switzerland, Holland, England, Scotland, and America, and for a time challenged the supremacy of the Catholic religion in his own France.

He rejected all belief not explicitly found in the Bible. His church buildings were plain and white without altars, statues, images, organ music, or stained glass windows. All vestiges of Catholicism, except the Bible, were stripped away. His most widely debated doctrine was predestination. He taught that man, as a result of Adam's fall, has no freedom of will, but is an absolute slave of God. God has predestined each one of us, some to hell and some to heaven, irrespective of our merits, so that if we are predestined for heaven, we cannot be lost.

Eventually Calvin settled in Geneva in 1536. It was still largely Catholic but it became the future "Rome of Protestantism," and before his death in 1564, he succeeded in having his religion adopted in many of the cantons of Switzerland. These reforming movements not only split the Church but they also caused serious social upheaval and new political alliances in Europe. Within two decades the fate of the Catholic Church was sealed in Sweden and Norway and there were no Catholics left in those countries. It was then decreed in 1555 that each state will adopt the faith of its ruler. More than four hundred years later, that historic decision still has an affect on the religious and political geography of today's Europe.

Henry VIII and The Anglican Church

Meanwhile, in 1509, England's Henry VIII succeeded his father Henry VII on the throne of England. In the same year, he married his deceased brother's widow, Catherine of Aragon, after obtaining the papal dispensation required for such a marriage. He publicly burned the writings of Luther and in 1521, he wrote a book against him entitled *The Defence of the Seven Sacraments*, which won for him the title of Defender of the Faith from Pope Leo X (1513–1521), to whom the book was dedicated.

Indeed, at one time England was referred to as the "Dowry of Our Lady," and it was England's St. Simon Stock who is said to have received the devotion of the Brown Scapular from the Blessed Virgin on July 16, 1251.

However, it was this same King Henry who tore the English Church from Rome and it was his English people who in less than a hundred years turned Protestant almost to the last man.

In 1527, he had a violent passion for Anne Boleyn, maid of honour to the queen, and he was determined to marry her. He applied to Pope Clement VII (1523–1534) for a declaration that his marriage to Catherine of Aragon was null and void on the grounds that marriage with a deceased brother's wife was forbidden by Divine Law (Lev. 18:16), and consequently, that the dispensation given by Pope Julius II (1503–1513) was worthless. When Pope Clement VII refused to grant him a divorce, Henry broke completely with the Holy See and in November, 1534, a subservient Parliament enacted the Act of Supremacy, namely, that "the king, his heirs, and successors should be taken and reputed the only heads of the Church of England."

Most of the cowardly bishops and priests proved unfaithful to their trust, took the prescribed oath, expunged the name of the Pope from the liturgical books, preached against the tyranny of Rome, and extolled the virtues and prerogatives of the new "Vicar of Christ." Of all the bishops of England, only one refused to take the oath before Henry. He was John Fisher, Bishop of Rochester, a man of seventy-seven years. "If I were to consent," he declared, "that the king is head of the English Church, I should be guilty of tearing the seamless robe of Christ, the one Catholic Church." For this fearless confession of faith, John Fisher was executed in 1535 by beheading. Anne Boleyn, the Queen of England and the second wife of Henry, eventually met the same fate. She was beheaded in the Tower on June 19, 1536.

The total number of men and women, priests, and monks, who suffered death in England for the Catholic faith from 1535 was over six hundred. All the laymen of England also gave their loyalty to Henry VIII above their loyalty to the Pope, except Sir Thomas Moore. He had been Chancellor of England, the trusted friend and counsellor of Henry VIII, who had often visited his house and walked arm-in-arm with him in his garden. When, however, he refused to subscribe to the laws proclaiming the king's spiritual supremacy, he was thrown into prison, and after all attempts to make him change his mind proved unavailing, he was beheaded on July 7, 1535. His head was fixed upon London Bridge!

Pope Paul III (1534–1549) excommunicated Henry in 1538, and when Henry died in 1547, the Court orators forbade the people to weep for him, "because such a pious king must have surely gone straight to heaven."

Of course, this is only a very brief history of the origin of the Anglican Church in England, but as Fr. John Laux, instructor of religion and professor of psychology, Villa Madonna College, Kentucky, wrote in his book *Church History*: "What sinister power was it that made Protestants of a king and a nation who did not want to be Protestants at all, and brought hundreds of loyal Catholics to a cruel death? It was the demon of lust... All the world knows what happened to Anne Boleyn, for whose sake England was separated from the Holy See, and to the other wives of Henry." This is a very blunt statement on his part, however, whereas this is indeed the history of the beginning of the Anglican Church, nonetheless, history will also record the great number of devoted and devout Christians in this Church over the years.

It was around this European period of disunity and division in the Church, with the loss of millions of the Catholic faithful to the Protestant and Anglican fold, that the Blessed Virgin Mary appeared in the New World in 1531. Since then, there have arisen numerous Churches and religious organizations. For example, the Presbyterian Church was founded by John Knox in Scotland in 1560. The Methodist Church was launched by John and Charles Wesley in England in 1744, and the Mormons (Latter Day Saints) by Joseph Smith in Palmyra, New York, in 1824. Hundreds of other new Churches were founded by men in the 20th century. These include the Jehovah's Witnesses, the Church of the Nazarene, and the Pentecostal Churches, all challenging several aspects of the teachings of the Roman Catholic Church founded by Jesus Christ in 33 AD.

The Catholic Church has the largest number of followers, totalling just over a billion. However, as Fr. Kenneth Roberts wrote in his book *Proud To Be Catholic*: "The billion Catholics fall into three categories: cultural, habitual, and committed. The *cultural* Catholic is one who is usually born into the Faith, whose background is Catholic. He or she may have been educated in the Catholic school system, but that's where the affiliation ends. He or she probably has not been to church in years, except for an occassional Christmas or Easter liturgy, but if asked, will proclaim: 'I am Catholic, but I don't practice.'

The *habitual* Catholic attends church more often, maybe every Sunday, but really knows little about the Faith, and if put to the test, could not effectively defend it. Then there are the *committed* Catholics. They know their Faith, are faithful to the Church's teachings, and support the Church. More importantly, they have grown in their relationship with Christ through the sacramental life of the Church." He then ends his commentary, saying: "Catholics are not the only people who think about their religion this way!"

Chapter 6

A Brief History of the Aztecs

T he first major apparition of the Blessed Virgin
Mary in the New World was in Guadalupe, Mexico
in 1531. Because it was the primogenitus or first
born of her major apparitions in modern times, I decided
to research the history of the Aztecs and events in Europe
shortly before and around that time, in an attempt to
understand the full significance of this great visitation
of the *Mother of God* to that chosen country. It turned
out to be far more interesting and important than I ever
imagined.

According to a widely accepted theory, some 20,000
years ago, nomadic tribes of peoples of Siberian origin
crossed to the western hemisphere by a route not yet
determined, probably during a period of lowered sea level
when the Bering Strait was dry land. Gradually, over a
period of centuries, they made their way southward through
Alaska, Canada, the United States, and into Mesoamerica.
Mesoamerica is the term used by archeologists to refer to
central and southern Mexico, including the Gulf Coast and
Yucatan Peninsula, Guatemala, and parts of El Salvador
and Honduras.

Long before the birth of Christ, the central and southern regions of Mexico were inhabited by peoples thought to be descendants of those primitive nomads, who had reached a high degree of civilization. First in importance were the Olmecs from about 2000 BC to 200 AD, then the ancient Maya civilization which reached its peak around 300–800 AD. Classic Maya civilization collapsed, for reasons still unknown, between 800–900 AD Then, there were the Toltecs (900–1170 AD), and some 60 km north of Mexico City is the modern town of Tula, wherein can be seen the ruins of what was once the great Toltec city. Before those dates we have only vague semi-historical data on the events which took place in the Valley of Mexico.

Around 1200 AD, somewhere to the northwest of present-day Mexico City, a band of men, women, and children abandoned their ancestral homeland Aztlan, from which the name Aztec was derived. It was not until much later that these peoples assumed the name "Mexica." The cause of their departure, according to one Aztec version, was that their tribal god of war and the sun, Huitzilopochtli, ordered them to go forth in search of a "promised land" from where they would conquer the world. The sign of this "promised land" was to be an eagle standing upon a cactus in the midst of the waters of a lake.

Over one hundred years later, in 1325, the itinerant Aztecs eventually discovered the sign which they had been seeking. It was in the Valley of Mexico on a small island in the western half of Lake Tezcoco. There they saw an eagle perched upon a prickly pear cactus growing out of a rock, and it was there that they settled. They called the place Tenochtitlan. The name Tenochtitlan in their Nahuatl language referred to *telt* (rock), *nochtli* (cactus), and *tlan*, the locative suffix. We may surmise that all this took place in the area of the present-day cathedral of Mexico City, since it is built over the ruins of the ancient temple of Tenochtitlan.

The national emblem of today's Mexico, which appears on the Mexican flag and on their coins, displays the hieroglyph of the Aztecs; the eagle perched on a prickly pear cactus. However, the modification of the serpent in the beak of the eagle was introduced into the hieroglyph only after the Spanish Conquest, as the serpent to the Spaniards was a symbol more in keeping with the idea of evil being crushed by an eagle.

It is told that the Aztecs' first act was to build a temple to their god of war and the sun, Huitzilopochtli. The construction had begun in 1325 AD, and by 1400 AD, the temple of the rain god Tlaloc, the god of agriculture, shared the summit of the Great Pyramid with that of Huitzilopochtli. Tlaloc, on the northern side, was painted in blue and white. Huitzilopochtli, to the south, was coloured red and white, the symbols of war and sacrifice; these twin shrines signifying the vital importance both of agriculture and of war to the Aztecs. In front of the temple of Huitzilopochtli was the sacrificial stone for human sacrifice.

Over the centuries, the Aztecs devoted themselves to resisting attacks from Azcapotzalco, the Tepanec neighbour, who became increasingly powerful. Eventually in 1428, the Aztecs and their neighbouring tribes, the Texcocans and the Tacubans, formed a Triple Alliance which defeated the powerful and domineering Azcapotzalco tribe after a siege lasting 114 days. The Triple Alliance then became the "Aztec empire," but the Aztec tribe soon reigned supreme over its allies. It was an alliance encompassing almost 2,000 square kilometers and several million people.

The Reign of Emperor Moctezuma I

In 1440, the Emperor Moctezuma I succeeded the Aztec ruler Itzcoatl. Moctezuma I has generally been seen as the founder and father of Aztec greatness. However, his reign opened with a series of terrible catastrophes, famines, floods, and other calamities, and Aztec society was tottering on its foundation. The disasters were attributed to the gods' anger, and in order to appease the gods, regular warring campaigns were organized to capture the largest possible number of prisoners who were to become sacrificial offerings.

The Aztecs certainly did not invent human sacrifice. It was already practiced by other tribes thousands of years earlier and indeed in several other cultures in the world, even in the time of Abraham. However, the Aztecs sacrificed their victims on an unprecedented scale. These killings, they believed, provided the source of vital energy, of "precious water" (blood), which was indispensable for the working of the cosmos, and were performed in order to avoid, or more exactly, delay the disappearance of the world condemned to destruction.

In addition, human sacrifice was an instrument of government, upholding a policy of fear and terror, while at the same time ensuring the physical elimination of their most dangerous enemies. To this end, Moctezuma I started a perpetual war between the Triple Alliance and the peoples of the Valley of Puebla-Tlaxcala.

Moctezuma II

In 1502, ten years after Christopher Columbus discovered some of the islands of the West Indies and brought Christianity to the New World, Moctezuma Xocoyotzin, called Moctezuma II, began his reign. He was the seventh ruler of the Aztecs and is the best known of them all. He was a scrupulous observer of omens and rituals and was very superstitious. Indeed, the decade before the Spaniards arrived produced many reasons for him to be fearful.

Ten years before the coming of Cortez, a dazzling comet appeared and one of Moctezuma's soothsayers prophesied calamities which were to destroy the kingdoms. Other omens sowed seeds of impending defeat and of anxiety in his mind. The sanctuary of the great goddess Toci caught fire, the lake's water formed gigantic waves, despite the fact that there was no wind, and a woman's voice in the night announced death and destruction. Above all, he was unnerved by the prospect of the return of the legendary god Quetzalcoatl to reclaim the land and regain his lost throne.

Quetzalcoatl

Quetzalcoatl ("the Plumed Serpent") was also known as Topiltzin-Quetzalcoatl, the priest-king of the Toltecs of Tula (900–1170 AD). According to Mesoamerican mythology, from a Toltec ruler he was transformed to a new version of a deity by the Aztecs and other peoples of Mesoamerica, who combined the two images, that of man and of a god. In other words, he was considered to be a man-god. His arch rival was Tezcatlipoca, an omnipotent god, associated with fate, whom in later years the Spanish Christian missionaries associated with the devil.

Contrary to the writings of many, my recent research clearly shows that Quetzalcoatl was not an evil deity (the so-called dreaded serpent god) but was a good god. He was opposed to human sacrifice, recommending in its stead the sacrifice of fruits and flowers. He taught the people to live in peace and was known as the god of peace and also the god of civilization. Another of his titles was the "Morning Star" which appears in the east at the moment of dawn. He also taught them about a one true god called Ometeotl in Aztec mythology.

A very poetic Nahuatl text from an Aztec colonial manuscript known as *Anales de Cuauhtitlan* tells the legendary story of Quetzalcoatl, and relates how during his reign there were abundance and happiness, and marvelous birds of all colours singing wonderfully. His house was of jade, fine gold, and turquoise and was all enveloped in quetzal feathers. This was his house of fasting and prayer.

The legend is that the forces of darkness had triumphed during that period in Tula, and Quetzalcoatl eventually destroyed his house, abandoned Tula, and beckoned to the sweet singing birds to follow him. He then set out for the east in the direction of the Gulf Coast. According to several Indian and Spanish chronicles, Quetzalcoatl promised to return from the east some day to overthrow the cult of Tezcatlipoca and to inaugurate an era when the gods would again "accept sacrifices of flowers" and cease their clamour for human blood. It is said that he prophesied the year of his return. It was to be in a year Ce Acatl "1 Reed."

We will see in chapter 10 in what way this is related to the apparition of the Virgin Mary in Mexico in 1531.

Chapter 7

The Empire of Satan

As we shall also see later, when the Spaniards first saw the arena of the Great Temple in the Aztec capital, the horror of it convinced them that Moctezuma's empire must have been the empire of Satan himself, and this religious interpretation which I now record must be understood and appreciated in the context of Satan's obsession with being "like unto God." This I believe to be the true *raison d'etre* of the satanic practices in Tenochtitlan.

The Fall of Satan

Sin was introduced in the empyrean heavens when Satan, considering himself superior to man, was disobedient to God's command and refused to worship the Second Person of the Blessed Trinity, who was to be incarnated as the God-man. As related in the divine revelations given to the Spanish mystic Maria de Jesus de Agreda (1602–1665), and recorded in her monumental work *The Mystical City of God* (first written in 1637), Satan, in disorderly fury over this command, aspired to be himself the head of all the human race and of all the angelic corps, and if there were to be a hypostatic union, he demanded that it be consummated in him: "It is I, and only I, who will be like the Most High. All will render me honour," he boasted. Indeed, from the very beginning he craved for tribute and honour to be paid to him and he instigated the first war in God's creation. However, Jesus testified to his fate: "I saw Satan fall like lightning from heaven" (Luke 10:18).

But let us now see how this "ape of God" tried in Mexico to emulate the Lord and Creator who expelled him from heaven, his Paradise lost.

The Promised Land

Aztec legend teaches that Huitzilopochtli, their tribal god of war and the sun, ordered them to leave their ancestral homeland Aztlan in search of a place from where they were to conquer the world. And so, it was the ancient serpent leading his "chosen people" to the new promised land. It was the mimic of God, attempting to rewrite the story of Abraham and Moses in the Books of Genesis and Exodus. It was to be the Old Testament, "according to Satan," but enacted this time in the New World. That, I believe, is what it was all about.

About 2091 BC, God called Abraham when he was living in the city of Ur in Babylonia, near the Persian Gulf, significantly, in what is now Iraq. The people of Ur made idols and worshiped them, believing themselves to be especially favoured by the moon-god. God said to Abraham: "Leave your country and your kinfolk and your father's house, and go to a land that I will show you. I will make of you a great nation, and I will bless you and make your name great... Between you and me I will establish my covenant and I will multiply you exceedingly... You are to become the father of a host of nations... Kings shall stem from you... And I will be their God... I will bless you abundantly and make your descendants as countless as the stars of the sky" (Genesis 12-18).

And so, just as the Hebrew descendants of Abraham wandered through the wilderness of the Sinai desert for forty years, so did the Aztecs roam for years through the wilderness of the Valley of Mexico, a desert-like land where the cactus grows. In mimicry, I believe, of God's promise to Abraham, it is the Aztec legend that their god Huitzilopochtli spoke through his priest-mediums during their trek to their promised land and said: "We shall proceed to establish ourselves and settle down, and we shall conquer all peoples of the universe; and I tell you in all truth that I will make you lords and kings of all that is in the world; and when you become rulers you shall have countless and infinite numbers of vassals, who will pay tribute to you and shall give you innumerable and most fine precious stones, gold, quetzal feathers, emeralds, coral, amethysts, and you shall dress most finely in these... And all this you shall see, since this is in truth my task, and for this have I been sent here" (Hernando Tezozomoc, *Cronica Mexicayotl*, 1949).

It was the mimic promising his "chosen people" material wealth and kingdoms, and to match God's promise to Abraham of countless numbers of descendants like the stars, he, in turn, promised the Aztecs, not descendants (he cannot create) but innumerable precious stones and infinite numbers of vassals who will pay tribute to them. However, instead of having innumerable vassals, the Aztecs eventually became vassals themselves, vassals of Spain.

But let us not forget that Satan is the prince of this world (John 12:31), and the promise to make them "lords and kings of all that is in the world" was the same as his third temptation to Jesus when "he took him up to a very high mountain, and showed him all the kingdoms of the world, and the glory of them, saying: 'All these I will give to you, if you will fall down and worship me'" (Matthew 4:8-9). Even the saying "I tell you in all truth" was a characteristic quote borrowed from the words of Christ, but this time it was uttered by Satan himself, of whom it is said "the truth is not in him" (John 8:44).

The Eagle and The Rock

The Aztecs chose the eagle on a rock as the sign of the place where they were to settle. It was to be *their* promised land, Satan's Canaan. In my opinion, the significance of his choice of an eagle can probably be traced to this bird's symbolism in the deliverance of the Israelites and their trek to the promised land as recorded in Exodus 19:1-4: "Three months after they came out of the land of Egypt...the sons of Israel came to the wilderness of Sinai... Moses then went up to God, and Yahweh called to him from the mountain, saying: 'You yourselves have seen what I did with the Egyptians, how I carried you on eagle's wings and brought you to myself.'"

Now, the eagle stood on a rock. In the Old Testament the *Song of Moses* (Deut. 32:1-43) speaks about the Rock: "The Rock, his work is perfect, and all his ways are just." Here the Rock refers to the Lord. In the New Testament,

Peter is also referred to as "the rock": "You are Peter, and upon this rock I will build my church" (Matthew 16:18). And so, Satan chose as his insignia, an eagle standing on a rock, and upon the area of the rock he planned to build his church and his satanic capital, Tenochtitlan.

But let us now research the significance of the cult of human sacrifice by the Aztecs in Tenochtitlan.

Chapter 8

Aztec Human Sacrifice

The Temple Ceremonies in Tenochtitlan

Whereas the Spaniards were astounded by the splendour and beauty of Tenochtitlan (now buried under modern Mexico City), these favourable impressions rapidly vanished when they reached the ceremonial center. Indeed, it was really a "religious center." This immense enclosure, measuring 402 meters by 301 meters, contained several dozen temples. The highest and largest was the Great Temple. It was there that they experienced the visual shock of seeing the 114 blood-soaked steps of this lofty pyramid-mountain upon which stood two temples. One was dedicated to Huitzilopochtli, the god of war and tribute, the sun god, and the other to Tlaloc, the god of rain and fertility, the god of agriculture. In front of the temple of Huitzilopochtli was the sacrificial stone for human sacrifice. It was Satan's high altar.

The upper section of the temple of Huitzilopochtli was decorated with white stone skulls set against a deep red background. There were also several skull racks within the enclosure, structures consisting of a base with vertical wooden posts, and on bars between the posts were strung thousands of the skulls of the sacrificed like beads on a rod. Let us now see how Satan tried to mimic Biblical history in the ceremonial center.

This is My Beloved Son

The sacrificed prisoners were obtained through war and were called "victims," and when they fought each other, the Aztecs tried to keep their adversaries alive in order that they might be sacrificed in Tenochtitlan. When an Aztec took a prisoner, he said: "Here is my beloved son," and the captive replied: "Here is my revered father." This was, therefore, Satan's equivalent to God speaking lovingly about His Son after He was baptized by John in the River Jordan: "This is my beloved son in whom I am well pleased" (Matthew 3: 17).

This is Your God

Now, when the Hebrew people became aware of Moses' delay in coming down from Mount Sinai, they took off their golden earrings and brought them to Aaron, who accepted their offerings, and fashioning this gold with their tools, they made a molten calf. The Israelites had returned to their pagan worship which so angered Moses. Then they cried out to all the Israelites: "This is your God, Israel" (Exodus 32:1-4).

After they arrived at the Great Temple, the victims of the Aztecs were led up the stairs through thick clouds of incense. Running up to where those to be sacrificed were lined up, and then going from one side to the other, the Aztec high priest then showed the pagan image of Huitzilopochtli to each man, and exclaimed in like manner: "This is your god."

Blood, Sacrifice and Incense

The altar of sacrifice stood in the middle of the Priests' Court in front of the Temple in Jerusalem, and worship at the Temple was often a very bloody affair since it involved the killing of many sacrificial animals, including bulls, oxen, goats, and sheep. Indeed, when Solomon dedicated the Temple, 22,000 oxen and 120,000 sheep were sacrificed (1 Kings 8:63). Sacrificial altars had special channels for carrying away the blood, and in the southeastern part of the rock, now covered by the great Islamic Mosque of Omar, is a round hole about two feet in diameter, through which the blood of the animal victims was carried away from the Temple area by underground pipes to the Kedron (Black Valley). It was thus called because of its clotted blood.

Not so, however, with the Great Temple of the Aztecs. The sacrificial stone stood in front of the temple of Huitzilopochtli and gallons of blood from the thousands of sacrificed human victims openly flowed down the temple steps and were unaesthetically left there, unwashed and malodorous for long periods. It was the hallmark of Satan's uncleanliness and ungodliness.

While the animals were sacrificed in the outer court of the Temple in Jerusalem, incense was offered on the altar, and the smoke of incense ascending up before the Lord in the Temple typified the prayers offered up to the eternal Father. And so, during their human sacrifices, the Aztecs also smoked incense around the Great Temple in Tenochtitlan, offering it up to the pagan sun god.

The Sacrifice of Jesus and His Pierced Heart

During the preparation of the Passover meal, the Israelites "crucified" the lamb as detailed by Yahweh to them on the night of the Exodus. And so, Christ, the Lamb of God, was also crucified. His arms were stretched out horizontally and nailed to the Cross, and His two feet were pulled down and pinioned with a single nail. Just after He died, the Roman centurion, the "captain" of the army, thrust his lance through His widened rib space (caused by His excessive inspiratory efforts to breathe over three hours) and then straight into the heart of the Supreme Victim, Jesus. This death, this sacrifice, this torn heart was offered to God the Father for the redemption of the sins of mankind. It was the perfect sacrifice. It was the only human sacrifice acceptable to God. It was the immolation of the true Lamb of God, because animal or ordinary human sacrifice could not redeem mankind.

Aztec Sacrifice of the Victim

Sacrifice to the gods was one of the Aztecs' more sacred obligations, since by feeding blood and hearts to the gods, the world and the sun were kept alive. Hence, the Aztecs considered themselves the "People of the Sun." According to José de Acosta's *Natural and Moral History of the Indies*, written in 1590, the usual method of sacrifice by the Aztecs was performed in a similar outstretched fashion as that of Christ's crucifixion. Two priests held the victim's feet, another two his outstretched hands, and another one held his throat. The one who performed the ritual killing of the victim, the sixth of the group, was considered the supreme or high priest. He carried in his hand a big flint knife, very pointed and wide. The sacrificial stone was itself so pointed that when the victim was thrown on his back against it, he was bent over in such a way that his rib spaces were widened and it was then easy to introduce the knife into his chest.

With great skill, the Aztec high priest made an incision between the ribs on the left side below the nipple, then he plunged in his hand, and like a ravenous tiger (it is said that it took only fifteen seconds), swiftly tore out the living heart of the victim while still beating, and offered it to the sun god. Hearts were assembled in piles and placed in a large receptacle; then with a kick he threw the victim's body down the temple steps to be decapitated and dismembered.

Mount Calvary

Christ was sacrificed on a hill called Golgotha, a Babylonian word meaning "the Place of the Skull." The Romans called it "Calvaria" (Calvary). Inside the shrine of Huitzilopochtli on the summit of the Great Temple in Tenochtitlan was a rack where thousands of the skulls of the victims were displayed as public trophies. And so, the Great Temple mount was the mount of the skulls. It was Satan's Calvary.

It has been estimated that the number of sacrificial victims in the Aztec empire as a whole had risen to about 250,000 (hearts) a year by the beginning of the 16th century when Cortez came to Mexico. For what was this manic destruction of human life? According to Aztec tradition, it was done to delay the coming of the end of the world.

48

Human sacrifice atop the Great Temple in Tenochtitlan

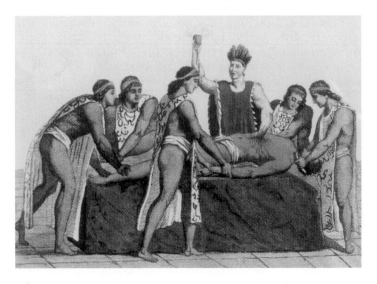

The skull rack in Tenochtitlan

50

Chapter 9

The Spanish Conquest of Mexico

Hernando Cortez (1485–1547) was seven years old when the Catholic King and Queen, Ferdinand and Isabella of Spain, conquered Granada in 1492 after the centuries-long battle to reclaim Spain from Islamic domination. As Richard Townsend in his book *The Aztecs* put it: "Christianity had taken on a militant guise, and war automatically assumed the nature of a *jihad*." When this last Mohammedan kingdom was vanquished, Spain, united and mighty, rose to the status of a world power. It was the same year that Columbus set out to discover the New World.

After two years as a student at the University of Salamanca, Cortez migrated to the Caribbean where he held the position of scribe to the colonists, landholder, and government employee in Santo Domingo and in Cuba. In 1519, Diego Velasquez, the Spanish governor of Cuba, because of his enterprising and determined character, chose Cortez to be in charge of an expedition to Mexico. Cortez sailed from Cuba with 10 ships carrying about 600 men, 16 horses, 32 crossbows, and 10 bronze cannons.

The expedition cruised around the Yucatan and reached the Vera Cruz coast in April of that year. It was on April 22, 1519. The date corresponded to the year Ce Acatl

"1 Reed" in the Aztec calendar, the exact date prophesied five hundred years earlier for the return of Quetzalcoatl. It was Good Friday! Coincidentally (or was it?), Veracruz means "True Cross."

For several years Moctezuma had been placing lookouts along the shores to watch for Quetzalcoatl's return. He knew that this would prove fatal to the worshipers of Huitzilopochtli, and the arrival of the bearded Cortez from the east brought fear and panic to the Aztec empire. It was his perception that Cortez was an incarnation of Quetzalcoatl. Moctezuma suddenly became an indecisive leader. Cortez and his army soon entered the region dominated by the Tlaxcalans, who decided to support the foreigners against the Triple Alliance. Continuing their march inland, they made further friendships and alliances with other enemies of Moctezuma, all thirsting for revenge.

Eventually on November 8, 1519, Moctezuma, with the image of Huitzilopochtli borne on a litter by several of the Aztec nobility, and surrounded by his court and a multitude of slaves carrying offerings for the gods, went to meet Cortez at the entrance of Tenochtitlan. Gold, turquoise, and jade were considered sacred, and Moctezuma was wearing his regal and iridescent green plumes of the Quetzal bird, a turquoise diadem, and golden jewelry signaling his royal status. Cortez, on the other hand, led his army of about 600 Spaniards in their shining armour, and with them were several thousand Indian allies. It was a scene that Cecil B. de Mille would have wished to have captured on film.

As Cortez himself wrote in 1519: "Moctezuma came to greet us and with him were some two hundred lords, all barefoot, and each one dressed in a different costume" (Letters from Mexico to King Charles V of Spain, translated by Anthony R. Pagden, 1972). It was the great meeting of the two worlds and the two cultures. Moctezuma greeted him in the name of his god Huitzilopochtli, and Cortez replied that he had come in the name of a powerful Lord, the one true God. The glittering procession then set off to Tenochtitlan while Moctezuma remained indecisive as to whether he should be aggressive or friendly.

The Magnificence of Tenochtitlan

On arriving in Tenochtitlan, the Spaniards were deeply impressed by the beauty, order, and cleanliness of this city of between 150,000 to 300,000 inhabitants, one of the largest metropoles in the world at the time. To quote the writing of Cortez himself: "This great city of Tenochtitlan is built on a salt lake. The city itself is as big as Seville or Cordoba. The main streets are very wide and very straight... Among the temples there is one, the principal one, whose great size and magnificence no human tongue could describe... There are as many as forty towers, all of which are so high that, in the case of the largest, there are fifty steps leading up to the main part of it, and the most important of these towers is higher than that of the Cathedral of Seville..."

In Bernard Diaz del Castillo's *The Conquest of New Spain*, written in 1568, he also described what he himself saw in 1519 as he accompanied Cortez into Tenochtitlan: "On reaching the market-place...we were astounded at the great number of people and quantities of merchandise, and at the orderliness and good arrangements that prevailed, for we had never seen such a thing before... Every kind of merchandise was kept separate and had its fixed place marked for it... After inspecting and thinking about all that we had seen, we turned to look at the great plaza and the multitude of people there, some buying and others selling... Among us were soldiers who had been in many parts of the world—in Constantinople, in all Italy, and Rome, and they said that they had never seen a plaza so large, so busy, and with so many people."

Cortez and his soldiers were then lodged in the palace of Axayacatl, but since the Aztecs had superior forces numerically, some Spaniards wanted to strike a sudden blow immediately. And so, after receiving reinforcements, they requested to be present at the ritual dances in celebration of the feast of Huitzilopochtli. This occasion provided them with an ideal opportunity to gather together and massacre the most eminent members of the Aztec nobility in a surprise attack. They are reported to have killed almost ten thousand Aztecs. Moctezuma himself was taken prisoner and he was later mortally wounded by one of his own people.

However, the surviving Aztec aristocrats did not throw in the towel and were determined more than ever to finish off the invaders. After Moctezuma's death, his brother and then his cousin, Cuitlahuac and Cuauhtemoc respectively, became the leaders of the Aztecs and continued the battle with vicious ferocity. More than half the Spaniards, and almost all their native allies, were massacred or taken prisoners, many of whom were sacrificed. Then on June 30, 1520, taking advantage of a moonless night and torrential rains, the Spaniards fled from Tenochtitlan. Eventually, it took repeated counterattacks, a famine, and an epidemic of small pox, a virus brought by the Europeans and a disease against which the natives had no immunity, to overcome Aztec resistance.

The city was eventually besieged by Cortez on May 30, 1521, and finally fell three months later on the *thirteenth* of the month. It was on August 13, 1521. As we shall see later, this date, the *thirteenth* of the month, was perhaps not without significance. And so, almost two years after Cortez entered Tenochtitlan, the pagan Aztec empire had collapsed. Cortez immediately set out to rebuild the capital and expand the conquest. A year later, in 1522, he became governor and captain-general of "New Spain," the new name given to the Aztec empire that was.

After the conquest, Cortez did not only impose submission to the Spanish Crown, he also demanded that the Indians convert to the Christian faith. He ordered an end to human sacrifice and cannibalism everywhere, and installed Christian images in the native sanctuaries— Christ, the Virgin, and other saints.

Serge Gruzinski in *The Aztecs: Rise and Fall of an Empire*, records: "The Indians were astounded by the violence and passion with which the conquistadors broke the statues of their gods. The Spaniards carried out raids against the temples, assassinated pagan priests, set fire to the pyramids, smashed the statues, and burnt codices covered in pictographs. Iconoclastic violence replaced that of the human sacrifices."

In fact, some historians and commentators have criticized the Spaniards for their ruthlessness. But was this not the command given by Moses to the Israelites in his final address to them about the pagans?: "These are the statutes and decrees which you must be careful to observe in the land which the Lord, the God of your fathers, has given you to occupy, as long as you live on its soil. Destroy without fail every place on the high mountain, on the hills, and under every leafy tree where the nations you are to dispossess worship their gods. Tear down their altars, smash their sacred pillars, destroy by fire their sacred poles, and shatter the idols of their gods, that you may stamp out the remembrance of them in any such place" (Deut. 12:1-3).

Indeed, the biblical account of the destruction by the Israelites of the Canaanite religious practices may sound cruel to readers only if they are unfamiliar with the salacious savagery of many pagan cultures of old. The Canaanite civilization (a word which does not necessarily connote 'civilized' behaviour) fell because the Israelites did away with the abominable Canaanite religious practices of human sacrifice to the god Moloch, the lewd rites demanded by the Canaanite god known as Baal, and the orgies and sacred prostitutions in the name of the goddess Asherah.

And so, the Christian zeal of Cortez and the missionary clergy was at times counterbalanced by the cruelty and excesses of the Spanish soldiers. God, glory, and gold were the motives of the Spaniards, but regrettably, not always in that order. Nevertheless, the European monks succeeding in winning over many of the people and part of the elite. Hundreds of thousands of baptisms were recorded but in certain areas resistance to Christianity lasted for years.

Cortez meets Moctezuma

Chapter 10

Enter Her Majesty, The Virgin Mary

It was Satan's empire, and the Woman of Genesis 3:15 came to Mexico to do battle with him. Luther had divided her Son's Church since 1517, and Henry VIII's passion for Anne Boleyn around 1527 led him to ask the Pope to annul his marriage to Catherine of Aragon. It was the beginning of the Anglican Church.

It was four years later. The year was 1531, ten years after the conquest of Tenochtitlan (now Mexico City). It was very early on Saturday morning, December 9, at that time the feast of the *Immaculate Conception*. A humble 57 year old Aztec, whose former name was Cuahatlatotzin, meaning "He who speaks like an eagle," and whose new Christian name was Juan Diego, was on his way to Mass on that great feast day of Mary. As he drew near to the little hill of Tepeyac, day was beginning to dawn. Much to his amazement, he heard singing on the hill. It was the singing of many birds, and their songs, extremely soft and melodious, surpassed that of the coyoltot, the tzinitzcan, and all the other precious birds of Mexico.

He looked towards the hill top, towards the easterly direction from which the sun was rising and from where the heavenly singing was coming. Suddenly the singing stopped. Then he heard someone affectionately calling to him from afar: "Juanito, Juan Diegoito," using the diminutive of his name. He ventured in the direction of the voice and when he had reached the top of the hill, he saw a brilliant white cloud surrounded by the arc of a rainbow, formed by rays of dazzling light streaming from the cloud.

A young lady of exquisite beauty, seemingly about 14 years old, then appeared in front of the cloud. The sun was not yet above the horizon, but when Juan saw her, her clothes were shining as bright as the sun with golden beams that rayed around her from head to foot. Indeed, so gloriously bright was she that her radiance seemed to turn rocks into pendants of jewels, cactus leaves into emeralds, and their trunks and their thorns shone like gold.

She came from the east, and arrived early in the morning when it was beginning to dawn. She appeared as bright as the sun. But isn't the sun a star? She appeared, therefore, as the *Morning Star!* But it was also a star from the east which announced her Son's birth: "Where is he that is born King of the Jews? For we have seen his star in the east, and have come to worship him" (Matthew 2:2). Solomon's *Song of Songs 6:10* was depicted by this apparition: "Who is she that comes forth as the morning star, fair as the moon, bright as the sun, terrible as an army set in battle array." It is the standard of the Legion of Mary. Indeed, she came forth to declare war on Satan, and Juan Diego was her first Aztec convert and warrior.

Now, as I previously said, according to the legend, Quezalcoatl, after he was defeated in Tula by Tezcatlipoca and the forces of evil, beckoned to the sweet singing birds to follow him and he promised to return one day from the east to regain his rulership. And so, the Virgin came from the east in the spirit, as it were, of Quezalcoatl. Quezalcoatl was also known as the "Morning Star!" The Aztecs would have understood that.

She beckoned to Juan to approach her and when he reached the spot where she was, he was filled with wonder, as her perfect grandeur surpassed all imagination. It was on a hill in Tepeyac where the Aztecs had once built a temple to the pagan mother-goddess Tonantzin. Tonantzin was reputed to be a mild deity who rejected human victims and was only to be appeased by the sacrifices of turtle doves, swallows, and pigeons.

Juan instinctively prostrated himself before her. It was then that she identified herself: "Know for certain, my dearest and youngest son, that I am the perfect and perpetual Virgin Mary, mother of the true God, through whom everything lives, the Lord of all things, who is master of creation and of heaven and earth. I ardently desire that a temple be built here for me where I will show and offer all my love, my compassion, my help, and my protection to the people. I am your merciful mother, the mother of all who live united in this land, and of all mankind, of all those who love me, of those who cry to me, of those who seek me, of those who have confidence in me. Here I will hear their weeping and their sorrow, and will remedy and alleviate their sufferings, their necessities, and their misfortunes. Therefore, in order that my intentions be made known, you must go to the house of the Bishop of Mexico City and tell him that I sent you and that it is my desire to have a temple built here..." Juan Diego replied: "My lady, my child, I am going right away to do your venerable word. I take my leave of you for the moment, I, your poor Indian."

"I am the perfect and perpetual Virgin Mary," she said. She thus confirmed the second Marian dogma, the Perpetual Virginity of Mary, proclaimed at the Lateran Council in 649 AD. "Mother of the true God," she also said, confirming the very first Marian dogma of the Council of Ephesus in 431 AD, which defined her as "Mother of God." In Guadalupe, however, she added "true," because the Aztecs worshiped false gods. "I am your merciful mother," she added, "mother of all who live united in this land," acknowledging the title given to her by St. Augustine in the 4th century AD, "Mother of Unity."

Juan called her "my child," and in similar fashion the Virgin had called him Juanito (little Juan) and Diegoito (little Diego). As I discovered in my research, it is because reverential diminutives were frequently used in the Nahuatl language. The well-bred person, for example, did not say "your house" but "your little house." This had nothing to do with actual size but was an expression of reverence and endearment (Fernando Horcasitas, *The Aztecs: Then and Now*). I could not but be deeply moved and amused at the obedience and humility of Juan Diego: "I, your poor Indian!"

However, understandably so, Bishop Juan de Zumarraga did not believe Juan Diego's message and very politely dismissed him. At the end of the day Juan returned to the little hilltop where the "mother of the true God" was waiting for him at the very spot where she had appeared the first time. "I beg you, my lady, my queen, my little one," he respectfully pleaded, "to entrust one of the nobles to bear your kind breath, your kind word; someone who is held in esteem, someone who is known, respected, and honoured, in order that he might be believed, because I am really just a man of the field, a *mecapalli* (a burden bearer), a *cacaxtli* (a back frame). I am a *cola* (a tail). I am an *alla* (a wing), a man of no importance. I myself need to be led, to be carried on someone's back. The place in which you sent me is a place where I am unaccustomed to going or spending any time. My youngest daughter, my lady, my little one, please forgive me..."

"The perfect and perpetual Virgin" listened to his plea with great sympathy and understanding, but implored him to go again to see the bishop on the morrow, and to tell him: "It is I, personally, the ever Virgin Mary; I, who am the Mother of God, who sends you." Juan obeyed and returned to the bishop. This time the bishop was more impressed, but he told him that the lady must provide some proof that she was really the Mother of God—a reasonable reaction, in my opinion!

At sunset, Juan Diego was back on the hill of Tepeyac where the lady was waiting for him and assured him that on the following day she would give him the sign which the bishop had requested. He went home to rest. However, when he reached home that evening, he found his uncle Juan Bernardino extremely ill, and rather than returning to Tepeyac, he spent the whole day caring for his uncle. During that night, Juan Bernardino thought that he was going to die and asked his nephew to go to Tenochtitlan to bring back a priest to anoint him.

The next morning, very concerned about his beloved uncle, Juan Diego set out on a different route around the hill of Tepeyac so that the lady, if she were there, would not detain him from his mission. However, she came down the side of the hill and intercepted him. Embarrassed and distressed that he had not kept his promise to her, he prostrated himself and greeted her with these words which must have caused the Queen to chuckle: "My young lady, youngest of my children, my child, I hope that you are happy. How are you this morning? Are you in good humor and health this morning, my lady, my little one?" With this flattery, he then told her about the plight of his uncle.

When Juan Diego's tale came to an end, the "merciful mother" consoled him: "Listen, do not be afraid or troubled with grief. Do not fear any illness or vexation, anxiety or pain. Am I not here, I who am your Mother? Are you not under my shadow and protection? Am I not the cause of your joy? Are you not in the folds of my mantle? In the crossing of my arms? What more do you need?" She paused for a while, and with a maternal and sympathetic smile, she gently added: "Do not let your uncle's illness worry you because he is not going to die. Be assured that he is already well."

As was later discovered, at that very moment Juan Bernardino had recovered. She then told Juan Diego to climb up the hill and that there he would find flowers in bloom which he should pluck and bring back to her. Juan climbed the hill with great alacrity and renewed vigour, and on reaching the hill-crest, his eyes opened in wonderment. There on the hill was a brilliant profusion of flowers. They were Castilian roses of exquisite fragrance, fresh, and glittering with dewdrops. Not only were they in bloom out of season, but it would have been impossible for any flowers to grow in such a stony terrain, which could only yield thistles and cactus plants.

Spreading out his tilma like an apron, he filled it with the colourful blooms, and with great joy he descended to where the lady was waiting for him. She then gave a feminine touch to the miraculous bouquet and carefully rearranged the flowers with her own hands, saying as she did so: "My youngest and dearest son, these flowers are the proof, the sign that you are to take to the bishop... You will be my ambassador, fully worthy of my confidence... Tell him everything... Tell him once again all that you have seen and heard here..."

Juan Diego returned to the bishop's house, opened his folded tilma and exposed the bouquet of roses, arranged *à la Maria*. They were Spanish Castilian roses for the Spanish bishop. But they were not just ordinary roses. Warren H. Carroll is a PH.D. in history from Columbia University. He is the President and Professor of History at Christendom College, U.S.A., and a convert to Catholicism in 1968. In his well-researched book *Our Lady of Guadalupe and The Conquest of Darkness*, he wrote: "When he arrived again at the bishop's house, Juan Diego was kept waiting a long time by the bishop's attendants, who eventually insisted on seeing the roses, but when they tried to take some of them they could not, because they became 'not roses that they touched, but as if they were painted or embroidered.'" He was quoting Charles Wahlig's *Past, Present and Future of Juan Diego*. Indeed, they were mystical roses from the *Mystical Rose* herself!

But after the roses cascaded to the floor, another and greater shock was in store for Bishop Zumarraga. There upon the tilma was a full portrait of the "Mother of the true God" as Juan Diego had seen her. All the people in the room fell to their knees. Full of awe, the bishop, weeping and sorrowful, begged her forgiveness for not having complied with her wishes. It was Tuesday, December 12, 1531. Two weeks later, a triumphant procession of Aztecs followed by Franciscan and Dominican missionaries, carried the sacred image to a small makeshift chapel on Tepeyac hill, singing exultantly: "The Virgin is one of us! Our Sovereign Lady is one of us!" They learned this from Juan.

Chapter 11

What the Tilma Said to the Aztecs

Aztec writing was a combination of several systems and the most elementary was the pictograph, so that if, for example, a writer wished to indicate a house, he drew a conventional picture of a house, and for concepts difficult to express by simple pictures, the Aztecs used an ideographic system. For instance, the verb "to speak" was shown as a scroll emerging from the individual's lips. "To speak harshly" was shown as a scroll with thorns on it, and "to speak softly" was expressed by a feather scroll. And so, the "painting" on Juan Diego's tilma was much more than a mere portrait. It was a pictograph which the Aztecs were able to read and understand.

A Woman Clothed with the Sun

The full length of the image was four feet eight inches (the Aztecs were a medium-height people). The Virgin of Guadalupe was surrounded by numerous rays of the sun. Indeed, she was as bright as the sun. Her most beautiful and serene face, olive in complexion, was serious, yet her expression was ever so tender, so amiable, so noble. Her head was slightly inclined to the right, her eyes cast down in an expression of humility. Her mantle was turquoise blue, edged in gold, and there were many golden stars, sprinkled seemingly randomly on it. It reached down to her feet and fitted well on her head, but fully revealed her face and the front of her black hair. She was a beautiful figure of purity and a mirror of modesty.

Turquoise, rose, and gold were considered sacred by the Aztecs and were colours of royalty, therefore, Juan Diego knew that she was a queen. She was standing on the moon, and the stars on her gown told them that she was a "celestial queen." Yet she could not be a goddess since her hands were joined in prayer, obviously to One greater than she.

The gown beneath her mantle was rose in colour and was embroidered with various flowers of different sizes, all with gilt edges. Like the mantle, it, too, fell to her feet. Under her gown she wore a soft white inner garment, barely seen, and closely fitting her wrists and the nape of her neck. In the center of the golden neckline of her gown hung a brooch with a black Cross. It was identical to the Cross on the banner and helmets of the Spanish conquerors, telling them that her religion was that of the Spaniards.

Standing on the Moon

The portrait was first seen on December 12, 1531. It was the winter solstice (a time in the year when the sun is at its greatest distance south of the equator and when it enters the sign of Capricorn) and at that time the moon in the sky was a crescent moon. The Virgin of Tepeyac stood on a crescent moon. The moon for the Aztecs was also a symbol of the earth, and so, it was a depiction of the Woman of the Apocalypse: "Now a great sign appeared in heaven: a woman clothed with the sun, standing on the moon..." (Revelation 12:1). It was a crescent moon. It was the dark side of the moon. In other words, it was that segment of the moon which does not reflect the light of the sun. In short, this was the woman who would crush the head of the serpent (Genesis 3:15).

Pregnant yet Virgin

The sash around her waist was blue and the tassels on it signified to the Aztecs that she was pregnant. At the same time, let us recall that she identified herself to Juan

Diego as "the perfect and perpetual Virgin Mary." Pregnant, yet perpetually a virgin? This would not have been so strange to the Aztecs as they were taught about the legend of their sun god Huitzilopochtil and his mother Coatlicue. The legend said that one day the goddess Coatlicue was sweeping the shrine at the mountain top when she was miraculously impregnated by a ball of feathers that fell from the sky, the result of which was the supernatural conception of Huitzilopochtli.

The Golden Shoe

Her left knee was flexed in a posture of walking, but only one foot was seen in the portrait. It was her right foot in a golden shoe. Now, according to the research of Duran, as recorded in Townsend's *The Aztecs*, when a new king or *tlotoani* was initiated into office, a crown of stones, all worked in gold, was placed upon his head during the investiture and the coronation. He was shod with golden sandals and clad with a precious mantle of henequen-like fiber, all gilded and painted with elegant pictures. And so, the Virgin was seen wearing a golden shoe on the tilma. It was one more sign of her royalty.

The Flowers on Her Gown

The flowers on her gown were also very meaningful. To the Aztecs, flowers were considered to be the "embodiment of God and earth." They mirrored the beauty of God and His creation. In fact, flowers were of such importance to the Aztecs that there was a special "god of flowers," Xochipilli, the flower prince. His image was studded with flowers in the shape of what appears, in my opinion, to be marigold flowers.

There were several multi-petalled flowers on her gown. They also seem to me to be marigold flowers, called in Mexico "Aztec marigold" or *cempoalxochitl*. It means "flower of many petals." The leaves also vary in size and form; some may be heart-shaped like the ones on her gown. The Oxford Dictionary speaks of the marigold as "golden or bright yellow flowers" (Middle English for *Mary* probably the Virgin + dialect *gold*). In addition, the marigold was associated with lineage and constituted a sign of office and rank. The flower also symbolized fertility and rulership. In this respect, the Virgin was pregnant and was also a queen! Moreover, during the coronation of the *huey tlatoni* (the king), marigold flowers were also worn as garlands on the women.

The Young Boy on the Tilma

There have been several interpretations of the "young boy" under the image of the Virgin, and whose body is seen only down to his chest. This, in my opinion, was solely an artistic necessity so that the image would be properly proportioned, thus giving preeminence to the queen. There are those who interpret him as being an angel and some go as far as to identify him as the Archangel Michael. However, the concept of angels was not known to the Aztecs at that time, and I believe that it is much more likely that this "young boy" is meant to be a representation of Juan Diego. In other words, it was "little Juanito," who was given the privilege of bearing the heavenly queen, just as the Aztec king was borne on a litter by his subjects.

The robe of the young boy was red with a golden collar. He was bedecked with eagle wings of long feathered plumage of green, white, and red (which are the national colours of Mexico). This depiction of the young boy's outfit was very similar to the feather outfit of the Aztec eagle-warrior, except that the tip of the feathers of the latter were pointed upwards. But Juan was a different type of eagle warrior (his original name was Cuahatlatozin or "He who speaks like an eagle"). He was a warrior of Mary.

The Burden Bearer

According to one Mexican author, Miguel Guadalupe, during his conversation with the "lady" on Tepeyac hill on December 9, 1531, Juan described himself to her thus: "I am a *mecapalli* (a burden bearer), a *cacaxtli* (a back frame). I am a *cola* (a tail), I am an *alla* (a wing), a man of no importance. I myself need to be led, to be carried on someone's back." Now, in those days, although the Aztecs were advanced in their knowledge of astronomy and many other sciences and arts, they had not as yet invented the wheel, and lowly Indians were used as vehicles to carry loads and people on their backs. I, therefore, believe that the humble Juan Diego was literally a burden bearer.

And so, Her Majesty portrayed him as her *mecapalli* and *cacaxtli*. Little Juan Diegoito is seen on the tilma with one hand holding the *cola* or the tail of her mantle, and the

66

other, the *alla* or the wing of her gown. He was carrying the queen as if on a litter. Note also that whereas her gown and its shadowing are depicted as being a soft material and the impression of her bent left knee is clearly seen through it, the lower end of her gown is folded like a stiff cuff, seemingly unyielding enough to act as a "litter."

The Portrait and Columbus' Ships

As Miguel Guadalupe cleverly observed, when we consider the names of Columbus' three Spanish ships the Pinta, the Niña and the Santa Maria, we note a hidden providence with respect to the miraculous image of *Our Lady of Guadalupe*. The Spanish word "Pinta" is a derivative of the verb "pintar," meaning "to paint." "Niña" means "Young girl," and "Santa Maria" is "Holy Mary." The Santa Maria was the flagship. In short, Mary led the way. The first island discovery was named El Salvador (The Saviour). It was a symbolic depiction of "to Jesus through Mary."

And so, I have attempted to interpret in some detail the meaning of the pictograph on Juan Diego's tilma. But what does science have to say about this tilma?

Our Lady of Guadalupe of Mexico

The hand of Rembrandt   The hand of God

68

A depiction of the miracle of the roses
on Tepeyac hill

The Aztec burden bearer

A sculpture of an Aztec warrior found by archeologists

Chapter 12

The Verdict of Science

The image was "painted" on the tilma of Juan Diego which was made of ayate fibre, derived from the threads of the maguey cactus plant. The life span of the ayate fibre is approximately 20 years, yet, to the wonderment of all artists and scientists, the tilma still shows no sign of decay after over 465 years. Under high magnification it also shows no detectable sign of fading or cracking, an inexplicable and unprecedented phenomenon after so many years.

Fibers from the tilma were sent to the 1938 Nobel Prize winner Richard Kuhn, then Director of the Chemistry Department of the Kaiser Wilhelm Institution (now the Max Planck Institute). He found that the chemicals used to colour the tilma were neither animal, vegetable, nor mineral dyes, and were unknown to science.

Yet another factor pointing to the supernatural origin and protection of the sacred tilma has been its miraculous preservation, in spite of several disasters that had threatened it over the centuries. In 1791, for example, a workman accidentally spilled some nitric acid on the tilma. It left only a barely discernible mark on the fibre. Then, on November 14, 1921, a powerful time bomb was concealed in a large vase of flowers under the tilma. It was during the period of the anti-Catholic despotic rule of Plutarco

Calles. The bomb exploded causing serious damage to the sanctuary, even twisting a sturdy iron crucifix on the altar to an arc of thirty degrees or so, but when the cloud of smoke and dust was lifted, the miraculous tilma was seen to be completely unscathed, and the thin protective glass covering it at that time was not even cracked. This twisted iron crucifix can still be seen in a glass cabinet in the basilica for all pilgrims and researchers to see.

That the sacred tilma is a "painting" was rejected in 1946 when a microscopic examination revealed that there were no brush strokes, and to date, the image has consistently defied an exact reproduction, whether by brush or camera. In 1954, Francisco Ribera also performed exhaustive studies on the tilma and concluded that he could find "no brush strokes." Indeed, in his book *The Wonder of Guadalupe*, Francis Johnston quotes the great Mexican painter Ibarra: "No painter has ever been found capable of sketching or copying *Our Lady of Guadalupe*... Its singular uniqueness proves the picture to be the invention, not of a human artist, but of the Almighty."

Now, infrared photography can unmask such things as brush strokes and expose the existence of any preliminary drawing underneath, an essential prerequisite for nearly all paintings at that time. In May 1979, Professor Phillip Callahan of the University of Florida, considered to be a world authority on infrared radiation, and Professor Jodi Smith of Pensacola, Florida, a Methodist and Professor of Philosophy and Religion, using infrared photography, found no evidence of brush strokes nor any preliminary artist's drawing under the picture.

Powerful lenses also revealed the astonishing fact that the coarse weave of the tilma had been deliberately used in a precise manner to give depth to the face of the image. Scientists believe that it is impossible that any human painter could have used a tilma with the imperfections of its weave so precisely positioned as to accentuate the shadows and the highlights in order to convey such realism. Indeed, a Painters' Commission, established to examine the tilma, concluded: "It is humanly impossible for any artist to paint or produce a work so excellent on something so coarse as is the tilma on which appears the divine picture."

Examinations done in 1951 by a draughtsman, J. Carlos Chavaz, using a powerful magnifying glass, and in 1956 by Dr. Rafael Lavoignet, an ophthalmologist, using an ophthalmoscope, showed that a human bust was seen in the cornea of the eyes. It was as though a man, who was facing the Blessed Virgin in the room with Bishop Zumarraga, was reflected in the cornea of her eyes. In fact, the cornea is a clear transparent tissue which truly acts as a mirror and reflects a luminous image. This reflection was later identified to be Juan Diego from an old contemporary painting of him. More recently, however, macrophotography and digitized computer amplification have astonishingly found a total of twelve persons imprinted in the eyes of the Virgin of Guadalupe (Miguel Guadalupe, *The Seven Veils of Our Lady of Guadalupe*, 1995).

Dr. Enrique Graue, Director of the Ophthalmology Hospital, Nuestra Señora de la Luz, in Mexico City, had this to say: "I was dumbfounded. The eyes displayed depth and curvature and reflected light exactly like living eyes. In the eyes of the image were reflected twelve people who were present in the courtyard on the day Juan Diego opened his cloak, and the amazing fact is that the same figures appeared in both eyes at precisely the positions expected by the law of optics and twin-eyed physiology." And as Dr. Charles Wahlig, an optometrist in Mexico, stated: "It was as though it were part of a plan to represent the portrait of Our Lady to all living in our era as being a scientifically validated supernatural phenomenon."

But science was to be humbled even further. The stars seen on the Virgin's mantle corresponded exactly to part of the constellation of stars in the sky that day. This inspired intuition of Fr. Mario Sanchez was arduously researched by Dr. J. Canto Ylla and Dr. Armando Garcia de Leon of the National University of Mexico, who showed that the winter solstice, normally due to occur on December 22, happened to occur at 10:40 a.m. local time (90 West of Greenwich) on Tuesday, December 12, 1531, the exact day and perhaps the exact time of the actual miracle on the tilma in the presence of Bishop Juan Zumarraga. It was the sky of the winter solstice at 19 degrees latitude, the geographical correspondent of present-day Mexico City. When the image was inverted with respect to the star map, it was then that the mind-boggling correlation was found.

As Bishop Renfrew of Scotland once said: "These mysteries level us all, the brainy and the brainless, for they save us from self-esteem and pride." And as Professor Phillip Callahan conceded: "It may seem strange for a scientist to say this, but as far as I am concerned, the original picture is miraculous. Studying the image was the most moving experience of my life. Just getting that close, I got the same strange feeling that others had, who worked on the Shroud of Turin. I believe in logical explanations up to a point. But there is no logical explanation for life. You break life down into atoms, but what comes after that? Even Einstein said: 'God.'"

This then is the verdict of science. To me, the "painting" on the tilma is the world's greatest work of art and far surpasses in beauty and artistry, in tenderness and perfection, all other great paintings. It is God's "Mona Lisa." It is the only Marian shrine where the Virgin has left a lasting testimony of her presence and no critic of the authenticity of the apparitions in Guadalupe is worthy of an audience unless he can successfully refute the scientific evidence cited above. But, he could not possibly do so! The Virgin is "one of us" and she did appear in Guadalupe, Mexico, in 1531.

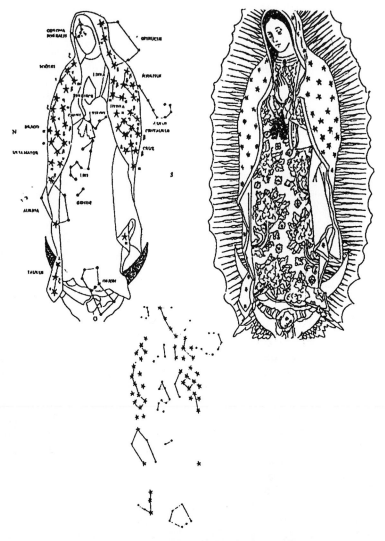

The winter solstice on December 12, 1531

Chapter 13

Why Guadalupe?

B ishop Zumarraga soon began to consider the erection of a suitable shrine on Tepeyac hill in compliance with the Virgin's request. Already numerous Aztec pilgrims were climbing the slopes to pray at the site of the apparitions and a temporary chapel was built without delay until such time as a permanent edifice could be constructed. The bishop then placed Juan Diego in charge of the chapel, to which a room was added for his accommodation.

Juan settled down at Tepeyac and devoted the rest of his life to the custody of the new shrine and to propagating the story of the apparitions. He laid great stress on the significance of the fact that "*the Mother of the true God*" had chosen to come to the previous site of the temple of the pagan mother-goddess Tonantzin, which the Spaniards had since destroyed. Moreover, the fact that she said to Juan Diego: "Am I not here, I who am your Mother?" made such an impact on the Aztecs that, for years after the apparition, they still referred to the sacred image as Tonantzin ("Our Mother") and Teonantzin ("Mother of God").

According to Francis Johnston in his well-researched book *The Wonder of Guadalupe*, many Aztecs had initially resisted the advances of the missionaries since, among other things, embracing Christianity would have entailed the abandonment of polygamy. However, as the cult of *Our Lady of Guadalupe* began to spread throughout the country, increasing numbers of Aztecs of all ages and classes queued for baptism. The trickle of conversions soon became a flood, and in a few years there were over eight million Aztec converts following the apparition.

No doubt, Juan Diego played a major role. He was the ideal evangelist, for not only was he a Christian convert but he spoke the Nahuatl language, repeating the story over and over again, thousands and thousands of times until everyone knew it very well. It is said by one researcher, Helen Behren, that when the Indians eventually presented themselves to the missionaries, "they had already been converted by Juan Diego."

Meanwhile, Juan remained in Tepeyac, living a life of great austerity and humility in his hermitage on the hill. The sacred image was enthroned over a tiny altar and he was the devoted custodian. He could thus be likened to the Hebrew high priest guarding the *Ark of the Covenant* in the Holy of Holies in Solomon's Temple.

Juan Diego died on May 30, 1548. He was 74 years old, and according to tradition, the Queen of heaven, his mother, who had once called him "dearest of my sons," appeared once more and consoled him on his death bed. The term of office of the "Ambassador" had come to an end. Juan's room in the chapel then became a baptistry and the commemorative plaque which was placed on the wall simply read: "In this place, *Our Lady of Guadalupe* appeared to an Indian named Juan Diego, who is buried in this church"—a humble epitaph for a humble son of a humble Queen.

Bishop Zumarraga died just three days after Juan Diego. Several years later, in 1570, the Archbishop of Mexico ordered a copy of the tilma to be painted and sent to King Phillip II of Spain. The king gave it to Admiral Andrea Doria, where it was placed in the cabin of his flagship during the Battle of Lepanto in 1573. It was a battle of decisive importance in safeguarding Christian Europe from invasion by the Islamic Turks and it was the occasion when Pope Pius V rallied all Christendom in Europe to pray the Rosary for victory. Against all odds, the battle was miraculously won and after remaining in the Doria family for several centuries, this replica of the tilma was eventually donated in 1811 to the shrine of *Our Lady of Guadalupe* at San Stefano d'Aveto in Italy, where it remains an object of veneration to this day.

During the ensuing decades, the little chapel at Tepeyac underwent several structural changes and renovations and the fabric of the sacred image remained exposed on a damp stone wall by the altar, where it was touched and kissed by literally millions of ardent pilgrims, without incurring the slightest damage. In 1622, the chapel was further extended to become a fair-sized church.

However, with the passage of time and the increasing number of pilgrims, the people of Mexico felt once again that the existing shrine at Tepeyac hill was too small and they were determined to erect a magnificent basilica for the Virgin. Nothing was too much for Her Majesty. The foundation stone of the new basilica was laid in 1695, and on April 30, 1709, there was a most impressive ceremony for the installation of the sacred image in its new home at the bottom of the hill. It was the most magnificent church in the Western Hemisphere.

As the centuries rolled by, the old basilica eventually began to tilt after the lakes surrounding Mexico City were drained as the city grew, and a larger and more modern building was in the hands of the architects. On October 12, 1976, the imposing new Basilica of *Our Lady of Guadalupe*, a modern circular edifice, was sufficiently completed to enable the sacred image from the old baroque shrine (which is still left tilting on the sinking ground) to be transferred to its new home.

In 1754, Pope Benedict XIV declared December 12 a holy day of obligation in Mexico, and decreed that *Our Lady of Guadalupe* be honoured as Patroness and Protectress of Mexico. Referring to the portrait on the tilma, he quoted from Psalm 147: "To no other nation has such a favour been done." October 12, 1895 was the date of the first coronation of the sacred image by Pope Leo XIII. It was on the feast of El Pilar (*Our Lady of the Pillar*), the greatest Marian feast in Spain which celebrates the apparition of the Virgin in Saragossa to St. James in 40 AD.

In 1945, once more on October 12, Pope Pius XII proclaimed *Our Lady of Guadalupe*, Patroness of both continents (North and South America). Paul VI, another great Marian Pope, was not to be outdone. On May 31, 1966, he sent a most beautiful golden rose to Her Majesty which is kept in the Basilica of *Our Lady of Guadalupe*.

But one of the greatest days in the history of Guadalupe was in 1979 when, about four months after his election, Pope John Paul II, the pilgrim Pope, personally visited the shrine. It was proper papal protocol that his first pilgrimage outside of Italy should be to the first shrine of Her Majesty in the New World, an event which occurred in 1531, hundreds of years before Lourdes and Fatima.

John Paul II beatified Juan Diego on September 8, 1992. It was the feast of the *Nativity of the Blessed Virgin Mary* and she must have been very happy over this recognition of her ambassador, her "poor little Indian." Indeed, it may be said that it was her birthday gift from John Paul II and today Guadalupe is the greatest Marian shrine in the whole world, visited annually by up to 20 million pilgrims, many more than visit St. Peter's or Lourdes yearly.

But why the name "Guadalupe?" It is said that the Virgin had told Juan Diego's uncle Juan Bernardino that she should be called *Santa Maria de Guadalupe*. However, there is a counterclaim by many that the Virgin may not have said "Guadalupe," since it was not an Aztec word. They believe that the word "Guadalupe" stemmed from a phonetic misinterpretation of the Nahuatl word "Coatlaxopuh," meaning, "She who crushes the stone serpent" and which sounds like the word "Guadalupe," the famous shrine of Mary in Spain. However, I do not share this opinion. Historical records are said to reveal that Queen Isabella gave her consent to Columbus' voyage on condition that his voyage be under the auspices of none other than *Our Lady of Guadalupe* of Spain. Columbus not only consented, but changed the name of his flag ship to "Santa Maria."

The statue of *Our Lady of Guadalupe*, carved of Oriental stained wood, was given by Pope Gregory the Great (590–604 AD) to Bishop Leander of Seville. It was lost for 600 years but was 'miraculously' in perfect condition when it was found 600 years later. A chapel was later built by order of King Alfonso XI, and the statue was enthroned therein. It was named "Guadalupe," the name of the village near the place of discovery. According to Joan Carrol in her book *Miraculous Images Of Our Lady*, the faithful always maintained that the image was a symbol of the Virgin's royal maternity, since the statue holds in its left hand the Child Jesus, while the right hand clasps a scepter. Royal maternity! The image of Our Lady of Guadalupe on Juan Diego's tilma was that of a queen. She was pregnant!

The popularity of the shrine was at its highest during the time of Columbus, who reportedly carried a replica of the statue with him. Furthermore, it is said that he prayed at the shrine before making his historic voyage and that upon discovering the West Indian island of Karukere on

November 4, 1493, he renamed it "Guadalupe" in honour of the Blessed Virgin. It is now named 'Guadeloupe' since the French colonization.

The ship's records also showed that the crew sang hymns to the Blessed Virgin every evening and that the first official words spoken in San Salvador after they erected the Cross were: "Hail, Holy Queen, Mother of Mercy..." It was the *Salve Regina.* And so, it is my viewpoint that the Virgin did say "Guadalupe," deliberately referring to her shrine in Spain and that it was her intention that Catholic Spain should bring Christianity and Marian devotion to Mexico. Indeed, Tenochtitlan's name was changed by the Spaniards to "New Spain."

80

Our Lady of Guadalupe of Spain

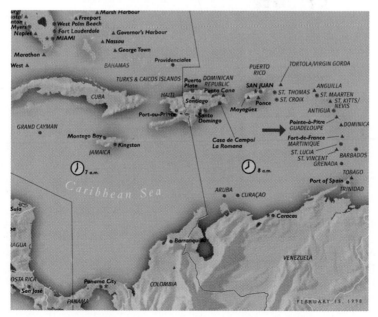

The island of Guadeloupe in the West Indies

Chapter 14

The Sacred Heart and Margaret Mary Alacoque
1673–1676

The sacrifices of the Aztec captives and the offering of their hearts to the sun god by the Aztec priest had come to an end after the Spanish conquest, and converts to Christianity accelerated after the apparition of the *"Mother of the true God"* to Juan Diego.

Meanwhile in France, the religious passions of the Catholics and Protestants were threatening to tear the country apart. In July 1593, King Henry IV of France rejected Protestantism and was received into the Catholic religion. However, it was with the hard-won knowledge that he would never be recognized as the true king of France without becoming a Catholic.

Several years later, in 1610, Francis de Sales founded the Order of the Visitation in Annecy, France, with the help of the Baroness de Chantal, now St. Jane Frances de Chantal. Francis did not want a strict enclosure of nuns, and allowed them to visit the sick and the poor, hence the name "Visitation" given to the new community. Notably, the Visitation Order had for its crest the hearts of Jesus and Mary united together.

Soon, postulants came in large numbers and the grain of mustard seed grew into a large tree. In 1613, the first daughter-house of Annecy was founded in Lyons, and in 1618, in an attempt to convert Protestants in the area to the Catholic faith, Fr. DeBarry, a Jesuit, asked the Superior of the Visitation Order in Lyons to establish a foundation in Paray le Monial. Fifty-three years later, in 1671, Margaret Mary Alacoque, the future saint of Paray, entered the convent. It was this nun who eventually became the great apostle of the devotion to the Sacred Heart of Jesus.

Now, symbolically, the organ of love is the heart. This tireless pump, about the size of a clenched fist, and weighing only slightly more than half a pound, unceasingly beats more than 2.5 billion times in seventy years. In the Bible, the heart is also used to symbolize what is deepest in a man, what is most profound in him, what is most personal and intimate in him—his innermost thoughts, desires, feelings, and wishes.

In fact, it is the word which has been used most often in the Bible. It occurs about seven hundred times, even more than the word "God" or "Lord." The first time that it is mentioned is in Genesis 6:5-6: "The Lord saw that the wickedness of man was great on the earth... It grieved him to his heart." The last time is in the Book of Revelation 2:23: "It is I who searched the heart and loins and give each of you what your behaviour deserves."

But just as the physical heart is an "untiring" organ incessantly beating during life, the heart of Jesus as an object of devotion is a reflection of His untiring and indefatigable love for men. It is His physical heart which during His mortal life did beat in His breast, and still beats in His glorified body in heaven.

In her diary, Margaret Mary Alacoque records as many as thirty accounts of apparitions and revelations which she received from Jesus during 1673–1676. But, as is the case with many favoured visionaries, she endured great suffering because of her singular privilege, including the pain of the questioning of her authenticity. She even experienced long spells of spiritual dryness. But her spiritual suffering far surpassed all the pain of opposition. However, as promised by Jesus, she received great support and consolation from the Jesuit, Fr. Claude de la Colombière, who was canonized in 1992.

The first message she received was on December 27, 1673. Significantly, it was at that time the feast of St. John the Evangelist, often referred to as the "Apostle of love." It was then that Jesus first spoke of His great love: "*My divine heart is so inflamed with love for men, and for you in particular, that it is unable any longer to contain within itself the flames of its burning love. It needs to spread them abroad through you and so manifest itself to them, in order to enrich them with the precious treasures which this heart contains, graces of holiness and salvation, which are necessary to withdraw them from the abyss of perdition. I have chosen you, in spite of your unworthiness and lack of knowledge, for the accomplishment of this great design, so that it may better appear that it has been done by myself.*"

Thereupon He asked her for her heart which she then implored Him to take. In a mystical transaction of which only God is capable, He took it from her breast and planted it into His own heart. Then, withdrawing it as a burning flame in the form of a heart, He replaced it in her breast. A surgeon may well say that it was the first heart transplant! But it was just the antithesis to the crude surgical incision of the Aztec priest who savagely tore out his victim's heart in the satanic rite to the pagan god in Tenochtitlan.

There was visible proof that this mystical transaction had taken place, for there was a closed wound in Margaret's side, which opened on the first Friday of each month. This extraordinary physical evidence left no doubt as to the authenticity of her revelations. Of relevant interest, many historians believe that the Crucifixion took place on the first Friday of the month of April.

The "Great Revelation," as it is called, was the occasion in June, 1675, when Jesus appeared in all His splendour and said to her: "*Behold this heart which has so much love for men, that it spared nothing, even to exhausting and consuming itself, in order to give them testimony of its love. If only they would give me some return for my love, I would think but little of all that I have done for them and would wish, were it possible, to suffer still more. But in return I mostly receive only ingratitude, through their irreverence and sacrileges, and through the coldness and scorn that they have for me in the sacrament of Love.*"

Then He added: "*But what gives me most sorrow is that there are hearts consecrated to me who treat me thus. Do you at least console me by making up for the ingratitude as far as you can. Therefore, I ask of you that the first Friday after the octave of Corpus Christi be set apart for a special feast in honour of my heart, by communicating on that day, and by making solemn reparation to it by a solemn act, in order to make amends for the indignities which it has received during the time it has been exposed on the altars. I promise you that my heart shall expand itself in abundance the influence of its divine love upon those who shall thus honour it, and cause it to be honoured."*

Indeed, with regard to the ingratitude which men shower on Our Lord, one would think that ingratitude was one of the commandments! As St. Peter Julian Eymard (1811–1868) once wrote: "Our coldness, our ingratitude are Satan's triumph over God."

Not unexpectedly, and understandably so, her mission was not an easy task, particularly in the Europe of that time which was experiencing the repercussions of the Reformation. However, she was consoled by Jesus who assured her: *"I will reign through my heart despite Satan and his agents...in spite of all those who oppose this devotion."* Indeed, by the time of Margaret Mary's death on October 17, 1690, the devotion was spread worldwide, particularly by the Jesuits.

However, the forces of darkness were certainly not inactive, and in the following century, St. Peter Julian Eymard, known as the disciple of the Eucharist, lamented: "In many countries the feast of Corpus Christi has been suppressed. Jesus Christ cannot show himself in public. Men are ashamed of him. *Non novi hominem!* 'I know not the man!'" He then continued: "...A cloud of desolation has passed over Europe. Jesus has been driven out of his temples and profaned on his altars. It is alarming today to see Jesus Eucharist abandoned and left alone, absolutely alone, in so many cities. And in our rural districts, the churches are closed for fear of thieves and lack of worshippers... Catholics have much reason to blush for their lack of respect in Our Lord's presence. Enter a synagogue; if you speak or do not behave properly, you are expelled. Before entering a mosque, you are requested to take off your shoes. They all have nothing real in their temples. In spite of that, their respect far surpasses ours..." This was said around 1860! Undoubtedly, this is as true today as it was then, if not more so.

She gave birth to Him, and it is to Mary, therefore, that we owe the heart of Jesus. Thanks to her consent, He took upon Himself a human heart. There was no human father in that conception. But at the same time, it is to Jesus that we owe the heart of Mary. And so, in a sense, the two hearts are one heart and they are one in their love; *unus in suis amore.*

Our Lady of the Sacred Heart

Before the 13th century, I could find no trace of any special devotion to the heart of Mary as a symbol of her love and sorrows. In the 14th century, however, St. Bridget of Sweden had a great devotion to the heart of Mary and it is claimed that she learned from Jesus Himself about the loving identity and *oneness* of the two hearts: "*The heart of my mother*," he said to her, "*was like mine. Therefore, I confirm that we worked together for the salvation of mankind. I, by the sufferings endured in my body, she by the sorrows of the love in her heart.*" In other words, salvation came from the love and suffering of Jesus Christ intimately joined with the love and sorrows of His mother. He was referring to the Redeemer and the *Coredemptrix*.

Francis de Sales, in his famous treatise *On the Love of God*, elaborated on Mary's love: "Since eternal love is the most ardent of all forms of love, and is an indefatigable and insatiable love, how much must it have been in the heart of such a mother and for the heart of such a Son?" But, whereas Francis promoted the devotion to the heart of Mary in 1622, it is to St. John Eudes (1601–1680) that is due the honour of having given the decisive impulse to the devotion in 1680. Through his preaching, he propagated it throughout France and wrote his great work *The Admirable Heart of the Holy Mother of God*, a result of almost twenty years of study and research. This was completed on July 25, 1680, three weeks before he died. In fact, St. John Eudes wrote many books on the heart of Jesus and Mary. He never used the plural, as he preached that "*the heart of Jesus and Mary is one.*"

As we shall see later, several events gave added impulse to the popularity of the devotion to the heart of Mary. One was the apparition of the Blessed Virgin to St. Catherine Labouré, a Sister of Charity, in the Rue du Bac on November 27, 1830, in Paris. It was the occasion of the origin of the *Medal of the Immaculate Conception*, colloquially called the Miraculous Medal. It was on that occasion that the Blessed Virgin showed Catherine the vision of a medal, bearing on one side a representation of herself with the inscription: "O Mary, conceived without sin, pray for us who have recourse to thee," and on the other side, a large **M** surmounted by a Cross, beneath which were two hearts close to each other; one was surrounded with a crown of thorns and the other was pierced by a sword. It was an image of the Sacred Heart of Jesus and the Sorrowful and Immaculate Heart of Mary.

But there was yet another devotion to emanate from France in the 19th century. It started in Issoudun, France, situated in the heart of France and in the diocese of Bourges. This region had suffered deeply from the effects of the French Revolution, then came on October 14, 1854, a young priest called Jules Chevalier, who at that time was thirty years of age and only three years a priest.

Aware of the great indifference and unbelief which were rooted in all social classes in France since the years of the Revolution, Fr. Jules sought a remedy for this and thought that he could find it only in the "heart of Jesus." Reflecting on the grave problems in France, he felt another inspiration, namely, to found a Congregation of Missionaries who would bring back the faith to dechristianized France. Coincidentally, the Missionaries of the Sacred Heart was born eventually on December 8, 1854, the same day that Pope Pius IX proclaimed the dogma of *the Immaculate Conception.* Its aim was to have a special devotion to the Sacred Heart of Jesus and to give to Mary a very special honour.

Through this love for the heart of Jesus, Fr. Chevalier made a pilgrimage to the tomb of St. Margaret Mary Alacoque in Paray le Monial and prayed to St. Margaret to obtain for him a deep love for the heart of Jesus.

Three years later, in May 1867, he was moved to promote a new title for the Virgin, namely, *Our Lady of the Sacred Heart.* He felt that Mary would truly receive new glory and would bring all men to the heart of Jesus. He wrote: "Pronouncing the name of *Our Lady of the Sacred Heart,* we would thank and glorify God for having chosen Mary among all creatures to form in her virginal womb the adorable heart of Jesus... We ask this compassionate Virgin to lead us to the heart of Jesus."

Pope Puis IX was very pleased with what Fr. Chevalier was doing and he even expressed a desire to be a member of the Congregation of Missionaries, adding to his signature: "Pius IX, who desires to love the Blessed Virgin Mary." Within a short time, this new title given to the Virgin aroused the same enthusiasm in Italy as it did in France and elsewhere, and by 1972, there were at least forty-five Italian bishops who recommended the devotion to *Our Lady of the Sacred Heart.*

The Sacred Heart appears to St. Margaret Alacoque

The incorrupt body of St. Margaret Alacoque
in Paray le Monial

Our Lady of the Sacred Heart

Mother of Divine Love

Chapter 15

The Origin of the French Revolution
1789—1830

The seventeenth and eighteenth centuries are often called the Age of Enlightenment. One aspect of the "Enlightenment" was the advance of science and a new view of the order of the universe. Nicholas Copernicus (1473–1543) proposed that the sun is the center of the planetary system and the earth revolves around it. Although this overturned the traditional view of the Greek astronomer Ptolemy, Galileo Galilei (1564–1642) demonstrated through observation that Copernicus was correct. The modern science of astronomy was born.

Not long afterwards, others, such as the Englishmen Sir Isaac Newton and Robert Boyle, were pioneering the new sciences of physics and chemistry. These sciences not only revolutionized the understanding of the physical universe, but they also gave birth to the application of science to technology which led to an industrial revolution in England and eventually in all Europe. Progress based on science and technology became a major focus of Western society.

Another aspect of the Enlightenment was a new approach to philosophy based solely on human reason.

The Frenchman René Descartes (1596–1650) taught that every concept should be questioned or doubted until reason could prove its validity. Rationalism was the name given to this philosophy, emphasizing the ability of human reason to determine the truth of all things.

Faith of any sort, including Christian faith, was rejected as a component of philosophy. For many of these philosophers, people who based their lives on beliefs primarily on faith were unenlightened or living in the past age of human development. Christian religion was not abandoned as such but relegated to the private sphere of one's personal life. There was the exclusion of religion from the public life of society, including politics, philosophy, science, literature, the arts, and the public media. This secularization process is still going on, but it found its roots in the so called "Enlightenment" of the seventeenth and eighteenth centuries.

According to Alan Schreck in *The Compact History Of The Catholic Church*, the people of Europe were tired of wars, and philosophers argued that the only basis for restoring unity and peace to Europe was to find a common basis of agreement either in a "reasonable religion," purged of all divisive dogmas, or in reason itself. Indeed, Immanuel Kant (1724–1804) wrote: "Have courage to use your own reason. That is the motto of enlightenment." Some philosophers, such as the German Gottfried Leibniz (1647–1716), were also optimistic about the prospect of discovering a "rational religion" that would again unify Europe.

The Englishman Lord Herbert presented five propositions that would be the substance of a new religion of reason, popularly known as Deism. According to the Deists, God established the laws of the universe and set it in motion like a clockmaker winding up his clock, but after that, He does not interfere directly in the affairs of His creation. Of course, this directly contradicts Christian belief in the divine revelation of miracles worked by God and the Incarnation of God in Jesus Christ. Yet, some Deists claimed that they were still Christians!

Other philosophers launched a direct attack against the Catholic Church and Christianity. The French satirist and philosopher Voltaire (1694–1778), more than any other person, made it fashionable to be a mocker of Christianity in a cynical way, especially regarding the Catholic Church. As a result of Voltaire's approach, a gentlemen's society of free thinkers, called Freemasons, arose in France and even attracted some priests. Unfortunately, there were no Catholics in France or elsewhere who had the charisma or ability to successfully criticize Voltaire, Diderot, and later philosophers who were undermining Christianity.

Eventually, however, while rationalism was making inroads into theology, there was also an upsurge in religious life, with the practices of Eucharistic adoration, devotions to the Child Jesus, the Sacred Heart, and to Mary. The Catholic Church was beginning to appear strong and influential again in the eighteenth century. However, Catholic Reformation had largely died away by 1750, and the internal weaknesses caused by the Enlightenment and the rise of nationalism began to be manifested in this century.

Two revolutions profoundly transformed Europe in the years from 1789 to 1850: the great French Revolution and the Industrial Revolution. The Industrial Revolution was a process of change from an agrarian to an industrial economy. It began in England about the year 1800 and was caused by the discovery of electricity and petroleum, and the invention of the steam engine and machines for mass production. Religion had no place. It was seen by many as an outworn superstition which impeded the attainment of universal happiness for mankind. Faith must give place to science.

French society was officially divided, as it had been for centuries, into three Estates. The clergy constituted the First Estate, the nobility the Second, and the Third Estate included all the rest of the population, an estimated eighty percent. By the end of the eighteenth century these class tensions were aggravated by rising food prices and a marked growth in the peasant population. The French Revolution then exploded in Paris on July 14, 1789 with the storming of the Bastille, which was the symbol of royal tyranny. Its purpose was to get rid of the *ancien regime*, the regime of the nobility and the clergy, and to establish a new social order based on *liberty, fraternity,* and *equality.*

Charles Dickens (1812–1870), in his literary classic *A Tale of Two Cities,* wrote a social commentary of the times. His "Tale" and its people were based closely on his research on Thomas Carlyle's *French Revolution* and other literature of the time. He began his novel describing *The Period*: "It was the best of times, it was the worst of times; it was the age of wisdom, it was the age of foolishness; it was the epoch of belief, it was the epoch of incredulity; it was the season of light, it was the season of darkness; it was the spring of hope, it was the winter of despair..."

It was during this period that the Bourbon King Louis XVI was eventually overthrown and guillotined by the Revolutionary Government, and in 1793, it began to dechristianize France and set up a new religion. All Christian holidays, including Sundays, were suppressed and Catholic churches were turned into "Temples of Reason." The orgy of blasphemy was crowned on November 10, 1793, by placing a girl of ill repute on the altar of Notre Dame Cathedral in Paris, and worshipping her as the Goddess of Reason.

On December 2, 1804, Napoleon Bonaparte crowned himself emperor of France in a magnificent ceremony in Notre Dame Cathedral in Paris. Pope Pius VII had been persuaded to conduct the ceremony, but Napoleon arrogantly placed two laurel wreaths on his own head and then crowned his wife, Josephine. The Pope, the head of Catholic Christendom, had traveled from Rome to bless a self-made emperor. It was in this fashion that the monarchy returned to France, almost eleven years after Louis XVI's gory head was shown to the crowd in the Place de la Revolution.

Napoleon invaded Russia in 1812. However, the greatest army he ever led crumbled into ruins in the snows of the Russian winter. He was defeated by "General Frost." In fact, Tchaikovsky's 1812 *Overture* was written to commemorate Napoleon's famous retreat in the winter of that year. The music opens with a Russian hymn *God, Preserve Thy Pope*, and the greater part of the work is devoted to a description of the battle, its progress indicated by the relative dominance of music based on the French and Russian (Czarist) national tunes.

Nationalism in Europe was given an immense fillip by the Napoleonic era, and historians commonly use the term "Restoration" to characterize that era in European history following the downfall of the Napoleonic empire. The period's end is placed at 1830 in some nations, and at 1848 in others. Hereditary monarchy was regarded by the then statesmen as one of the fundamental institutions to be restored, for they felt that it was the only form of government capable of showing continuity and stability in human affairs. Indeed, in almost every country in Europe, the Restoration brought a revival in the status of the nobility, and the Bourbon monarchy was restored in France in 1814.

Along with the monarchy and the aristocracy, the Church regained its influence during the Restoration. Indeed, by 1815, it was viewed as one of the bulwarks of the social order and once more enjoyed a position of favour with European rulers. However, many resented legislation which favoured the nobility and the clergy, and some of the bitterest political struggles in 1830 took place in France. It was against this background that the Blessed Virgin appeared in Paris in that year.

Chapter 16

The Medal of
the Immaculate Conception
1830

The first of the apparitions of the Blessed Virgin in modern times took place in France in the 19th century. On a midsummer's night on July 18, 1830, significantly, the eve of the feast of St. Vincent de Paul, the Blessed Virgin came to a humble and narrow back street in Paris called the Rue du Bac. It was in the chapel of the Mother House of the Sisters of Charity, founded by St. Vincent de Paul, that she appeared to a nun, Sr. Catherine Labouré.

The Virgin descended the altar steps and then seated herself in a chair. Catherine rushed to her and knelt, resting her hands on the Virgin's lap. It felt solid! She said to Catherine: "My child, the good God wishes to charge you with a mission." She went on to tell of God's plan for her, to warn her of the trials that would come upon her, and to show her how she should bear them: "You will be given graces. Have confidence. You will see certain things. Give account of what you see and hear... The times are very evil and many sorrows will come upon France."

She then began to specify the sorrows and dangers. She spoke in broken sentences, in halting phrases, fighting back the tears that glistened her eyes: "There will be victims... There will be victims among the clergy of Paris. Monseigneur the Archbishop..." She could not finish because of weeping. "My child, the Cross will be treated with contempt. They will hurl it to the ground. They will open up again the side of Our Lord. The streets will stream with blood. Monseigneur the Archbishop will be stripped of his garments..." Once more she could not go on. Tears choked her voice, and her lovely face was contorted in sorrow. She could only add: "My child, the whole world will be in sadness." Catherine understood that these events would all come to pass within forty years, that is, by 1870.

All too soon, the prophecies began to be fulfilled. On July 27, 1830, just one week later, a revolution erupted in fury in Paris. It was the beginning of a series of woes for France and the world. Barricades were thrown across the narrow streets. Boulevards and alleys echoed to the rattle of musketry and drunken cries of looting, burning mobs. The Bourbon Charles X had brought it upon himself. He had failed to measure the temper of the times. He failed to realize how very deeply the ideas of the French Revolution of 1789 had taken root in France. His futile attempt to restore the "divine right" monarchy of Louis XIV came to a precipitous climax on July 26, 1830, when he dissolved the Chamber and muzzled the press. The constitutional monarchists, the middle-class shopkeepers, the extreme radicals, and the Parisian mob then all united against him.

In the three days of that July Revolution, Charles X was toppled from his throne. The Church, however, did prosper under Charles. Indeed, "For Throne and Altar" had been the motto of his reign, but with his fall, the Church felt the wrath of his enemies. Bishops, priests, and members of religious orders, were imprisoned, beaten, or killed. Godlessness ran wild, desecrating churches, pulling down statues, trampling the Cross underfoot, as prophesied by the Blessed Virgin to Catherine.

As the Virgin also foretold, Monseigneur Hyacinth de Quélen, Archbishop of Paris, had much to suffer at the hands of his people when they revolted against the oppression of selfish rulers. Although he was considered a true father of his people and shepherd of his flock, like many other innocent men, he was forced to suffer with the guilty. In fact, he had to flee twice for his life. However, he was saved from the maelstrom and spirited away by the quick thinking of one of the Sisters of Charity in the Rue du Bac. Soon afterwards, Charles X escaped to England and Louis Phillipe, who belonged to a younger branch of the Bourbon family, was accepted as his successor on August 7, 1830.

When peace and stability were restored in France, a general election was held and Prince Louis Napoleon, nephew of Napoleon Bonaparte, who had returned from exile in England, gained the most votes and was elected President of the Second French Republic (1848–1871) in December, 1848. He soon persuaded the senate to vote for a Bonapartist restoration and was then proclaimed as Napoleon III on December 2, 1853 (Napoleon's only son, the Duke of Reichstadt, had died in 1832, and the Bonapartists had regarded him as Napoleon II). France's Second Republic was thus transformed into an Empire.

Louis Napoleon was the nephew of Napoleon I. His father was Louis Bonaparte, Napoleon I's third brother. His mother was Hortense, the daughter of Napoleon I's wife, Empress Josephine, by her first husband. His great appeal unquestionably lay in the magic of his name. Like his famous uncle before him, he saw himself as an instrument of destiny, and he was determined to make himself the master of France.

However, all his life he was an intriguer rather than a governor. Also described by some historians as a plotter rather than an administrator, this was the impression he made upon those who came to know him. Prince Albert of Piedmont called him "an amateur," and Lord Palmerston of England considered that "his mind was full of schemes as a warren is full of rabbits." Victor Hugo also dismissed him as *Napoleon le petit.*" Within two years of the proclamation of the Second Empire, Napoleon III was involved in the Crimean War of 1854–1856, and France lost about 95,000 men.

On November 27, 1830, Her Majesty appeared once more in the convent. Catherine saw the Virgin standing on a globe with her foot on the head of a green and yellow serpent. Her eyes were lifted to heaven, and in her hands, which were raised to the level of her heart, she held a globe surmounted by a Cross.

She said to Catherine: "The globe which you see represents the whole world, especially France, and each person in particular." All at once, the globe disappeared and she lowered her hands. Each finger was then seen to be covered with three rings set with precious stones, from which sprang rays of such brilliance that her feet and robe were then no longer visible. "Behold," she said, "the symbol of the graces which I bestow on those who ask for them." Then she added: "The gems from which rays do not fall are the graces for which souls forget to ask."

An oval frame then appeared around the image, and forming a semicircle inside the frame were the words written in gold: "O Mary, conceived without sin, pray for us who have recourse to thee." She then requested: "Have a medal coined upon this model. Those who wear it around their necks will receive great graces." The frame then appeared to turn around and Catherine saw a large **M** surmounted by a Cross and beneath were two hearts, one with a crown of thorns and the other pierced by a sword. Around the edge of the frame were twelve equally-spaced stars.

Now, because the other side of the frame was surrounded by the words: "O Mary conceived without sin...," Catherine asked "the apparition" what should be written on the back of the medal. "The **M** and two hearts say enough," was the Queen's gentle response"—a response which, in my opinion, has not been given enough emphasis and publicity. Indeed, it says more than enough. In fact, all the mysteries of Mary are found in the symbols on the *Medal of the Immaculate Conception*, as it was originally called, but because of the miraculous favours which many people experienced in those early days of its distribution, it was popularly called the Miraculous Medal. However, by so calling it, we obscure the true theological significance and message of the medal. It is the *Medal of the Immaculate Conception*!

The Virgin, standing on the globe with her foot on the serpent's head, signified the new Eve, who will crush the serpent's head as promised by God in Genesis 3:15: "*I will put enmity between you and the woman, between your seed and her seed; (s)he will crush your head.*" He was referring to the second Eve, who gave birth to the second Adam, the Redeemer of mankind.

The rays emanating from the rings on her fingers signified that she is also the *Mediatrix of Graces*. Grace, as Augustine of Hippo put it, is a supernatural gift of God bestowed upon us through the merits of Jesus Christ for our salvation, and all graces came to mankind through the suffering and resurrection of Christ. But as St. Pius X added: "It cannot be denied that the dispensing of these gifts, graces, belong by strict and proper right to Christ for they are the exclusive fruit of his death. Nevertheless, by this union in sorrow and suffering which existed between the mother, who at the foot of the Cross of Redemption died a martyr's death without dying, and the Son, it has been allowed the august Virgin to be the most powerful *Mediatrix* between Jesus and man."

There were three rings on each of her fingers. In biblical history the ring is a symbol of delegated authority, and so, the Pharaoh gave it to Joseph (Genesis 41:42), and the father placed the ring on the finger of the prodigal son on his return to the household (Luke 15:22). She is the daughter of the Father, the mother of the Son, and bride of the Holy Spirit, and the three rings on each finger reflected her relationship with the Trinity, from whom she received her authority as the *Mediatrix of Graces*.

In confirmation of this, Fr. Stefano Gobbi, founder of the Marian Movement of Priests, testified that these were the words of the Blessed Virgin given to him in an inner locution. Referring to the title *"Mediatrix of Graces,"* she is alleged to have said: "This is a natural consequence of my divine motherhood. In my virginal womb this first act of my mediation was carried out. As your mother, I was the means chosen by Jesus, and through me, all of you may reach him. My task is that of distributing grace to all of my children, according to the particular needs of each one, which the mother is very good at knowing." I need to stress, however, that it is my interpretation that the graces are also distributed by her Son.

"O Mary conceived without sin" was this time the *written* confirmation of her *Immaculate Conception*, which she had *inferred* when she first appeared in Guadalupe on December 9, 1531, at that time the feast of the *Immaculate Conception*. See how she unfolds it all to us! Now, *Immaculate Conception* means that from the very first moment of her own conception, through the anticipated merits of her divine Son, she was preserved by special grace from the stain of original sin. This Immaculate Queen was the singular exception to the universal law for, as I said, how could God abide in a womb which was once under the dominion of Satan, even for a moment. The law was not made for her.

"Pray for us who have recourse to thee" signified that she is our *Advocate* with the Son, and pleads to him on our behalf. Indeed, her first public manifestation of such a role was during the wedding feast in Cana (John 2:1-11). In the Old Testament, the queen mother brought the petition needs of the people of Israel to the throne of her son, the king (1 Kings 2;19). In like manner, the Church teaches that Mary is the new Queen Mother and Advocate in the Kingdom of her Son, and brings the petitions of her children to the throne of Christ the King.

The **M** surmounted by a Cross, all in one unit, signified the *Redeemer* on the Cross and the *Coredemptrix* beneath the Cross. St. Therese of Lisieux once said that there can be no great love on earth without great sorrow. Indeed, the two hearts which were side by side below the **M** were not only symbols of their love but also of their sorrow. One was seen with a crown of thorns, the other was pierced by a sword.

The twelve stars signified that she was the Woman of the Apocalypse, the Woman of the end times: "The temple of God in heaven opened and the ark of the covenant could be seen inside it...then a great sign appeared in heaven, a woman clothed with the sun, standing on the moon and with twelve stars on her head for a crown" (Rev 11:19; 12:1). The twelve stars represented the twelve tribes of Israel and the twelve apostles, for she is the Woman of Israel and the Queen of the apostles, a title bestowed upon her in the Litany of Loreto.

Undoubtedly, John was not seeing the ancient *Ark of the Covenant* of Mosaic times. That has since been lost somewhere on earth. He was obviously referring to the living *Ark of the Covenant*, Mary, the womb of the Mediator of the new Covenant. He was referring to Her Majesty, the Tabernacle of the Most High. And just as the ancient *Ark of the Covenant* contained the two tablets of stone with the Ten Commandments, she contained in her blessed womb, not the tables of the Law, but the Lawgiver Himself. And just as the ancient Ark was made of incorruptible acacia wood, so is Her Majesty incorrupt, incorruptible, and immaculate, for she is the *Immaculate Conception*.

This Miraculous Medal, the Medal of the Immaculate Conception, is therefore inextricably linked to the proposed dogma of the Coredemptrix, Mediatrix, and Advocate. And so, the mother of the second Person of the Blessed Trinity has herself a trinity of gifts and titles.

On February 11, 1836, a canonical inquiry into Catherine's apparitions was conducted. The findings of the inquiry completely validated Catherine. The court extolled her character and virtue, and placed wholehearted credence in her visions. Overjoyed at the findings of the court,

Archbishop de Quélen gave free rein to his lifelong devotion to *the Immaculate Conception* of the Blessed Virgin. In a series of pastoral letters he promoted this devotion to his people, and consecrated himself and his diocese to *the Immaculate Conception*. Indeed, through his efforts, the invocation "Queen conceived without sin" was inserted in the Litany of Loreto, and in 1854, Pope Pius IX declared belief in Mary's *Immaculate Conception* a dogma of the Catholic faith.

Catherine had fulfilled her mission as best as she could. Hundreds of millions of medals have been stamped and diffused since the Virgin designed it and showed it to her. "Have a medal coined upon this model," she said. "Those who wear it around their necks will receive great graces." It was the promise of *the Immaculate Conception*.

When her body was exhumed in 1933, 57 years after her death, a gasp of astonishment ran through the crowd. Catherine's body was as fresh and serene as the day she was buried. Her skin had not darkened in the least. Her eyes were as intensely blue as ever, and her arms and legs were as supple as if she were merely asleep. Her preserved remains can be seen today in the chapel of the Rue du Bac in Paris.

The Virgin appears to St. Catherine Labouré

The Medal of the Immaculate Conception

The incorrupt body of St. Catherine Labouré
in the chapel of the Rue du Bac

Chapter 17

The Mother of
Sorrows in La Salette
1846

O f all the Marian apparitions of the last two centuries, the apparition at La Salette is certainly not the most celebrated, as the fame of Lourdes and Fatima has overshadowed it. Commenting on it, however, Giovanni Ricciardi wrote in the magazine *Thirty Days*: "The La Salette apparition is unique, not only in terms of the message Our Lady gave to the two French shepherds, but also because of the very special human circumstances of the visionaries and the endless polemics over the "secret" the Virgin left with them that became the object of a whole series of Vatican interventions in the years that followed. It is a complex affair..."

This complex affair began on a September day in 1846, when the Blessed Virgin appeared to two children, Melanie Calvat and Maximin Giraud, in the French village of La Salette in the Alpine mountains, and expressed her sorrow that people had drifted away from prayer and the sacraments. It was on a Saturday, the eve of the feast of *Our Lady of Sorrows* (celebrated at that time on September 20), that she appeared to the children, weeping copiously.

Maximin's innocently mischievous nature was characteristically manifested during the vision. As the two children, fearful and overawed, approached the "beautiful lady," Maximin reassured his companion: "Keep your stick ready. I will keep mine ready, too, and if she does anything to us, I will hit her with it!" However, they soon realized that there was no need to be fearful of her. It was, indeed, Mary.

The two youngsters, aged 15 and 11, had not been given any kind of education, religious or otherwise, at the time, and what struck people most was that neither of them had normally much of a memory, but when they had to relate the message of the apparition, they were able to repeat it word for word. Moreover, at no time did they contradict each other, even when they were questioned individually.

Describing the appearance of the weeping Madonna, whom they saw on September 19, Melanie wrote: "Her face was majestic and imposing. She compelled a respectful fear but at the same time as Her Majesty compelled respect, it was mingled with love and she drew me to her. Her gaze was soft and penetrating... The holy Virgin was all beauty and all love, and in her finery as in her person, everything radiated the majesty, the splendour, the magnificence of a queen beyond compare. Her voice was soft, enchanting, ravishing, and warming to the heart. It soothed and softened. The clothing of the most holy Virgin was silver-white and quite brilliant, and the crown of roses which she wore upon her head was so beautiful that it defies imagination. It formed a most beautiful diadem which shone brighter than the earth's sun."

Now, the word Rosary is derived from the Latin *rosarium,* meaning a crown of roses or sometimes, a garden of roses. In short, the colourful crown of roses on her head which is depicted in drawings with the colours red, yellow, and white, was the first of her apparitions with a "Rosary." It was represented by a crown of roses on her head!

Melanie continued: "She had a most pretty Cross hanging around her neck. It was Our Lord on the Cross. At one end of the Cross there was a hammer and at the other end, a pair of pincers. The Christ was flesh-coloured and at times He appeared to be dead. His head was bent forward and His body seemed to give way as if about to fall, had He not been held back by the nails which held Him to the Cross. At other times, He appeared to be alive. His head was then erect, His eyes open, and He seemed to be on the Cross on His own accord. At times, too, He appeared to speak and He seemed to show that He was on the Cross for our sake, out of love for us, to draw us to His love.

"The holy Virgin was crying nearly the whole time that she was speaking to me. Her tears flowed gently, one by one, down to her knees, then like sparks of light they disappeared. These tears of our sweet mother, far from lessening her air of majesty of a queen, seemed on the contrary to embellish her, to make her more beautiful, more powerful, more filled with love, more maternal, more ravishing. Is it possible to see a mother cry, and such a mother, without doing anything possible to comfort her and change her grief into joy?"

Here now are some extracts of the messages and prophecies given to Melanie by the Virgin of La Salette and which were eventually published in their entirety in 1879: "If my people do not wish to submit themselves, I am forced to let go of the hand of my Son. It is already so heavy and weighs me down so much, I can no longer keep hold of it." She then lamented the lack of observation of Sunday as the day of the Lord, and also the frequent swearing, using the name of her Son: "When you found bad potatoes, you swore oaths and included the name of my Son... They will continue to go bad." She prophesied the potato famine and that by Christmas (1846) it would reach its peak. It did.

Indeed, apart from the famine in France and Central Europe, the fungus *Phytophthora infestans* also caused a potato blight in nearby Ireland. It was a famine which killed over a million people and drove as many more to emigrate to America. She also added: "The nuts will go bad, the grapes will rot." They did.

She proceeded to scold and warn of impending disasters if mankind continued on the path of godlessness: "Melanie, what I am going to tell you now will not always be a secret. You will make it public in 1858. The priests, ministers of my Son, the priests, by their wicked lives, by their irreverence and their impiety in the celebration of the holy mysteries, by their love of money, their love of honours and pleasures, they have become cesspools of impurity. Yes, the priests are asking for vengeance, and vengeance is hanging over their heads. Woe to the priests and to those dedicated to God who by their unfaithfulness and their wicked lives are crucifying my Son again! There are no more generous souls; there is no one left worthy of offering a stainless sacrifice to the Eternal for the sake of the world...

"May the Vicar of my Son, Pope Pius IX, never leave Rome again after 1859. May he, however, be steadfast and noble. May he fight with the weapons of faith and love. I will be at his side. May he be on his guard against Napoleon III. He is a man of duplicity, and when he wishes to make himself pope as well as emperor, God will soon withdraw from him. He is the eagle who, always wanting to rise higher, will fall on the sword he wished to use, to force his people to be raised up...

"France, Italy, Spain, and England will be at war. Blood will flow in the streets. Frenchmen will fight Frenchmen, Italians will fight Italians. A general war will follow which will be appalling, and for a time God will cease to remember France and Italy because the Gospel of Jesus Christ has been forgotten...

"There will be a series of wars until the last war, which will then be fought by the ten kings of the Antichrist, all of whom will have one and the same plan and will be the only rulers of the world, but before this comes to pass, there will be a kind of false peace in the world. People will think of nothing but amusement and the wicked will give themselves over to all kinds of sins. But the children of the holy Church, the children of the faith, my true followers, they will grow in their love for God and in all the virtues most precious to me..."

She also made somewhat complicated revelations about the Antichrist and his rise and fall. Then she said: "And then water and fire will purge the earth and consume all the works of men's pride and all will be renewed. God will be served and glorified." Finally, she ended her long discourse, saying: "And so, my children, you will pass this on to all my people."

Following the news of the apparition, more and more pilgrims began visiting the site of the apparition and drinking from a well which had started to gush without ceasing since the vision happened, and which was bringing about numerous inexplicable cures. Christian practices were again being observed by most of the people in the area and by the end of that first year, twenty-one miraculous healings through the intercession of the Virgin of La Salette had been certified.

At first, the Church was very prudent. The Bishop of Grenoble then formed two commissions to study the phenomenon and he appointed two trusted ecclesiastics,

Fr. Orcel and Fr. Rousselot, to carry out an inquiry and draw up a report, which was submitted to the bishop at the end of 1847. At the end of the inquiry, Rousselot and Orcel declared in favour of the apparition's supernatural nature, and after an extensive examination, the commissions reached the same conclusion, despite the opposition of the lay press and some of the French clergy.

Eventually, after five years of careful examination of the facts, the Church authorized the cult of Our Lady of La Salette. The decree of the Church's approval of the event of La Salette as supernatural is dated September 19, 1851, the fifth anniversary of the apparition. It states: "We judge that the apparition of the Blessed Virgin to two shepherds on September 19, 1846 on a mountain in the Alps in the parish of La Salette...shows all the signs of the truth and the faithful have grounds for believing it indubitable and certain."

But Melanie's messages, their prophetic language, the heart-rending appeal to the clergy, and the announcements of fearful punishments were found to be very severe and accounted for the clear hostility of the French church hierarchy against her. Indeed, she would say later on in one of her letters to a Mr. Schmid on June 25, 1897: "There are people who believe it is their duty to see that Almighty God does not say things that are too severe or too shocking when he lowers himself to talk to his creatures. They allow the Good Lord to complain about farmers working on Sunday, blasphemy or the omission of Mass...but they do not allow him to complain about the clergy..."

However, in a letter written to her parish priest Fr. Mesiere on December 14, 1904, she showered her personal blessing on the clergy. Melanie Calvat died on the following day, December 15, 1904. She had lived a long life of sorrow, frustrations, disbelief in her messages, and humiliations. Yet she persevered. What is probably little known is that at certain times, particularly on Fridays and during Lent, she experienced the stigmata of Christ and bled profusely, but in her humility she begged that the pain remain just as violent but that the outward signs should disappear. These mysterious wounds, however, reopened a number of times and some of her last letters carried the stains to prove it. This was confirmed by Abbé Combe, her spiritual director, who was also the parish priest for the last years of her life.

Some time after her death, permission was given for the disinterment of her virginal corpse. Fourteen years later, on December 19, 1918, the ceremony took place at 3:00 a.m. The body was found to be intact. After Mass, the precious remains were removed to a small room adjoining the garden before being placed in a magnificent tomb in the middle of the church which was dedicated to *the Immaculate Conception*. Indeed, it was appropriate for her incorrupt earthly remains to rest in the bosom of the Church of *the Immaculate Conception*.

On the occasion of the 150th anniversary of the *Mother of Sorrows'* appearance at La Salette, Pope John Paul II issued this address from the Vatican on May 6, 1996: "This year the diocese of Grenoble, the Missionaries of La Salette and many faithful throughout the world will celebrate the one hundred and fiftieth anniversary of the apparition of the Blessed Virgin on this peak of the Alps in which her message has been unceasingly heralded... In this place, Mary, a mother filled with love, manifested her sadness in the face of the moral evil of humanity. Her tears help us understand the painful gravity of sin, the denial of God, as well as the passionate fidelity that her Son, the Redeemer, maintains towards her children, despite a love wounded and rejected.

"The message of La Salette was given to two young shepherds at a time of great suffering. People were scourged by famine, subjected to many injustices, and indifference and hostility towards the Gospel message worsened. As she appeared bearing on her breast the likeness of her crucified Son, Our Lady showed herself associated with the work of salvation, experiencing compassion for the trials of her children, suffering when they strayed from the Church of Christ as they forgot or rejected the presence of God in their lives, the blessedness of his name.

"The wide diffusion of the event of La Salette bears convincing attestation that the message of Mary is not contained within the suffering expressed by her tears. The Virgin begs us to regain our spiritual composure. She invites us to penance, to perseverance in prayer, and especially to fidelity in the observance of Sunday. Through the witness of the two children, she asks us that her message be made known to all her people... Mary is as present in the Church today as she was on the day of the Cross, on the day of the Resurrection, and the day of Pentecost. She will never abandon the people created in the image and the likeness of God. May she lead all the nations of the earth to her Son."

A large church has been built on the site of the apparition and attracts thousands of pilgrims every year. My first visit to the shrine was in August, 1993. From ground level it took my taxi about twenty minutes to course the long and winding uphill road to reach the shrine high on the alpine hills.

La Salette was the first major apparition in which the *Mother of God* openly shed tears copiously. They were ordinary tears, not tears of blood. These were to be shed many years later. Let us now see in the following chapters how the prophecies of the Virgin of La Salette, the *Mother of Sorrows*, came to pass over the years, albeit not yet fully fulfilled at the time of writing.

110

Maximin and Melanie

Melanie Calvat in later years

The Virgin of La Salette
as she appeared to the visionaries

The Mother of Sorrows weeps copiously

112

The church in La Salette built at a level of 1400 meters

The author stands at the original site of the apparition

Chapter 18

Pope Pius IX
1846 – 1878

B ut who is this Pope, Pius IX, about whom the *Mother of Sorrows* spoke so endearingly in La Salette? I researched him. Pope Leo XII was succeeded by Cardinal Francisco Castiglione, an elderly stopgap, who took the name of Pius VIII. However, he only reigned for eighteen months. Cardinal Giovanni Maria Mastai-Ferretti, Bishop of Imola, was elected Pope on July 17, 1846, two months before the Virgin appeared in La Salette. He took the name of Pius IX in memory of Pius VII, the heroic opponent of Napoleon, whom he excommunicated in 1809.

It was then that Napoleon I scornfully remarked: "Does the Pope think that the weapons will fall from the hands of my soldiers because of his excommunication?" A few years later, an army report from the icy plains of Russia read: "The weapons are falling from the hands of our soldiers." The report was referring to the ignominious defeat of the French army when Napoleon was forced to a disgraceful retreat from Moscow. The year was 1812.

In 1846, there was a call for Italian unity and Pius IX faced the real prospect of the Papal States being swept away altogether by a tidal wave of Italian nationalism. During his reign there were anticlerical excesses, including the murder of priests. The continuing threat to the Church's position was illustrated by the long and harrowing tussle in which he was engaged after 1850 with the government of Piedmont, which had adopted a provocatively anticlerical policy involving, among other measures, the suppression of many religious orders.

The Virgin of La Salette had told Melanie: "May the Vicar of my Son, Pius IX, never leave Rome again *after* 1859." Indeed, he did leave Rome in 1849 and returned on April 12, 1850. Plans were being made by King Emmanuel of Piedmont to unite the whole of Italy under himself with Rome as capital, but the French had come to the help of the Pope. They marched into Rome and reestablished order in the city. But Napoleon was two-faced and his real motive was his desire to win the support of French Catholics for his regime.

Let us remember that the Virgin had described Napoleon III as "a man of duplicity." Indeed, Pius' most delicate problem was his relationship with the French, to whom he owed his restoration and on whom his security depended. At the same time, he was resolved not to allow Napoleon III to lay down conditions as the price of the continued presence of his troops. He insisted on retaining sole authority in political as well as ecclesiastical matters.

1860 was a year of vast upheaval in Italy. The reasons for the Virgin's concern were now quite clear. The Piedmontes army hovered on the papal frontier and small revolutionary bands roamed the papal state. In 1861, Cavour made a speech recommending the advantages of "a free Church in a free State," that is, of a system under which the Pope would lay down his temporal power in return for strict safeguards for the Church's independence in the religious sphere.

However, Pius IX was deeply convinced that his spiritual and temporal powers were inseparable. He felt that he could not effectively fulfill his mission as Head of the Church unless he could at the same time act as an independent territorial sovereign. It was not enough for the Pope to be Bishop of Rome. In order to stand up to the world's pressures and to deal on equal terms with Napoleon III, he needed to have a temporal base of his own.

He also fought against false liberalism which threatened to destroy religion. In 1865, he compiled a list of modern "errors and false doctrines" to be condemned and refuted. The decision to make the list public seems to have been prompted by Pius' irritation with Napoleon's jibe that the

Papacy was not in step with the enlightened conceptions of the nineteenth century.

No less than eighty propositions, religious, philosophical, ethical, social, and political, were condemned outright, but they were all summed up by the eightieth proposition, which read: "The Roman Pontiff can and should reconcile and concern himself with progress, liberalism, and recent civilization." Inevitably, his list ran into a storm of criticism and alienated many whom it had been designed to rally.

Pio Nono, as he was sometimes lovingly called, summoned a General Vatican Council for 1869. It was to meet on December 8, *the feast of the Immaculate Conception*. It was attended by about seven hundred bishops drawn from all five continents. One of the main issues to be debated was the dogmatic definition of Papal Infallibility. However, there was a determined resistance from a minority. Those who were opposed to a dogmatic pronouncement did not necessarily reject infallibility as such; they questioned the wisdom of defining it publicly because it would excite objections from governments and lay opinion generally, and offend Christians of other denominations.

Eventually, on July 18, 1870, the formula to be voted on declared that the Roman Pontiff is infallible "when he speaks *ex cathedra*, that is, when in the exercise of his office as pastor and teacher of all Christians, he defines by virtue of his supreme apostolic authority, doctrine concerning faith and morals to be held by the universal Church." In the final reckoning, 533 bishops voted in favour and only two against. But they, too, eventually submitted. The Dogma of Infallibility received the Council's approval.

Three days after the adoption of the dogma, Napoleon declared war on Prussia, thus ensuring his own downfall. Immediately afterwards, Napoleon III, now a prisoner of the Prussians, the Italian government brusquely informed the Pope of its intention to send troops into the Patrimony. Soon afterwards his temporal power came to an end. The crisis that abolished papal sovereignty was played out at a dizzy speed. All of a sudden Pius found himself confined to the Vatican. By 1876, the country acquired a left-wing administration, headed by the Freemason Depretis, which was not only anticlerical but frankly antireligious, and the official Italian attitude towards the Holy See was changing from benevolence to nagging hostility.

Pius IX died on February 8, 1878. However, he left the Church in a far healthier condition than in the earlier half of the century, largely owing to his own courageous stands in matters of principle. He was succeeded by a 68 year-old aristocrat, Vincenzo Gioacchino Pecci, who reigned as Leo XIII (1878–1903).

Throughout this pontificate, left-wing governments under Depretis continued to harass the Holy See. They were egged on by Masonic and other anticlerical groups. The worst of these was a riot which interrupted the solemn transfer of the remains of Pius IX from St. Peter's to the Basilica of San Lorenzo Fuori le Mura. Stones and mud were hurled at the procession and priests were insulted or assaulted. A similar and perhaps more dangerous attack was launched against the Church's position in France and was sustained until, in the year of Pope Leo's death, it resulted in the separation of Church and State.

The 1848 Revolutions

But the Virgin's prophecies in the Rue du Bac concerning the woes for France were not fully fulfilled by the events of the 1830 Revolution, nor were they meant to be. Louis Philippe became bored with being a figurehead king and his Bourbon blood had begun to show in a series of high-handed actions that smacked of a return of absolutism, and so, on February 22, 1848, there erupted another very bloody Parisian battle. Louis Phillipe then abdicated on February 24 and fled to England, landing in New Haven under the name of Mr. Smith.

Food prices, particularly the price of bread, the staple diet of the lower classes, rose remarkably during 1847. It was the year after the Virgin's apparition in La Salette when she warned of famine and the potato blight. The crisis had its origin in low grain production in Britain and Europe in 1845 and 1846, and in the failure of the potato crop in Ireland. In France, where industrial expansion had not been accompanied by a corresponding development of new markets, this led to falling prices for manufactured goods, business failures, and widespread unemployment.

By 1848, the price of wheat had more than doubled, and as bread became dearer, the industrial depression grew worse. This was the case in the rest of Europe, but conditions in France were much worse. Rioters, waving red flags, appeared in the streets. However, the National

Guard, when it was called out, was reluctant to support the monarchy against the demonstrators and the violence of the mob increased.

Four months later, another bloody three days' battle was fought on June 24–26. Some 20,000 workers barricaded off the large industrial districts of Saint-Marcel and Saint-Antoine in Paris. The artist Meissonier wrote about how he "saw defenders shot down, hurled out of windows, the ground strewn with corpses, the earth red with blood..." Those three days of rioting in Paris had brought the monarchy to an end. The revolt was finally put down by General Louis Cavaignac, but not before Monseigneur Affré, the Archbishop of Paris, who had succeeded Archbishop de Quélen, died by an assassin's bullet on the barricades. The Virgin's prophecies were all coming to pass.

James Derum, in his book *Apostle in a Top Hat*, records the events leading to the death of the Archbishop in the uprising of 1848: "A sacrifice hastened the end of the fighting. The insurrectionists realized that the Archbishop had offered his life for peace, and the fact that he had been stricken in the cause of peace softened their hearts. Following his death, most of the insurgents fought with little heart for slaughter."

Unfortunately, events in Paris encouraged uprisings and demonstrations in other parts of Europe. Revolts broke out in Germany, Austria, and especially in Italy. Italians were fighting Italians, as the Blessed Virgin had predicted. There were rising food prices and increased unemployment. Papal finances could afford only a few public works to relieve this, and there was continuous unrest and outbreaks of violence during which the rioters shouted: "Death to the priests!" Soon afterwards, Pope Pius IX, dressed as a simple priest, left Rome and took refuge in a castle at Gaeta. He said that he had gone into exile "in order not to compromise our dignity or by our silence appear to approve the excesses that have taken place and might take place in Rome."

Pope Pius IX

Chapter 19

I Am The Immaculate Conception
1858

Following the apparitions of the Blessed Virgin to Catherine Labouré in 1830 and during the reign of Pius IX, an event of momentous importance in Church history took place. The year was 1858, two years after the end of the Crimean War. France was still in political and religious turmoil, and on February 11, the Blessed Virgin appeared in the little town of Lourdes. It was a few weeks after a bomb was thrown at the carriage of Napoleon III and his wife Eugenie, as they drove to the Opera House in Paris. Neither of them was hurt but eight bystanders were killed and up to one hundred injured.

Now, at the foot of the Pyrenees, on the banks of the Gave, the town of Lourdes lies where the mountains come down to meet the plain. As early as 56 BC, the Romans, realizing the strategic importance of the site, built the first fortress at the top of the limestone spur. From the 5th to the 7th centuries, the fortress was altered a number of times by different peoples—Vandals, Alans, Visigoths, Vascons, and Franks, who successfully invaded the area. Later, the town was occupied by the Saracens.

In 778 AD, the year of the Battle of Roncevalles, the Emperor Charlemagne besieged the fortress of Lourdes. As starvation threatened, an eagle fortuitously dropped a trout at the feet of the Saracen commander, Mirat. Cunningly, Mirat had the fish sent to Charlemagne to give him the impression that he still had plenty of food. Charlemagne was about to lift the siege when the Bishop of Le Puy, who was with him, had an inspired thought. Mirat should be asked to surrender, not to the Emperor, but to the Queen of Heaven. This was because the Koran speaks highly of Mary: "And remember the angels' words to Mary. They said: 'God has chosen you. He has made you pure and exalted you above womankind'" (Koran 3:40-45).

This idea appealed to the Saracen who laid down his arms at the feet of the statue of the Black Virgin of Le Puy. He was eventually baptized as Lores, and his name was given to the town, which in time became Lourdes. Since then, its coat of arms bears an eagle holding, not a snake, but a silver trout in its beak, an interesting difference from the Aztec coat of arms.

The Blessed Virgin chose the humble grotto of Massabielle near the river Gave to appear to a fourteen year-old peasant girl, Bernadette Soubirous, on the Thursday before the Mardi Gras. It was to be the first of eighteen apparitions which would end on July 16, 1858, significantly, the feast of *Our Lady of Mount Carmel*.

Bernadette was in the grotto collecting wood. A gust of wind was suddenly heard but not a leaf moved. Her attention was drawn to the cleft of the rock of Massabielle, from which hung the flexible and shaking branches of a wild rosebush. In fact, this spot was very reminiscent of the cleft in the rock fashioned into the sepulcher where Jesus was buried. The mystic Maria Valtorta described it in her diary *The Poem of the Man-God*: "Eventually they rolled the heavy sepulchral stone into its lodging. Some long branches of a ruffled rosebush hanging from the top of the grotto towards the ground seems to be knocking at the stone door. They seem to be weeping tears of blood as they shed their red petals, and their corollas lie along the dark stone." The revelance of this did not escape my attention.

Bernadette then saw a golden-coloured cloud which preceded a light. It was a light "more brilliant than the sun." In the midst of this supernatural light a young lady appeared in an instant—shades of Guadalupe! She seemed to come out of the depth of the niche cut into the rock. She was dressed in a white garment that also shone brilliantly, with a long white veil which, covering her head, came down over the shoulders. Her garment was gathered at the waist by a blue cincture fastened with one bow. Her feet, resting on a carpet of grass and twigs, were bare, but on each one there was a golden rose. This was the panorama which Bernadette experienced and never forgot up to the day she died.

J. B. Estrade, a government official, had faithfully recorded the actual words of Bernadette during her investigation by the French authorities in 1858: "Without thinking what I was doing, I took my Rosary in my hands and went on my knees. The lady made a sign of approval with her head and took into her hands a Rosary which hung on her right arm (In La Salette she wore a crown of roses). When I attempted to begin the Rosary and tried to lift my hand to my forehead, my arm remained paralyzed, and it was only after the lady had signed herself that I could do the same. The lady left me to pray all alone. She passed the beads of her Rosary between her fingers but she said nothing; only at the end of each decade did she say the 'Gloria' with me."

As has been observed by a few biographers of Bernadette's life, this last detail, which Bernadette in her simplicity could not have invented, reveals a deep theological truth. The *Gloria*, which is a hymn of praise to the Trinity is indeed the only part of the Rosary which is suitable to the Virgin. The *Our Father* is certainly not for one who had no need to pray for her daily bread. As for the *Hail Mary*, the angel's greeting, this could only be recited by Bernadette, as the apparition had no need to greet her own self.

On March 25, 1858, the sixteenth apparition, Bernadette asked the lady her name. She had previously done so on three occasions, but this time the Virgin, who until then had kept her hands joined together that day, opened her arms and lowered them, as she appeared on the *Medal of the Immaculate Conception*, thus causing her Rosary to slip down towards her wrists. Then she joined her hands again, brought them above her breast, raised her eyes to heaven in an expression of reverential gratitude and said: "*I am the Immaculate Conception.*" Then she smiled, spoke no more, and disappeared smiling. It was something to smile about!

It was in this cleft in the rock in Massabielle that the lady with the lovely face and sweet sounding voice made that historic announcement. The scene immediately brings to mind the words of the *Song of Songs 2:13-14*: "Arise my love, my beautiful one, and come! O my dove in the cleft of the rock, in the secret recesses of the cleft, let me see you, let me hear your voice, for your voice is sweet, and you are lovely." And so, the wise Virgin shows a cleft in the rock of Massabielle!

Now, she never said that she was "Our Lady of Lourdes." Neither did she say: "I am the result of an Immaculate Conception," nor "I am she who was conceived immaculately." She said: *"I am the Immaculate Conception."* As W. R. Ainsworth once said: "To those who have difficulty with this form of expression, it may well be said that it runs in the family, as it was her Son who said: *'I am the resurrection and the life'"* (John 11:25).

It was an identity which she had *hinted* in Guadalupe in 1531 when she appeared on the feast of *the Immaculate Conception,* and which she *wrote* on her *Medal of the Immaculate Conception* in the Rue du Bac, Paris, in 1830. But it was in Lourdes that she chose to *speak* to Bernadette the words which to this day reverberate throughout its hills and valleys: *"I am the Immaculate Conception."* It was on March 25, 1858. It was the feast of the Annunciation of the Lord when she accepted the invitation of Ambassador Gabriel to be the Mother of the Redeemer. But to be the Mother of the Redeemer, Mother of the Word, she had to be *the Immaculate Conception!*

On Monday July 16, 1858, the feast of *Our Lady of Mount Carmel,* the Blessed Virgin appeared to Bernadette for the last time. As we shall see later, this feast is of extreme importance. There was no spoken message. It was her eighteenth apparition to the little French girl. It was a silent farewell. Bernadette, when twenty-two years old, then disappeared into a life of silence and prayer on July 9, 1864, and she donned her nun's habit as Sr. Marie-Bernard of the Sisters of Charity of Nevers.

When, on July 19, 1870, France declared war on Prussia, the Mother Superior put her convent and her Sisters at the disposal of the Ministry of War and Sr. Marie-Bernard worked in the infirmary after it had been turned into a military hospital.

On April 16, 1879, at the age of thirty-five, Bernadette died after a long painful illness. Thirty years later, in 1909, as part of the procedure to canonize her, Pope Pius X instituted an enquiry into her "reputation of holiness." During the course of the enquiry on September 9, 1909, Bernadette's body was exhumed in the presence of the Bishop of Nevers, the Mother Superior of the convent, the civil authorities, and two forensic medical experts. Bernadette's body appeared to be intact!

In 1923, Pope Pius XI ordered a final examination of her body before declaring her "Blessed." On April 18, 1925, forty-six years after her death, Bernadette's body was exhumed once more. This time the autopsy revealed the perfect condition of her internal organs. The surgeon, Dr. Comte, noted, in particular, the astonishingly well-preserved state of her liver, which is the organ most subject to decay.

She was canonized in 1933 by Pope Pius XI. Over a hundred years after her death, Bernadette, looking healthier than many of us, lies in a glass casket in the chapel of St. Gildard's convent in Nevers. On three separate occasions, I visited the chapel and beheld this miracle which defies all scientific explanation. But the Virgin's apparitions in Lourdes were not to be the last of her apparitions in France during the nineteenth century.

Pope John Paul II praying at the grotto in Lourdes

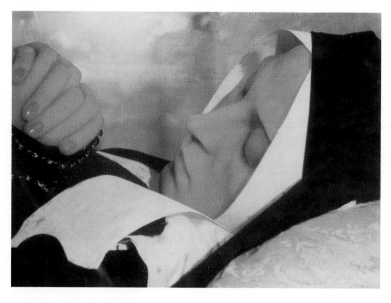

Incorrupt body of St. Bernadette in Nevers

Chapter 20

The Virgin Appears in Pontmain, France
1870–1871

"There will be a series of wars until the last war," the Virgin of La Salette had told the two little shepherds in 1846. Now, prior to 1870, Prussia was an independent power which, from a small duchy in the sixteenth century, rose to dominate the whole of central Europe and to become one of the most powerful empires of recent European history. In 1861, King William I (1797–1888) had appointed Otto von Bismarck to head the Ministry of Foreign Policy and obtain the submission of Parliament. Indeed, Bismarck, at the very beginning of his ministry, informed the Diet that "the question of the day was not to be decided by speeches and majority votes, but by blood and iron."

He then built up the Prussian economy and the military and financial power. From 1868 onwards, he set about to accomplish the unification of Germany, if necessary, in a war of all the German states against France, while Emperor Napoleon III sought, through military preparedness and alliances, to defeat Prussia and recover part of the Rhine frontier. Bismarck eventually provoked a conflict with France, and on July 19, 1870, the French were foolishly taunted to declare war on Prussia.

To Bismarck's great satisfaction, the south German states, regarding France as the aggressor, at once came to his support. It was the beginning of "a series of wars," as predicted by the Virgin. The Prussian army was superior to the French in almost every respect and the Germans won a decisive victory at the battle of Sedan on September 1–2, 1870. Napoleon was taken prisoner.

This unification of Germany ended centuries of disunity and division, and is regarded as one of the most significant events of the 19th century. German unity had been brought about by bringing all the separate states within Prussian control, for Prussia was greater in area and population than all the rest of the German empire together, and the Prussian capital, Berlin, was also the imperial capital. The German empire was, therefore, in reality a Prussian empire. It led to a complete change in the European "balance of power."

France of 1870–71 was a country that bothered little at that time with matters of the spirit and the churches were empty. However, Pontmain, a village of about 500 people, was a fortunate exception to the rule of religious indifference. Pontmain's people were farmers and devout believers. In 1870, when the Franco-Prussian War had begun, thirty-eight young men from Pontmain had been conscripted and were serving in the defense of their homeland. Their families and friends were desperate with fear and concern for them and for the nation.

On January 17, 1871, the Prussians were closing in on Laval, the capital of the region in which tiny Pontmain was situated. On that morning, even as the Prussian General Schmidt was leading his soldiers closer and closer, the parish priest of Pontmain, Abbé Michel Guèrin, was offering prayers of hope: "Let us add penance to our prayers," he said, "and then we may take courage... God will have pity on us; His mercy will surely come to us through Mary."

It was no more than eleven hours later that his words began to be fulfilled for Pontmain. It was a wintry day. About six o'clock in the evening and twenty feet above the roof tops, two children saw a beautiful lady with her hands stretched out in a gesture of welcome. She wore a blue dress studded with golden stars. This star-studded tunic without a belt fell straight down to her feet and barely covered her gold-ribboned slippers. She also wore a black veil which hid her hair and her ears, and at the back reached down to her waist. On her head was a plain crown widening towards the top. It was without decoration except for a red band almost midway around it. This is what the children, Eugène and Joseph Barbedette, saw. A little later, two other children, Françoise Richer and Jeanne-Marie Lebossé, also witnessed the apparition.

Around the upper half of her body were three white stars disposed in the shape of a triangle, one above her head and the other two to the right and left of her waist line. An oval frame of the same blue colour as her dress surrounded the vision. Inside the frame four candles stood on horizontal ledges, two at heart level and the other two around knee height. Then, from beneath the oval frame, the children saw a little star move from candle to candle, lighting them on the way before it rested in a position directly above the frame.

It seems to me that the four candles surrounding the vision can be interpreted as signifying that her Son, the Redeemer, is the "Light of the world," who lights the four corners of the globe and who, in what seems to be the darkest hour of night, brings light to a new dawn, and in what seems to be an hour of despair, turns it into a day of hope.

Little by little, the villagers gathered and they, too, saw the three stars, but not the Virgin. The parish priest invited the crowd to say the Rosary, and the Virgin's expression showed how attentive she was to the prayer. As the Rosary was completed, Abbé Guèrin began to recite the *Magnificat*. The old man's heart was full of emotion. Devotion to the *Mother of God* had been a passion all of his life. Soon, under her feet, a scroll unrolled, on which, one by one, gold letters slowly appeared. They were spelt out excitedly in a loud voice by the children and in the end, the sentence read: "But pray my children. God will answer you in a short while. My Son will respond to your prayers."

As the people rejoiced over this news, the Virgin smiled gloriously in response. A small red Cross then appeared over the lady's heart, and the vision grew larger in size as the prayers were being said. How significant! The stars on her gown seemed to multiply so fast that she seemed clothed in gold rather than navy blue. After a momentary silence the priest suggested that they sing the hymn "Mother of Hope." At the end of the hymn, the banner bearing the inscription vanished, and a large blood-red crucifix was then seen in front of the vision bearing the body of Christ of the same colour.

She held it in both hands, slightly tilted towards the children, and at the top of the Cross was an inscription in large red letters against a white background—**JESUS CHRIST**. She showed it to the children with a look of such deep sorrow that the children's faces suddenly became sad as they saw the sorrowful expression of the beautiful lady. The Blessed Virgin kept looking at the Cross of her Son.

Indeed, all his life Joseph Barbedette remembered that moment, as it made a deep impression on him. He wrote in his diary: "Her face was marked with a profound sorrow... The trembling of her lips at the corner of her mouth showed a deep feeling... Yet, no tears ran down her face... A few months later, I saw my own mother overwhelmed with grief when my father died. One knows how such a sight can affect the heart of a child. Nevertheless, I remembered thinking that my mother's sorrow was nothing in comparison with that of the Blessed Virgin. It was truly the Mother of Jesus at the foot of her Son's Cross."

The crowd prayed fervently and started to sing the hymn *Ave Maris Stella*. The blood-red crucifix then disappeared and the Virgin extended her hands again towards the people, and smiled ever so sweetly. At the same time, two small white crosses appeared on her shoulders. Once more her face lit up with joy and then the vision slowly vanished. It was almost 9 o'clock in the evening.

On the day after the vision, January 18, 1871, the relentless advance of the German troops which had reached the gates of Laval, suddenly stopped, and following instructions from higher authorities, General Schmidt and his German troops unexpectedly withdrew without fighting and abandoned the country. Eight days later, on January 28, Paris surrendered, the armistice was signed, the war was over, and the thirty eight soldiers who had been conscripted from the parish of Pontmain all returned home unscathed.

In gratitude, the prayers which the Virgin requested continued to grow in fervour and crowds from many miles around the village flocked to Pontmain. Many conversions followed and the parish church was no longer big enough to house the faithful. A huge basilica now stands in its place, and there some two hundred thousand pilgrims go each year to pray to *"Our Lady of Hope,"* the lady who came to save a little village which prayed and had *hope* in her. The Basilica was later called the Basilica of *Our Lady of Hope*.

As for the children, they were thoroughly examined by three doctors, who ruled out any question of hallucination and other neurotic factors to explain their testimony. It is all described in great detail in *Pontmain Histoire Authentique* by Fr. R. Laurentin and A. Durand. After an extensive enquiry, on February 2, 1872, Mgr. Wicart, Bishop of Laval, came to this decision: "We judge that the Immaculate Virgin Mary, Mother of God, truly appeared on the 17th January, 1871, to Eugène Barbedette, Joseph Barbedette, Françoise Richer, and Jeanne-Marie Lebossé, in the hamlet of Pontmain."

The Barbedette brothers became priests. Eugène was curate and then parish priest in the diocese of Laval. Joseph became an Oblate of Mary Immaculate, the order which had taken charge of the shrine, and Jeanne-Marie Lebossé became a nun with the Sisters of the Holy Family of Bordeaux. Francoise Richer lived a humble life as assistant teacher of junior children and later became priest's house keeper to Eugène Barbedette.

The Virgin appears in Pontmain

The visionaries of Pontmain

The Basilica of Our Lady of Hope

Our Lady of Hope

Chapter 21

After the Franco-Prussian War

Napoleon III was taken prisoner by the Prussians after
the Battle of Sedan. The Franco-Prussian War
brought the Second Empire to an end but
Napoleon's reputation suffered beyond his lifetime. Karl
Marx once said that the comparison between the First and
Second Empires of France showed that history repeats
itself, first as a tragedy and then as a farce. He was
considered to be a pale imitation of his great uncle, and
his rule was regarded as a period of disastrous tyranny for
France.

The German Empire, on the other hand, was in reality
a Prussian empire. Though the Empire did not include the
Germans within the Austrian Empire, it was now the
strongest power on the continent and was inevitably to be
the center of European politics during the coming years.
This caused an upheaval in international relations that can
be seen to have resulted in the Great War of 1914–1918,
later called the First World War. In fact, most Europeans
in the first half of the twentieth century saw the newly
created Germany as responsible for both that war and the
Second World War.

Many people believed that the disasters of the war were
due to the widespread laxity of thought and morals under
the Second Empire of Napoleon III. With such thinking,

religious orders multiplied, and so did their schools, orphanages, and hospitals. Among the most prominent of these orders were the Assumptionists, founded at Nimes in 1843, who sought to popularize devotion to the cult of the Sacred Heart of Jesus to gain pity for the sorrows of France, which was predicted by the Blessed Virgin.

The symbol of this in Paris was a great new Church of Sacré-Coeur on the dominating heights of Montmartre. It was built in 1873 by public subscription on the authority of the National Assembly, by way of expiation of the nation's sins. Thousands of pilgrims were also carried by rail to visit Lourdes and other shrines as an act of penitence. The Government supported the Church in its activities and gave it privileges, particularly in finance and education, which were greater even than those it had enjoyed during the Second empire. The result, however, was to increase the anti-clericalism of the Republicans.

The revolutionary song, *La Marseillaise*, was the national anthem, and the 14th of July, the anniversary of the storming of the Bastille, was made a public holiday. In 1881, steps were taken to protect the Republic against monarchical revival, and in 1886, all members of such families were expelled from France.

The Republicans believed, however, that the most important task immediately before them was to limit the power of the Church. Ever since its suffering at the hands of the revolutionaries, who had sought to abolish religion in France, the Church had largely been on the side of conservatism and monarchism, and since 1870, this connection had become even closer. During the election campaign of 1878, Gambetta conducted a vigorous attack on clericalism and the influence of the clergy in politics. "Clericalism, that is the danger," he declared.

With the discoveries and inventions of the Industrial Revolution, in such a new world religion had no place. It was seen as an outworn superstition which impeded the attainment of the universal prosperity now being offered to mankind. Faith must give place to science and reason!

In 1880, the Jesuits and several other religious orders were dissolved and their members were forbidden to teach in state schools, and in 1882, religious instruction was removed from all state schools. These measures were accompanied by the abolition of chaplains in the armed forces and the removal of nursing nuns from hospitals. However, since France was still mainly a Roman Catholic country, the enforcement of this policy met with much

134

opposition. Some four hundred magistrates and officials resigned rather than enforce the laws, and troops had sometimes to be called in. This legislation was the prelude to the separation of Church and State in France, which was to be enacted early in the next century, and it was the beginning of a bitter political dispute which lasted almost as long as the Third Republic.

Germany in 1859

Germany in 1871

Napoleon III

Bismarck—The Iron
Chancellor

Napoleon III surrenders to the Germans
after the Battle of Sedan

Chapter 22

World War I
1914–1918

F ollowing the German victory over France in the
Franco-Prussian War of 1870–71, the powerful force
influencing Europe during the nineteenth century was
nationalism. But European nationalism in its modern sense
was initially a product of the French Revolution, which had
destroyed the concept of a French kingdom possessed and
symbolized by the monarchy, and had replaced it by the
complete identification of the French nation with the
French state.

In Germany, for instance, *Grimm's Fairy Tales* (1824)
was part of a movement to recover the old folk stories and
myths of the German past. It was political, seeking to
create a nation State that would preserve the national
identity of the country. Thus, Leopold von Ranke wrote in
1830 that Germans should "create the pure German state
corresponding to the genius of the nation."

Meanwhile, Mazzi, the prophet of Italian unity, also
proclaimed that "every people has its special mission,
which will cooperate towards the general mission of
humanity. That mission is its nationality. Nationality is
sacred." Eventually, nationalism and liberalism came into
conflict with each other, and liberalism was to be the loser.
Indeed, in the following years German nationalism parted

company with liberalism and became antidemocratic and warlike.

When in 1870 Germany toppled France, it was one of the greatest upsets of the century, in fact, in modern history. The astonishing speed with which France, regarded as the greatest of European powers, was soundly defeated by Prussia indicated that the new German state might soon be in a position to dominate the continent, and the feeling that Europe was heading for "Armageddon" grew more acute throughout the rest of the 19th century.

In 1879, a Dual Alliance of Austria and Germany was established. It was a defensive arrangement in which each of them promised to assist the other if either were attacked by Russia, or to provide assistance in the case of an attack on one of them in which Russia actively cooperated or undertook menacing military measures. When Italy joined Austria and Germany three years later in 1882, the arrangement was transformed into a "Triple Alliance." It was not the first "Triple Alliance" in world history. In 1428, a "Triple Alliance" of the Mexica, the Texcocans, and the Tacubans finally succeeded in breaking Tepanec power. That "Triple Alliance" was to become the satanic Aztec empire!

There was also a "Dual Alliance" of France and Russia. However, the British did not wish to be permanently allied with anyone, adhering strictly to Lord Palmerston's stand: "We have no eternal allies and we have no perpetual enemies. Our interests are eternal and perpetual, and these interests it is our duty to follow." However, by 1907, such was the pressure of European events, that Britain, France, and Russia were for practical purposes allied against the Triple Alliance of Germany, Austria-Hungary, and Italy. The sides were drawn for a major war, greater than the Franco-Prussian War. It was to be the second of "a series of wars," as predicted by the Virgin of La Salette in 1846.

The second half of the nineteenth century also witnessed the rise of the "Slavic idea" which saw Russia as a state culturally and politically distinct from the states of western and central Europe. Russia also had an historic mission to protect all Slav peoples, which meant defending the interests of Bulgarians, Serbs, and Montenegrins. This commitment was a more extreme, modernized version of the older notion of an Orthodox brotherhood of believers.

Now, as Turkish power receded in the Balkan peninsula, a multisided wrangle developed to see what would replace it. The indigenous Balkan peoples wished to be independent and to go their separate ways, but regrettably they all hated each other—Serbs disliking Bulgarians, Bulgarians despising Greeks, Greeks distrusting Albanians, and so on around the circle. As these people were Orthodox Christians, Orthodox Russia had declared herself to be their protector, a pose which neatly dovetailed with the ancient Russian ambition to spread into the Mediterranean.

When, in 1908, Austria proclaimed the annexation of the provinces of Bosnia and Hercegovina, which she had occupied militarily ever since 1878, these two provinces remained a troublesome area for Austria. Their chief city was Sarajevo, and Serbian nationalists hostile to Austria-Hungary were highly active there.

Franz Josef I, Emperor of Austria and King of Hungary, was 84 years old in 1914, and on the morning of June 28, the heir to the Austria-Hungarian empire, Archduke Franz Ferdinand, and his wife, paid their official visit to Sarajevo. As they proceeded through the town in an open car, a Serbian nationalist, 19 year old Gravilo Princip, stepped on the running board of the car and fired two shots. They were both assassinated. Princip was a member of a terrorist group called the Black Hand, whose ambition it was to incorporate all Serbian peoples within the Serbian state.

Many Austrian officials regarded the nationalism of these minority groups as the greatest threat to the continuing existence of the Habsburg monarchy. As a consequence, at 11:00 a.m. on July 28, Catholic Austria-Hungary declared war on Orthodox Serbia. On July 30, Russia ordered a full mobilization in support of Serbia. War between the Russians and the Austrians now appeared to be inevitable. Consequently, Germany, a member of the "Triple Alliance" with Austria-Hungary and Italy, then ordered her army to mobilize and dispatched an ultimatum to Russia, demanding the immediate cessation of all military measures against its ally, Austria-Hungary within twelve hours.

When the Russians failed to reply to this ultimatum, the Germans declared war on them at 6:00 p.m. on August 1. France, Russia's Dual Alliance partner, then ordered a general mobilization on the same day. The Germans declared war on them two days later. On the morning of August 4, German troops crossed the Belgium frontier and by midnight Germany and Great Britain were at war. It was all precipitated by a young Serbian assassin.

The violation of Belgium's neutrality by Germany on August 4, had provided a convenient justification for those in the British Cabinet who had already reluctantly decided that intervention was inevitable. In fact, Britain's entry into the war had little to do with Belgium. Britain would have intervened in any case, believing that this was essential to preserve the balance of power and prevent German domination of Europe.

Britain, independent of the alliance's system, joined the Dual Alliance of France and Russia against the Triple Alliance of Germany, Austria, and Italy. However, Italy was not drawn into the conflict as a result of her prior commitment, and on August 3 she declared her neutrality. In any event, her partners in the Triple Alliance had practically ignored her during the crisis, not only because they distrusted her, but also because they had a low opinion of her abilities as a great power. Eventually, however, Italy went to war in 1915 against her former allies!

Pope Benedict XV (1914–1922) was not long elected Pope when the war began, and as Sir Nicholas Cheetham in his *History of the Popes*, commented: "How ought the Holy See to react to a murderous conflict in which Catholic Austria-Hungary and partly-Catholic Germany stood initially opposed to an alliance of Catholic, but officially irreligious, France with Orthodox Russia and Protestant Great Britain? That was the problem, shortly to be complicated by Italy's entry into the war, which confronted Pope Benedict XV."

Thus, it may be legitimately argued that the underlying cause of the war was nationalism in general, and in particular the demand for unified, independent states in the Balkans and the threat this posed to the socio-political structure of Austria-Hungary. Russia's historic mission was the emancipation of the Christian peoples of the Balkan peninsula from Turkish yoke and the protection of Orthodox Serbia. But nationalism, when carried to extremes, becomes racism, and extreme nationalism leads to the kind of thinking that causes people to rejoice at the prospect of war.

This was the Europe of 1914. There was dancing in the streets and spontaneous demonstrations in support of governments throughout Europe. Men flocked to recruiting offices, fearful that the war might end before they had the opportunity to fight. There was a spirit of festivity and a sense of community in all European cities, a display of patriotic fervour.

World War I also incorporated the Bolshevik take over in Russia. It was a military insurrection led by Vladimir Lenin, which overthrew the Czar and introduced the Communist regime. In November, the Bolsheviks came to power in Russia with the popular slogan, "Peace, land, and bread and all power to the Soviets." However, it was not part of Lenin's plan to fight Germany, and almost immediately after he had seized power, he offered the Germans an armistice. On March 3, 1918, the peace treaty was signed. Russia's war with Germany was over, but the Allies were furious and regarded the Bolsheviks as traitors to the great cause.

The Bolsheviks then sought to overthrow all organized church life and to extirpate all religious belief. Atheism was taught in every school and by every teacher. Former churches were turned into "museums of religion and atheism," and all active Christians were to be classified as "counter-revolutionaries" and treated accordingly.

It will never be known how many of the clergy and the laity suffered imprisonment or death because of their Faith, but it is calculated that since 1917, among priests alone, at least twelve thousand and possibly far more, were executed or died through ill-treatment. As the Archpriest Avvaqum said: "Satan has obtained our radiant Russia from God, that she may become red."

The United States entered the war on April 2, 1917, and eventually the evidence coming from the battlefields was of a German army emaciated by nearly four years of bloodshed, with its morale plummeted by news of unrest at home, and unable to cope with the fierce determination of the British and French and the keenness of the Americans.

The end of World War I, when it came, took many by surprise. Shortly before dawn, in a railway carriage in the forest of Compiégne in France, Field Marshal Ferdinand Foch, Commander-in-Chief of the allied forces, and the British Admiral Wemyss, received a German delegation, including two generals and a Catholic politician. Six hours later, at 11:00 a.m. on the 11th day of the 11th month, the armistice took effect. The year was 1918. By month end, order and discipline for which the Germans were known throughout Europe vanished virtually overnight in the wake of defeat in war. The Kaiser fled to Holland, disheveled sailors and disillusioned soldiers mutinied, and angry political agitators roamed the streets.

The Treaty of Versailles was eventually signed in the Hall of Mirrors of the Palace of Versailles on June 28,

1919. It imposed heavy penalties on Germany. The Rhineland was to be demilitarized and the Czar controlled by the League of Nations. With the breakup of the Habsburg and Turkish empires following the end of the war, four new nations came into being—Austria, Hungary, Czechoslovakia, and an enlarged Serbia called Yugoslavia. However, Winston Churchill, one observer with foresight, knew that the treaty would breed a thirst for revenge in the proud Germans.

The economic hardships and depression following the war were horrendous. Reckoning in 1918, the total cost of the war had been estimated around 350 billion U.S. dollars, and Europe's place in the world economy was seriously impaired. The human cost is even harder to assess. More than 10 million Europeans had died in battle, as well as 150 thousand Americans. At least twice that number had been wounded, many of them left to live out their lives as cripples, and thereafter millions of mutilated walked the streets of Europe as reminders of the ravages of war. France lost half its men between the ages of 20 and 32, and suffered almost as much in casualties. The armistice was signed but the end of the war did not bring peace.

While the Great War was estimated to have claimed 10 million lives, nature was even more disastrous. In 1918, a pandemic of a type of influenza, which was called "the Spanish flu," killed 10 million more people than the war, and heralding things to come in the following years of the century. Experiments in 1919 at Manchester University by Professor Ernest Rutherford culminated in a process for "splitting atoms." An important ingredient of World War II was in the making.

Archduke Ferdinand and his wife
moments before their death

The assassin strikes

Chapter 23

Berthe Petit

It was in the year of the Franco-Prussian War that a special soul was born. On January 23, 1870, at Enghien, Belgium, Jeanne Petit gave birth to a baby girl whom she named Berthe Frances Maria. This child eventually became a mystic who enjoyed the highest esteem of cardinals, theologians, and other members of the hierarchy.

In later years Berthe had invisible stigmata which caused her much pain, but in her humility she had begged Our Lord not to impose any visible stigmata on her. However, on Good Friday and many Fridays throughout the year, she endured great pain in the palms of her hands and soles of her feet and also in her side. The suffering in her head, similar to that caused by a crown of thorns, was with her continually and she hardly ever slept.

But it was not until she was thirty-nine years old that the first indication of her mission was revealed to her. She was attending Christmas midnight Mass in 1909 when she saw the wounded heart of Jesus and closely adherent to it was the heart of Mary pierced with a sword. Then she heard these words: "Cause my mother's heart, transfixed by sorrows that rent mine, to be loved." It was Jesus speaking. Indeed, this brief statement summarizes her special mission of spreading the devotion to the *Sorrowful and Immaculate Heart of Mary.*

On February 7, 1910, she then saw the hearts of Jesus and Mary "interpenetrating" each other, and hovering over the hearts was a dove. Jesus then spoke to her: *"You must think of my mother's heart as you think of mine; live in this heart as you will seek to live in mine; give yourself to this heart as you give yourself to mine. You must spread love of this heart so wholly united to mine."* A few weeks later, He said to her: *"The world must be dedicated to the **Sorrowful and Immaculate Heart** of my mother as it is dedicated to mine. Fear nothing, no matter what suffering or obstacles you may meet. Think only of fulfilling my will."*

On September 17, 1911, the "mother" herself appeared to Berthe, and revealed in a symbolic way the bloodless martyrdom which she suffered at the foot of the Cross. Berthe saw her with her forehead pierced and bleeding and her hands and heart pierced. Mary then said: "Now you can understand the sorrows which my heart endured, and the sufferings of my whole being for the salvation of the world."

In fact, in one of His communications with Berthe, Jesus also made this significant remark with respect to His mother's role as *Coredemptrix*: *"It is in **coredemption** that my mother was above all great. That is why I ask that the invocation, as I have inspired it, should be approved and diffused throughout the Church... It has already obtained grace. It will obtain more until the hour comes when, by consecration to the **Sorrowful and Immaculate Heart** of my mother, the Church shall be uplifted and the world renewed."*

At a Holy Hour devotion, during the night of March 24–25, 1912, the eve of the feast of the Annunciation, the Blessed Virgin spoke again of her sorrowful heart: "I am called *the Immaculate Conception.* With you, I call myself the *Mother of the Sorrowful Heart.* This title that my Son wants is the dearest to me of all my titles and it is through it that shall be granted and spread everywhere graces of mercy, of conversion and of salvation."

The renowned Cardinal Désiré Mercier of Belgium was deeply impressed by Berthe's heavenly communications and readily promoted the devotion to the *Sorrowful and Immaculate Heart of Mary.* He then approached Pope Pius X and attempted to win his approval for the devotion. Seventeen petitions were made to the Pope, but he did not find it appropriate to approve the new devotion at that time. However, it certainly was never condemned on doctrinal grounds.

July 12, 1912, marked the beginning of a different phase in the mystical experiences of Berthe Petit. Until that time, her heavenly communications dealt solely with religious matters, but on that day she received the first of several revelations concerning political matters and world events. They were similar to the messages of a political nature, which were given by His mother to St. Catherine Labouré in 1830, and to the children of La Salette in 1846.

Jesus told Berthe that the heir to the Catholic empire of Austria-Hungary would be assassinated: "*A double murder,*" He said, "*will strike down the successor of the aged sovereign, so loyal to the faith.*" He was referring to the aged Franz Josef I (1830–1916) who was eighty two years old at the time. He added: "*It will be the **first** of those events, full of sorrows, but from whence I shall still bring forth good and which will precede the chastisement.*"

His prophecy was fulfilled a little less than two years later, on June 28, 1914, when Archduke Franz Ferdinand, the heir to the Austria-Hungarian empire, and his wife Sophia, the Duchess of Hohenburg, were assassinated by Gavrilo Princip, a Serbian nationalist. The following day, June 29, Jesus said to Berthe: "*Now begins the **ascending** curve of preliminary events which will lead to the great manifestation of my justice.*" In my viewpoint, He was prophesying that the preliminary events of the Franco-Prussian War and World War I would eventually lead to World War II and then probably to World War III.

Berthe spent the years of World War I in Switzerland, where she was constantly told in advance of the calamities that would befall the Allies. On August 4, 1914, the Germans entered Brussels and violated Belgium's neutrality. According to Berthe, just as He harshly criticized the Scribes and the Pharisees as recorded in the Gospels, Jesus had harsh words to say of the German invaders: "*The proud race and its hypocritical and ambitious ruler* (Kaiser William II) *would be chastised on the very soil* (Belgium) *of their unjust conquest.*" Later on, Jesus said to Berthe: "*The worst calamities which I had predicted are unleashed. The time has now arrived when I wish mankind to turn to the **Sorrowful and Immaculate Heart** of my* *mother. Let this prayer be uttered by every soul: '**Sorrowful and Immaculate Heart of Mary,** pray for us'...so that it may spread as a refreshing and purifying balm of reparation that will appease my anger...*"

The two Cardinals who cooperated most closely with Berthe Petit were Cardinal Désiré Mercier, the Primate of Belgium, and Cardinal Francis Bourne, the Primate of England and Archbishop of Canterbury. Cardinal Mercier was also Berthe's spiritual director for several years. But it was the English Cardinal Bourne who went furthest in complying with the wishes of Our Lord in regards to this new devotion. The revelations of Berthe Petit were first brought to his attention on May 1, 1916, and in that year he issued two pastoral letters and consecrated England to the *Sorrowful and Immaculate Heart* of Mary. He then prescribed the prayers to be said on Friday, September 15, 1916, the feast of *Our Lady of Sorrows*. That day, September 15, marked the greatest success of the British Army!

Indeed, recalling the tender devotion of the English people throughout the Catholic centuries before the era of Henry VIII, Cardinal Bourne once said: "Nowhere in Christendom should honour be paid more readily to the *Sorrowful and Immaculate Heart of Mary* than here in England. Of old, in the days of united faith, her purity and her sorrows were ever held in love and veneration. In those days, England was in truth Our Lady's dowry..."

World War I ended on November 11, 1918, and Jesus said to Berthe: "*Had I not intervened in answer to the recourse to the **Sorrowful and Immaculate Heart** of my mother, and through the leadership of my apostle Francis, victory would have been on the side of those who strained every nerve during so many years to prepare and organize a great war for the attainment of their own ambitions. Material strength would thus have prevailed over justice and right. For why should I come to the help of the people of a France intent on persecuting my Church... That is why trials will continue until the day, when humbly acknowledging her errors, this nation will render me my rights and give full liberty to my Church.*"

However, it was in October 1920 that Jesus exalted the merits of the sorrow of His mother to Berthe, in a most powerful and significant way: "*The title **Immaculate** belongs to the whole being of my mother and not specially to her heart. This title flows from my gratuitous gift to the Virgin who has given me birth. However, my mother has* acquired for her heart the title **Sorrowful** by sharing generously in all the sufferings of my heart and my body from the crib to the Cross. There is not one of these sorrows which did not pierce the heart of my mother. Living image of my crucified body, her virginal flesh bore the invisible marks of my wounds as her heart felt the sorrows of my own. Nothing could ever tarnish the incorruptibility of her immaculate heart. The title of **Sorrowful** belongs, therefore, to the heart of my mother, and, more than any other, this title is dear to her because it springs from the union of her heart with mine in the redemption of humanity. This title has been acquired by her through her full participation in my Calvary, and it should precede the gratuitous title 'immaculate' which my love bestowed upon her by a singular privilege."

As the late Fr. Joseph A. Pelletier once wrote: "The 'Co-redemption' of Mary is the doctrinal truth expressed by the title 'The Sorrowful Heart of Mary' and is what Our Lord wants recognized in the Church on a worldwide basis." Fr. Louis Decorscant, Berthe's spiritual director, transmitted her latest revelations to Rome, but the Vatican remained silent. Then in 1922, Jesus told Berthe: "My apostle will arise at the predestined hour...when the appalling cataclysm which approaches will have overset all the present calculations of mankind and their deplorable policies. My will concerning my mother's glory will not be fulfilled at present."

Mlle. Berthe Petit

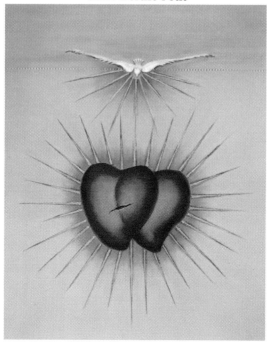

Berthe's Vision

The Sorrowful and Immaculate
Heart of Mary

Chapter 24

Our Lady of the Rosary of Fatima
1917

On August 20, 1914, Pope Pius X died, and on September 3, Giacomo della Chiesa was elected Pope. He chose the name Benedict XV. In his first statement as Pope on September 8, 1914 (the feast of the Nativity of the Blessed Virgin Mary), Benedict XV mourned the bloodshed, and pleaded for a quick end to the war just begun. He denounced the war as a crime against religion, humanity, and civilization, waged as it was by Catholic countries. He blamed both sides equally for allowing it to happen and to continue. In his first encyclical *Ad Beatissimi*, issued on November 1, 1914, he criticized the warring Christian peoples. "Who could realize," he said, "that they are brethren, children of the same Father in heaven?" His encyclical closed with a call for prayer to Christ and to the Blessed Virgin Mary, "who bore the Prince of Peace."

On May 31, 1915, eight days after Italy had entered the war, Pope Benedict sent a letter to the Dean of the Sacred College, Cardinal Venutelli. It concluded with the following recommendation addressed to all the bishops of the world: "Let us send up our prayers, more than ever ardent and frequent, to Him in whose hands lie the destinies of all peoples; and let us appeal with confidence to the *Sorrowful and Immaculate Heart of Mary*, the most gentle mother of Jesus and ours, that by her powerful intercession, she may obtain from her divine Son the speedy end of the war and the return of peace and tranquility."

On May 5, 1917, in a letter to his Secretary of State, Cardinal Gasparri, he wrote: "Our earnestly pleading voice, invoking the end of this vast conflict, the suicide of civilized Europe, was then and has remained ever since unheard... Since all graces which the Author of all good deigns to grant to the poor children of Adam, by a loving design of His Divine Providence, are dispensed through the hands of the most holy Virgin, we wish that the petition of her most afflicted children, more than ever in this terrible hour, may turn with lively confidence to the august *Mother of God*."

He then directed that the invocation, "*Queen of Peace, pray for us*," be added permanently to the Litany of Loreto, and made his ultimate appeal to her: "To Mary, then, who is the *Mother of Mercy* and omnipotent by grace, let this loving and devout appeal go up from every corner of the earth from noble temples and tiniest chapels, from royal palaces and mansions of the rich as from the poorest hut, from every place where a faithful soul finds shelter from blood-drenched plains and seas. Let it bear to her the anguished cry of mothers and wives, the wailing of innocent little ones, the sighs of every generous heart; let her most tender and benign solicitude be moved and the peace we ask for be obtained for our agitated world."

Eight days later, on Sunday May 13, 1917, Her Majesty responded to the prayers of the Pope and the rest of the Catholic world. It was on a glorious spring day in Fatima, Portugal, that the Blessed Virgin Mary appeared to three children—Lucia, Jacinta and Francisco. Atop a small evergreen tree about three feet tall, they saw a ball of light, within which stood a lady clad in white. To quote Lucia's own words: "We beheld a lady all dressed in white. She was more brilliant than the sun and radiated a light more clear and intense than a crystal glass filled with sparkling water, the rays of the burning sun shining through it." Once more, "more brilliant than the sun!" It was the woman of Revelation 12:1.

She wore a white mantle falling to her feet, edged in burnished gold. A prominent star shone from the hem of her robe, while from her hand hung an exquisite Rosary of white pearls: "I come from heaven," she said. "I want you to come here on the 13th of each month until October when I will tell you who I am and what I want." She spoke to them about personal matters and of their own salvation. But in her last words to them on that day, she stressed the immense crisis which had brought her from heaven, and implored: "Say the Rosary to obtain peace for the world and the end of the war."

On June 13, the lady came back to the Cova da Iria. On that occasion she gave them a message which to date has not been revealed. *The Immaculate Conception* then showed them a vision of her immaculate heart, encircled by piercing thorns representing the sorrows she suffered and the sins that wounded her. She then said to Lucia: "God wishes you to remain in the world for some time because he wants you to establish in the world devotion to my immaculate heart, for the heart of Jesus wants my immaculate heart to be venerated by His side. I promise salvation to those who embrace it, and their souls will be loved by God as the flowers placed by myself adorning His throne." Other visionaries have also said that she places flowers before the throne of God everyday.

Soon after saying this, she departed into the east as before. The upper leaves in the oak tree remained for several minutes stretched and bending towards the east, as if bidding her farewell. I recalled that she also came from the east when she appeared to Juan Diego in Guadalupe in 1531. She came as the *Morning Star!*

On July 13, after showing the children a vision of hell, the Virgin said to Lucia: "You have seen hell where the souls of poor sinners go. To save them God wishes to establish in the world devotion to my immaculate heart. If people do what I ask, many souls will be saved and there will be peace. The war (World War I) is going to end soon, but if people will not stop offending God, another and more terrible war will begin during the reign of Pius XI... To prevent this, I shall come to ask for the consecration of Russia to my immaculate heart and the Communion of Reparation on the five first Saturdays. If my requests are granted, Russia will be converted and there will be peace. If not, she will scatter her errors throughout the world, provoking wars and the persecution of the Church. The good will be martyred, the Holy Father will have much to suffer and various nations will be annihilated. In the end my immaculate heart will triumph; the Holy Father will consecrate Russia to me. Russia will be converted and a certain period of peace will be granted to the world." It is important to note that Russia at that time was a very Christian country, mainly Orthodox.

Russia did indeed scatter errors, wars, and persecutions throughout the world. Mary's warning and her promise resounded down through years, and all over the world millions of people prayed the Rosary as she had asked, and pleaded for a rescue from heaven. Perhaps none prayed more devoutly and passionately than the victims of Communist rule in Eastern Europe and Russia, where, although the Fatima prophecy was never allowed to be publicly mentioned, it was very widely known.

On August 13, among other things, she said to the children: "I want you to continue praying the Rosary every day. In the last month (October), I will perform a miracle *so that all may believe*." On September 13, she also spoke very briefly: "Continue to say the Rosary to bring about the end of the war. In October, Our Lord will come also, as well as *Our Lady of Sorrows* and *Our Lady of Carmel*. St. Joseph will appear with the Child Jesus to bless the world. God is pleased with your sacrifices."

It was October 13. It was just past noon. The children saw the usual flash from the east. To quote Lucia's own words: "We saw the flash of light, and then Our Lady appeared on the holm oak. She said: 'I want to tell you that a chapel is to be built here in my honour. I am *the Lady of the Rosary*. Continue always to pray the Rosary every day. The war is going to end, and the soldiers will soon return to their homes.'"

Now, I wish to emphasize that she never called herself "Our Lady of Fatima." That terminology, as far as I am concerned, is only geographic. She said: "I am *the Lady of the Rosary*," and by calling her "Our Lady of Fatima," we obscure her true message.

Lucia also wrote: "After Our Lady had disappeared, we beheld St. Joseph with the Child Jesus and Our Lady, robed in white with a blue mantle, beside the sun. St. Joseph and the Child Jesus appeared to bless the world... When a little later, this apparition disappeared, I saw Our Lord and Our Lady. It seemed to me that it was *Our Lady of Sorrows*. This apparition also vanished, and I saw Our Lady once more, this time resembling *Our Lady of Carmel*."

Then, the sun was seen to move from its celestial abode, and came hurling down to the crowd only to retreat back to the heavens at the command of the Queen of the Universe. Twenty five miles away, the poet Alfonso Lopes Vieira saw the miracle of the sun from his own house.

Other distant witnesses of this event absolutely destroyed any theory of mass suggestion or hallucination generated by emotion and expectation among the crowd as an explanation of what was seen in the sky.

The Virgin requested Lucia to spread the devotion to her immaculate heart, but a Blue Army (a Catholic Marian organization in America) sponsored pamphlet, *Sorrowful and Immaculate Heart of Mary*, made these interesting observations concerning the devotion to the heart of Mary as manifested at Fatima and to Berthe Petit: "At Fatima, Our Blessed Lady asked that her immaculate heart, that free gift of God's grace, should be specially honoured. But it would not have been in accordance with her perfect humility had she exalted her own merits in proclaiming the glory of hcr sorrowful heart. It is, therefore, incumbent on the faithful, as it were, to complete the message of Fatima, by obtaining, through ardent prayer, the consecration of the world to the *Sorrowful and Immaculate Heart* of the mother of Our Saviour."

But why did Her Majesty choose Portugal for this important manifestation? It is because Portugal was officially consecrated to the Immaculate Virgin in 1646 by King John IV, the restorer of national independence, and on October 20, 1646, as a sign of his love and recognition, he laid down his royal crown at the feet of *Our Lady of the Immaculate Conception*. With all his nation reunited, he proclaimed her Patron of his kingdom. By this solemn act, Portugal, faithful to its old tradition, chose to consecrate itself to the Virgin Mary under the title of her *Immaculate Conception*, preceding by two centuries the infallible definition of Pope Pius IX. After that ceremony, no king of Portugal ever wore a crown. It was reserved for Her Majesty, the Queen of Heaven.

But when Mary came to Portugal in 1917, it was in a very sorry and pitiful condition. The Church had been persecuted in all sorts of ways. There was a rising belligerence of anticlerical and revolutionary parties, aided by the intrigue of the Freemasons. All these persecutions finally culminated in laws leading to the separation of the Church and State on April 20, 1911. The author of these laws, one Alfonso Costa, declared afterwards: "Thanks to this law of separation, in two generations Catholicism will be completely eliminated from Portugal."

The day after the great miracle of the sun on October 13, 1917 was a Sunday, and the date of the municipal elections. Comparing the results of the elections in

1911, the newspaper *O Dia* reported that the three main democratic, republican, and revolutionist parties had lost 95,000 votes to the Catholics in the capital alone. Furious at this setback, some fanatical Freemasons decided to ransack the place of the apparitions, and on the night of October 22 and 23, they demolished the primitive sanctuary which had been erected at the Cova da Iria.

Soon afterwards, a Masonic pamphlet was circulated to *all liberal Portuguese*: "Citizens! As if the pernicious propaganda of reactionaries were not enough, we now see a miracle trotted out in order further to degrade the people into fanaticism and superstition. There has been staged...a ridiculous spectacle in which the simple people have been ingeniously deceived by means of collective suggestion into a belief in a supposed apparition of the Mother of Jesus... As if, however, the declaration of these poor little dupes who affirm they have seen a "Virgin" who, however, nobody else can see; and if this were not sufficient, it is affirmed, or rather invented, that the sun, at a certain hour on 13th October, 1917, and in the height of the 20th century, was seen to dance a fandango in the clouds."

The pamphlet went on to recommend that there should be "an intensive and tenacious propaganda, which will rouse the mentality of one's co-citizens to the realms of truth, reason and science, convincing them that nothing can alter the laws of nature... Let the professors in the schools and colleges educate their pupils in a rational manner, liberating them from religious preconceptions as from all others, and we shall have prepared a generation for the morrow, happier because more worthy of happiness."

History, of course, has shown that this "propaganda" has not achieved its godless end and millions of people continue to journey to Fatima, some on their knees. On June 28, 1918, a communiqué announced the reconciliation of the Republic with Rome. Several years later, Cardinal Cerejeira was able to declare: "Since Our Lady of Fatima appeared in 1917 in the sky above Portugal, a special blessing of God has come down on our land. The violent cycle of religious persecution has stopped and a new era of peace and of Christian restoration has begun."

The authenticity of the Fatima apparitions has been confirmed not only by the Virgin's prophecies, which "came to pass," but also by the thousands of witnesses of the great miracle of the sun, which not only defied the laws of nature, but also defies the incredulity of any sceptic.

The three children of Fatima

Our Lady of the Rosary of Fatima

158

Pope John Paul II meets Sr. Lucia

Pope John Paul II in Fatima

The International Pilgrim Virgin Statue
(Courtesy Jackie Galley)

Chapter 25

Freemasonry

It is said that modern Freemasonry began in England in 1717, and just twenty one years later, Pope Clement XII issued the first formal prohibition of Masonry in 1738. However, since the time of its origin in the early 18th century, there has been continued opposition to the Catholic Church by Masonic societies.

In December 1901, Richard Davey, an English Protestant publicist, Freemason, and Grand Master, wrote: "Every single law directed against the Church, or rather Christianity, in France has sprung from and was endorsed by the Grand Orient. It is the duty of every good Mason to use all his influence to bring about the suppression of all ecclesiastical associations (conventual, educational, and charitable—authorized or otherwise), then to see that their property be confiscated by the state."

A circular was also sent to every Masonic lodge in France, demanding the name of every official, from prefect to postman, who dared to send his children to a Catholic school, or who attended any Catholic religious service. Davey next urged the lodges of Spain and Portugal to destroy the religious orders. The sending of this document by the Grand Master was followed by many disorderly scenes, in which nuns were insulted, churches and convents burnt, and literature of a most blasphemous and inflammatory character was distributed wholesale throughout the peninsula.

Senator Delpech, President of the Grand Orient in France, boasted on September 20, 1902: "The triumph of the Galilean has lasted many centuries, but now he dies in his turn... Brother Masons, we rejoice that we are not without our share in this overthrow of false prophets. The Roman Church began to decay from the day the Masonic association was established." In similar vein, the Swiss lodge declared: "We have one irreconcilable enemy—the Pope and clericalism."

Masonic documents, seized by the government of Italy, also declared that the ultimate idea of Masonry there was to destroy Catholicism and even the Christian idea altogether and in 1913 the Grand Orient of France admitted that "the aim of the Grand Orient is to crush Roman Catholicism in France first, and then elsewhere."

As Fr. Albert Shamon wrote in his booklet *Apocalypse, The Book For Our Time*: "It was Freemasonry which took the eldest daughter of the Church, France, away from Christianity." He also quoted Carlton Hays, the renowned historian, who once said: "In France, where Freemasonry was frankly atheistic in principle and practical tendency, almost every radical politician was a Freemason. Men like Garibaldi, Jules Ferry, Aristide Briand, George Clemenceau, and Emile Combes, a very active Freemason, created a godless France."

However, some Masonic journals in England at that time replied to these quotations by saying that English Masonry did not sympathize with such extravagant utterances, and that it had no opinions, political or religious. But to this, Albert Pike, an American Mason and Grand Commander of the Scottish Rite, replied: "It is idle to protest. We are Masons, and we recognize the French brotherhood as Freemasons in virtue of solidarity. Ours is a universal fraternity." In other words, what he has said is that once one is a member, one is part of the whole!

In 1917, the year that the Blessed Virgin appeared in Fatima, when Freemasons were celebrating the 200th anniversary of their founding, they held their major festivities in Rome. There, through the streets marched the Masonic groups with black banners bearing the image of Lucifer crushing St. Michael the Archangel under his feet (Satan always reverses everything that is holy). On the banners were written: "Satan must reign at the Vatican. The Pope will be his slave." This was in October 1917, a few days after the great apocalyptic miracle of the sun in Fatima.

As a consequence of this and other violations, the 1918 Code of Canon Law of the Vatican stated that anyone who joined the Masonic sect or other societies which plot against the Church incurred automatic excommunication. However, one interpretation was that membership in a particular Masonic group would be forbidden *only* when that organization opposes the Church by open prejudice or persecution, undermining civil authority, and so on.

In this respect, responding to the claim in its defense that Masons have many charitable institutions, in Volume I of *Radio Replies*, Frs. Rumble and Carty responded: "We do not condemn any good they are able to accomplish. Meanwhile, the Catholic Church has charitable works on a much more vast scale and she condemns the Masonic system, without casting reflection upon the sincerity of individual Masons or the good works of the Craft."

More recently, a Declaration on Masonic associations issued on November 26, 1983 by the Sacred Congregation for the Doctrine of the Faith, and published in *L'Osservatore Romano*, reiterates that "the Church's negative judgment in regard to Masonic associations remains unchanged since these principles have always been considered incompatible with the doctrine of the Church and therefore membership in them remains forbidden. The faithful who enroll in Masonic associations are in a state of grave sin and may not receive Holy Communion."

The statement continued: "It is not within the competence of local ecclesiastical authorities to give a judgment on the nature of Masonic associations which would imply a derogation from what has been decided above..." This Declaration was approved by Pope John Paul II and signed by Joseph Cardinal Ratzinger, Prefect of the Sacred Congregation for the Doctrine of the Faith, and by Fr. Jerome Hamer, O.P., Titular Archbishop of Lorium, and Secretary.

The declaration clearly intends to tighten up the Church's position on Masonic membership and seems to stress that nothing is changed, that the Church's negative position "remains unaltered" and that joining the Masons "remains prohibited" to all, 3rd degree or 33rd degree! Moreover, this new regulation of 1983 also seems to restrict the power of local bishops, and such bishops no longer have authority to judge whether a specific Masonic organization could be approved for membership.

Now, there are 33 degrees in Masonry, but most Masons only belong to the three basic degrees, namely, Entered Apprentice (First Degree), Fellow Craft (Second degree) and Master Mason (Third degree), and do not rise higher than the latter. Apart from the 32nd degree Southern Jurisdiction of the Scottish Rite, which often has been accused of actions and attitudes prejudicial to Catholics and the Catholic Church, Masonic organizations in the United States generally avoid the more sinister characteristics of international Masonry. In fact, in his encyclical of 1884, Pope Leo XIII also recognized that "there may be persons, and not a few, who, although not free from the guilt of having entangled themselves in such associations, are neither themselves partners in their criminal acts, nor aware of the ultimate object which they are endeavouring to attain."

However, the major objection of Christians against Freemasonry has been not only its sometimes anti-Catholic and antireligious activities, but perhaps, even more, its beliefs and quasi-religious character, many aspects of which seem contradictory to Christian doctrine. It was this objection in particular which inspired the strongest condemnation yet of memberships in Masonic organizations by the American bishops. A lengthy report from a committee of the U.S. National Conference of Catholic Bishops, released in June 1985, calls Freemasonry "irreconcilable" not only with Catholicism but with all Christianity. It stated: "The principles and basic rituals of Masonry embody a naturalistic religion, active participation in which is incompatible with Christian faith and practice."

In his book, Fr. Albert Shamon also claims that "Franklin Delano Roosevelt and Harry S. Truman, both 33rd degree Masons, packed the United States Supreme Court with Masonic judges. From 1941 to 1971, there were never less than five Masonic judges on the court, and in those critical years, these judges did to America what was done to 19th c?entury France—they secularized this once God-fearing America by raw judicial power. This Masonic Court outlawed prayer in schools, repeatedly denied aid to private schools, legitimized pornography, abortion, and so on."

However, Freemasonry membership includes even a few of the clergy! In an interview with *Inside the Vatican* in 1966, Abbot Boniface Luykx, an Archimandrite of the Ukrainian Catholic Church, remarked that "there have always been Freemasons among the high-ranking prelates of the Church since the time of Pius IX in the 19th century, and even under Pius X, the great opponent of modernism... You must understand the scope of Freemasonry. I have come to understand that Freemasonry is a power that is much bigger than we think. It seeks to change the nature of the Church, and in this way, to destroy her."

But it is not only the Roman Church which expresses concern about Freemasonry. The Free Presbyterian Church of Scotland in 1927 made abstention from the lodge a condition of its own membership. In the same year, the Wesleyan Conference in England declared that the Christian message "is wholly incompatible with the claims of Freemasons."

Fr. Stefano Gobbi, a member of the Company of St. Paul, holds a doctorate in sacred theology from the Pontifical University of the Lateran in Rome. His book *To the Priests, Our Lady's Beloved Sons* contains "interior locutions," messages which Fr. Gobbi is said to have been receiving from the Blessed Virgin since 1973. Belief in his authenticity is reflected by the membership of his Marian Movement of Priests, which number over 300 bishops and more than 60,000 priests. As to the laity, since there is no formal conscription, one cannot give even an approximate figure, although they certainly number in the millions.

In his recordings of his messages received between June 13–17, 1989, Fr. Stefano has disclosed the following remarks on Freemasonry said to be given to him by the Blessed Virgin: "Freemasonry has infiltrated into the interior of the Church, that is to say, *ecclesiastical* Masonry, which has spread especially among the members of the hierarchy. This Masonic infiltration in the interior of the Church was already foretold to you by me in Fatima, when I announced to you that Satan would enter even to the summit of the Church. If the task of Masonry is to lead souls to perdition, bringing them to the worship of false divinities, the task of *ecclesiastical* Masonry on the other hand is that of destroying Christ and His Church, building a new idol, namely a false Christ and a false church.

"The Church is truth... *Ecclesiastical* Masonry seeks to destroy this reality through false ecumenism, which leads to the acceptance of all Christian Churches, asserting that each one of them has some part of the truth. It develops the plan of founding a universal ecumenical Church, formed by the fusion of all the Christian confessions, among which is the Catholic Church.

"*Ecclesiastical* Masonry receives orders and power from the various Masonic lodges and works to lead everyone secretly to become part of these secret sects. Thus it stimulates the ambitions with the prospect of easy careers; it heaps up goods to those who are starved for money; it assists its members to exceed others and to occupy the most important positions, while it sets aside, in a subtle but decisive way, all those who refuse to take part in its designs."

166

Fr. Stefano Gobbi (2nd row center)
and some of his Marian priests in Germany

Fr. Stefano Gobbi with Pope John Paul II

Chapter 26

The Virgin Appears in Beauraing, Belgium
1932–1933

After Fatima, her next apparition was in Belgium. On August 2, 1944, I visited the quaint and quiet town of Beauraing in search of the shrine where the Virgin appeared in 1932. Beauraing is south of an imaginary line which bisects the nation of Belgium. North of that line, Belgians spoke Flemish, a language similar to Dutch. To the south, every tongue of the people spoke with a French dialect. It was a small insignificant town of about two thousand residents, and yet Beauraing was chosen as a place for a special blessing.

As a consequence of World War I, by February 1931, almost five million were unemployed in Germany. In mid 1931, the bankruptcy of Credit-Anstalt began the European financial collapse, and all the banks were eventually closed. The Allies then voted to ease Germany's economic crisis by suspending the repayments of the 1914–1917 war debts, but by 1932, five million unemployed Germans looked to Hitler's Nazi party to solve their problems.

Britain was also in deep industrial depression, and in October of that year hunger marchers, protesting unemployment, fought pitched street battles with the police. There were food riots in London, Bristol, and Liverpool, and more than two million Britons were out of work, relying on their "dole" money, twenty-nine shillings a week, to live. Throughout the western world unemployment had soared. In America, some fourteen million were also jobless. Unemployed executives and skilled workers begged on street corners and the smash hit song was: "Buddy, can you spare a dime?"

It was "the worst of times." In addition, the Belgians once more grew increasingly nervous about the belligerence of neighbouring Germany, especially of a demigod named Adolf Hitler. It was a very troubled Belgium in which the Blessed Virgin appeared in 1932, and a world which had even greater troubles in store for it.

The Communists were in firm control of Russia, and were spreading their godless socialism throughout the world. The Fascist Benito Mussolini was master of Italy and was also persecuting the Church. At the same time, Adolph Hitler was rising in Germany and would soon assume complete power within a few months. Communists, Fascists, and Nazis were all aided by the unrest caused by the worldwide depression. Indeed, the Labour Party, which was Marxist and anti-Catholic, had carried the district of Beauraing in the recent elections.

As in France, Belgian Catholics viewed the Catholic Church as the Church of their birthright, but the anti-clericalism which had poisoned France in the previous century also had its toll on Belgian piety. Once staunchly Catholic, Belgium had drifted away from the Roman Church after the Reformation, and a lukewarm, halfhearted practice of the faith was therefore the norm in Beauraing in 1932.

This was the world scene when on November 29, 1932, five little children in Beauraing testified that they saw the Blessed Virgin Mary. They were Fernande Voisin, Gilberte Voisin, Albert Voisin, Andre Degeimbre, and Gilberte Degeimbre. They saw the luminous figure of a lady. The vision was about three feet from the ground, below an arched branch of a hawthorn tree. Significantly, the word "Beauraing" is French for "Beautiful branch." Her Son once said: "I am the vine, you are the branches" (John 15:5). Indeed, she is the most "beautiful branch" of all.

She was seen walking in the air, and as she walked, they could see the movements of her knees through the folds of her robe. Her feet were partly hidden by a little cloud. Her hands were joined and her blue eyes were raised heavenward. She lowered her eyes to look and smile at the children and then opened her arms and disappeared.

A total of thirty three apparitions occured in Beauraing, from November 29, 1932 to January 3, 1933. In all the apparitions in Beauraing she always appeared in the same place, below the arched branch of the hawthorn tree. The children would always fall to their knees when the Virgin appeared and they would pray in a high-pitched voice, which was so different from their natural voices. They could not help going to their knees in this manner as soon as she appeared. It was an instinctive reaction, and as they crashed to their knees, the thud was heard by all the bystanders. Sometimes their stockings were torn in the fall, but their knees were never bruised. On the contrary, they said that they felt as if they were kneeling on cushions.

Another remarkable feature was the fact that they all hit the ground at exactly the same time. On several occasions they were deliberately separated and could not see each other, but they still hit the ground at the same time. This certainly rules out the possibility of hallucination or of deliberate deceit. These two phenomena, the sudden simultaneous falling to their knees, crashing to the ground, which should normally cause severe pain, and the praying of the *Hail Marys* in a voice different from their natural ones, tended to prove that something was happening which was beyond the natural powers of the children.

On December 2, 1932, she identified herself for the first time by nodding her head affirmatively when asked by Albert Voisin if she was "the Immaculate Virgin." She then spoke simply to the children, entreating them: "Always be good." She asked them to return on "the day of *the Immaculate Conception*," and also requested that a chapel be built. She made that similar request, of course, in Lourdes and Fatima. Notably, as in Lourdes she wore a Rosary with a gold chain on her right arm.

On December 8, the feast of *the Immaculate Conception*, the crowd was estimated at between ten and fifteen thousand. It was on that day that the medical profession had another opportunity of authenticating the ecstasy of the children. Dr. Maistriaux, who practiced medicine in

Beauraing and was one of the four doctors who had come
with the children, applied the flame of a match to the
underside of Gilbert Voisin's hand until half of the match
had burnt. Later examination revealed no trace of a burn
nor was there any expression of pain from this.

The same flame test was applied to the hand of Gilbert
Degeimbre, "long enough to cause a first-degree burn," the
doctor said. But there was no burn. The doctors also
pinched the arms, calves, and ear lobes of three of the
visionaries. There was no reaction from the children. Later,
no traces of redness or other marks of the pinching could
be found. Finally, a very strong flashlight was placed at
close range before the opened eyes of the children and
whereas the effects on the pupils appeared to be normal,
namely, a contraction of the pupils, the eyelids did not
move. This verification of the state of ecstasy by the
doctors greatly impressed the sceptics.

On December 29, some eight thousand people, including
thirty-seven doctors, were present for the apparition which
took place at 7:00 p.m. It was on that occasion that she
appeared with a brilliant heart of gold. The heart was near
the center of her chest and was surrounded by little golden
rays. It was meant to be the *Immaculate Heart of Mary*.
Indeed, she showed her heart of gold on five different
occasions in Beauraing.

In her last apparition on January 3, 1933, she
promised: "I will convert sinners." After that, she confided
a message to the children and then said: "I am the *Mother
of God*, the *Queen of Heaven*. Pray always." But it was
what she had already said to Juan Diego in the other side
of the world in Guadalupe, Mexico, in 1531: "I am the
perfect and perpetual Virgin Mary, *mother of the true
God*..." The colour of her robe also told the Aztecs that she
was a Queen. The robe was studded with stars and so she
was the *Queen of Heaven*.

Her last words to the children were: "Do you love my
Son? Do you love me? Then sacrifice yourself for me.
Farewell." And so, the substance of the message of
Beauraing, which was delivered in very few words, can be
reduced to four elements: prayer, sacrifice, the conversion
of sinners, and devotion to the Immaculate Heart of Mary.
Notably, these were also the essential messages of Fatima
in 1917.

On the last of her apparitions in Beauraing, Fernande
had a special vision that day. She alone saw a ball of fire
about five feet in diameter burst in the shrub. Sparks flew

high in the air somewhat like lightning, and then there was a loud noise which sounded like a clap of thunder. Then the Blessed Virgin appeared to her under the hawthorn tree. It was a depiction of Rev. 11:19: "Then the sanctuary of God in heaven opened, and the ark of the covenant could be seen inside it. Then there were flashes of lightning, peals of thunder and earthquakes, and violent hail." Indeed, the Blessed Virgin is *truly* the *Ark of the Covenant*.

As time went by, doubt and scepticism of the apparitions gradually disappeared as the facts of the story became known. Even hardened socialists were convinced, and some of them returned to the Church. In fact, the story of the apparitions caused a great sensation all over Europe and in 1933–34, it was fashionable to espouse Beauraing. Two million pilgrims visited the hawthorn in the year 1933.

On July 2, 1949, in a letter to the clergy in his diocese, the bishop said: "We are able in all sincerity and prudence to affirm that the *Queen of Heaven* appeared to the children of Beauraing during the winter of 1932–33 especially to show us in her maternal heart the anxious appeal for prayer and the promise of her powerful mediation for the conversion of sinners."

Twelve days after her last apparition in Beauraing, she appeared again in the Belgium hamlet of Banneux, fifty miles to the north of Beauraing, to eleven year old Mariette Beco. She was dressed in a garment similar to her Lourdes "outfit." A white Rosary also hung from her right arm. Then, on Wednesday, January 18, 1933, she identified herself: "I am the *Virgin of the Poor*." On Saturday, February 11, the 75th anniversary of her first apparition to Bernadette in Lourdes, she said to Mariette: "I have come to relieve suffering... I am the *Mother of the Saviour, Mother of God*. Pray much."

She came to Banneux as the *Virgin of the Poor* to console them during the height of the great economic depression which was a prelude to the emergence of Hitler's Third Reich.

The Pope prays at the shrine of Our Lady of Beauraing

The young visionaries of Beauraing

Chapter 27

World War II
1939—1945

It was just twenty five years later and Germany was once more the initiator of an even greater war. The foreign correspondent and historian, William L. Shrirer, wrote a monumental classic on the Nazi era and World War II in his book *The Rise and Fall of the Third Reich*. It records in detail the events of those most horrible and unspeakable years of violence in world history.

The First Reich had been the medieval Holy Roman Empire. The Second Reich had been that which was formed by Bismarck after Prussia's defeat of France in 1871. Both had added glory to the German name but the Weimar Republic (the new postwar German nation of 1919) had, as Nazi propaganda put it, dragged that fair name in the mud. Hitler's Third Reich was to restore it. His gospel was that the Versailles Treaty, the Communists, and the Jews had brought on the woes which had befallen Germany.

Democracy was out of the question and the author-itarianism of the Prussian Army was to be adopted by the Third Reich and his party, the **Nazi**onal Sozialistische Deutshe Arbeiterpartie, abbreviated to NAZI, became the only legal party in the land. It was all about the glorification of war and conquest, and the absolute power of the authoritarian state; the belief in the Aryans, especially the Germans, as the master race, the hatred of the Jews and Slavs, and the contempt for democracy.

The Nazi standard was taken from old Roman designs. It was a black swastika, a hooked cross on top, with a silver wreath surmounted by an eagle. The pagan Aztecs also had an eagle for their standard.

This Third Reich was born on January 30, 1933, soon after the apparitions in Beauraing and Banneux. Hitler boasted that it would endure for a thousand years. In Nazi parlance it was often referred to as the "Thousand-Year Reich." It was an apocalyptic number of years based on the Book of Revelation which foretold the thousand-year reign of Christ on earth (Rev. 20:1-6). However, in spite of his vain boast, it only lasted twelve years and four months, but in that space of time, Hitler succeeded in raising the German people to heights of power and plunging them to depths of depravity.

Exemplifying the interplay between politics and religion, Shrirer commented on the immense influence that Martin Luther had on the Germans and their subsequent history: "He left a mark on the life of the Germans, for both good and bad, more indelible, more fateful than was wrought by any other single individual before or since. Through his sermons and his magnificent translation of the Bible, Luther created the modern German language, arousing the people not only to a Protestant vision of Christianity but also to a heightened pitch of German nationalism and taught them, at least in religion, the supremacy of the individual conscience."

In the spring of 1936, Belgium, whose neutrality had been previously violated by Germany at the start of World War I, frightened by the re-militarization of the Third Reich, again sought refuge in neutrality. In fact, on October 13, 1937, Germany officially and solemnly confirmed its promise that under no circumstances would it impair the inviolability and integrity of Belgium.

On May 22, 1939, Hitler and Mussolini signed a military alliance, and on September 1, 1939, German troops invaded Poland. Two days later, England declared a state of war with Germany. Eventually, on May 10, 1940, Nazi troops broke across the borders of three small neutral states, Belgium, Holland, and Luxembourg, in brutal violation of the German word, solemnly and repeatedly given. It was on that day that Winston Churchill became the prime minister of England.

On June 4, 1940, the predicament of Great Britain was indeed grim. Dunkirk fell and the British Expeditionary Force had to evacuate from a devastating German onslaught. France was doomed. Unprepared as it was, Britain had no army to defend the island, and the Royal Air Force had also been greatly weakened from the battles in defense of France. Only the Navy remained and the Luftwaffe bombers were based just ten minutes away across the narrow English Channel.

On June 10, the French government hastily departed Paris, and on June 14, the great city, the glory of France, which was undefended, was occupied by General von Kuechler's Eighteenth Army. The Swastika was immediately hoisted on the Eiffel Tower and two days later, France asked for an armistice. France was out of World War II after only six weeks.

Hitler selected the place for the signing of the armistice. It was to be on the same spot where Germany, at the end of World War I, had capitulated to France and her allies on November 11, 1918, in the little clearing in the woods at Compiégne. There the Nazi warlord would get his sweet revenge. Hitler felt as Satan did after his victory in the Garden of Eden. It was on June 21, 1940. It was "the longest day" for France, literally and figuratively.

William Shrirer, as a foreign correspondent, was there for that historic event and his diary recorded the occasion: "When Hitler reached the little opening in the forest and his personal standard had been run up in the center of it, his attention was attracted by a great granite block which stood some three feet above the ground. Hitler, followed by the others, walked slowly over to it, and read the inscription engraved in French in great high letters: 'Here on the eleventh of November 1918, succumbed the criminal pride of the German empire vanquished by the free peoples which it tried to enslave.'"

Hitler and Goering read it and Shrirer looked at the expression on Hitler's face: "I have seen that face many times at the great moments of his life," he wrote, "but today! It is afire with scorn, anger, hate, revenge, triumph. Suddenly, he swiftly snaps his hands on his hips, arches his shoulders, and plants his feet wide apart. It is a magnificent gesture of defiance, of burning contempt of this place now, and all that it has stood for in the twenty two years since it witnessed the humbling of the German empire."

Hitler and his party then entered the armistice railway car, and the Fuehrer seated himself in the chair occupied by the French victor Marshal Foch in 1918. Adolph Hitler had reached his pinnacle. Pride was glorifying itself. Arrogance was asserting itself and saying "I will be like unto God." He then went off with his entourage to do the sights of Paris briefly and then to visit the battlefields of the First World War, where he had served as a dispatch runner. When in Paris he gazed down at the tomb of Napoleon I at Les Invalides, and he told his faithful photographer, Heinrich Hoffmann: "That was the greatest and finest moment of my life." Indeed, Hitler and Napoleon I had at least two things in common—nationalistic pride and an insatiable greed for power.

Three weeks later, on June 28, 1940, a confidential message arrived for Hitler from Pope Pius XII. Similar communications were addressed to Mussolini and Churchill, offering his mediation for "a just and honourable peace." Neither responded. Throughout the last fortnight of June and the first days of July, Hitler waited for word from London that the British government was ready to throw in the sponge and conclude a peace treaty. No such thing was on Churchill's mind.

On July 16, 1940, the feast of *Our Lady of Mount Carmel*, Hitler finally reached a fateful decision, which was to be the beginning of his downfall. He chose the wrong day! On that day he issued "Directive No. 16 on the Preparation of a Landing Operation against England." The code name for the assault was to be "Sea Lion." Then on July 30, 1940, General Jodl, Chief of Operations and Hitler's favourite strategist, wrote: "The final German victory over England is now only a question of time." The German Air Force and Navy were to be given the mission of carrying on alone the war against England. September 15, Hitler said, would be the earliest day for Operation Sea Lion to begin. It was also an important date in Catholic Marian history!

August 15, 1940, brought the first great battle in the skies. The Germans threw in the bulk of their planes, 801 bombers and 1,149 fighter aircraft, but were severely mauled by seven squadrons of British Hurricanes and Spitfires. Sunday, September 15, 1940, was certainly one of the most decisive battles of the war. Some 200 German bombers, escorted by three times as many fighters, appeared over the English Channel about midday, headed for London. On that day another small group of British pilots intercepted and destroyed 185 enemy aircraft intended to be the spearhead of the German invasion by sea, and before they reached the capital, many were dispersed and others shot down before they could deliver their bomb load.

Two hours later, an even stronger German formation returned and that too was routed. From that day onward, the daylight attacks of the Luftwaffe ceased. That being so, the prospect of an effective landing by sea by the Germans was dim and two days after that decisive air battle, the Fuehrer called off "Sea Lion" indefinitely. That September 15 was the turning point, "the crux," as Churchill later judged it, "of the Battle of Britain."

For the first time in the war, Hitler had been stopped, his plans of further conquest frustrated, and at a time when he was certain that final victory had been achieved, a handful of British pilots had thwarted his invasion. Britain was saved. As Churchill told the House of Commons in a memorable speech when the battle in the skies was still raging: "Never in the field of human conflict was so much owed by so many to so few."

Indeed, in another speech in the House of Commons on October 8, 1940, he also paid tribute to those great victories: "The three great days of August 15, September 15, and September 27 have proved to all the world that here at home over our own island we have the mastery of the air." August 15 was the feast of the *Assumption of the Blessed Virgin Mary* and September 15 was the feast of *Our Lady of Sorrows*, a feast day so dear to Cardinal Bourne of England. And so, one may well say that although it was the Virgin's victory, England claimed the credit!

Slave Labour

Germany made full use of slave labour during the war, and Martin Bormann, Hitler' party secretary, wrote a long letter reiterating the Fuehrer's views on the subject: "The Slavs are to work for us. Insofar as we do not need them, they may die. Therefore, compulsory vaccination and German health services are superfluous. The fraternity of the Slavs is undesirable. They may use contraceptives or practice abortion—the more the better. Education is dangerous. It is enough if they can count up to 100... Religion we leave to them as a means of diversion. As for food they won't get any more than is absolutely necessary. We are the masters. We come first."

Now, the obsession of the Germans with the idea that they were the "master race," including the idea that the

Slavic people must be their slaves, was especially observant in regard to Russia. Erich Koch, the Reich Commissar for the Ukraine, expressed it in a speech at Kiev during the war: "We are the master race and must govern hard but just... We are a master race, which must remember that the lowliest German worker is racially and biologically a thousand times more valuable than the population here."

By the end of September 1944, some seven and one half million civilian foreigners were toiling for the Third Reich as slave labourers. Nearly all of them had been rounded up by force, deported to Germany in boxcars, usually without food or water or any sanitary facilities, and they were put to work in the factories, fields, and mines.

During the first five years of the Nazi regime most concentration camp inmates were Christians. Jews were relatively late arrivals. Little needs to be repeated about the holocaust when six million Jews were exterminated in gas ovens by the Nazis. Six *million!* This extermination of Jewry was considered by Hitler and his Nazi party to be the "final solution of the Jewish question." An inexpensive, easy-to-manufacture gas known as Zyklon B, a hydrogen cyanide, was used in chambers built to resemble large shower rooms.

But this "final solution" also included the enslavement of "Christian subhumans" like Russians, Poles, Romanians, Hungarians, and Yugoslavs, and their reduction in number grew through a programme of planned extermination. As Max Dimont said in his book *Jews, God, and History*: "If the Christian reader dismisses what happened in Germany as something which affected a few million Jews only, he has not merely shown his contempt for the 7 million Christians murdered by the Nazis but has betrayed the Christian heritage as well."

In fact, the Nazi regime intended eventually to destroy Christianity in Germany, and substitute the old paganism of the early tribal Germanic gods and the new paganism of the Nazi extremists. The National Reich Church was to clear from its altars all crucifixes, Bibles, and pictures of Saints. On the altars there must be nothing but *Mein Kampf* and to the left a sword. The Christian Cross must be removed from all churches and must be superceded by the only unconquerable symbol, the Swastika.

Much of it is forgotten now, but the world knew no greater period of violence and of satanism than in the early 1940s, when the principalities and powers of the underworld reduced men into irrational beasts. Indeed, it would take an entire book to record the uncivilized atrocities perpetrated by this brutal and inhumane regime called the Third Reich. It surpassed the savagery of the Aztec empire four centuries previously.

On December 7, 1941, without warning or any declaration of war, Japan attacked the American fleet in Pearl Harbor and launched a campaign of conquest of the Pacific, transforming the European war into a global war. Initially very reluctant to become embroiled in the European conflict, the United States then entered the war on December 8, 1941. It was a most important helping hand to Britain on the feast of *the Immaculate Conception*. It was an entry which eventually led to the destruction of the Third Reich and Japan.

On April 28, 1945, the executed bodies of Benito Mussolini and his mistress, Clara Patacci, hanging upside down in the Pizza Loretto in Milan, provided a grisly monument to European Fascism and the end came quickly for the Third Reich in the spring of 1945 when the Russian, British, and the United States armies rolled into Berlin.

On April 30, 1945, as Red Army tanks and the Allied forces pounded Berlin into the dust, Hitler dictated a banal message in his bunker, blaming his own army as well as the Jewish-Bolshevik conspiracy for his failure. He then shot himself in the mouth. His recent bride, Eva Braun, swallowed poison instead. World War II had ended in Europe and on May 8, 1945, Field Marshal Keitel signed Germany's final act of surrender. And so, God who made the mighty, made the mightier yet. But the war in the Far East was not over. Enter the atomic bomb on August 6, 1945.

As World War II approached, Berthe Petit received frequent revelations concerning the dark days that awaited the world, and her heavenly communications continued during the course of the war. About the year 1942, she complained to Jesus: "Lord, how is it that while confiding this work to me, you permit it to be thwarted at every moment?" "You are astonished!" He replied. "Have you forgotten that my own acts were constantly thwarted and that my mother always lived in anxiety and suffering? Give time for the light to make its appearance."

On March 25, 1943, the feast of the Annunciation, when she was at the very threshold of death, Berthe spoke of the consecration of the world to the *Sorrowful and Immaculate Heart of Mary*, and said with a faint smile: "It will be accomplished." The next day she passed away very peacefully in her sleep. She was buried in the little village of Louvignies. It was difficult to find but I eventually found her burial place there on August 2, 1994. Very few people in the area knew about her when I enquired!

The surrender of Germany in 1918

June 1940.
Hitler visits the sights of Paris

Sir Winston Churchill

Chapter 28

Pope Pius XII
1939 – 1958

As Sir Nicolas Cheetham recorded in his classic book *The History of the Popes* that when the Nazis made very substantial gains in the autumn election of 1931, it was only a step towards Hitler's accession to office in January, 1933. Pius XI received the news with some equanimity. Whether or not he had studied *Mein Kampf*, he observed that Hitler's early public statements as Chancellor were not unfriendly to the Church but clearly hostile to Communism. Counselled by Cardinal Eugenio Pacelli, his Secretary of State, he decided he must have a concordat with the Reich.

But any optimism which the Pope and the hierarchy may have had about the future was soon dispelled as reports poured in of breaches of the concordat, both in letter and in spirit. The Nazis began to employ a regimentation and political indoctrination of the youth, the intimidation of parents who sent their children to Catholic schools, and the suppression of Catholic associations and trade unions. Moreover, all these were being aggravated by crude physical violence against Catholics, and scurrilous propaganda campaigns orchestrated by Goebbels and Streicher against religion and the papacy. Indeed, persecution of recalcitrant Catholics was beginning to resemble that of the Jews.

In January, 1937, the Pope received five leaders of the German hierarchy and it was after their talk that he circularized the encyclical *Mit Brennender Sorge* (With Burning Anxiety). It is now known that it was actually Cardinal Eugenio Pacelli, his Secretary of State, who drafted it. Published in German instead of the traditional Latin, it was conveyed secretly to Germany, printed, distributed and read out in all the churches on Palm Sunday. No epithets were omitted in its criticism of Nazism, Hitler himself being described as a "mad prophet possessed with repulsive arrogance."

The encyclical stated that the totalitarian and racist dogmas were incompatible with Christian teaching, and that the Nazis were violating Church rites. An infuriated Hitler then ordered priests to be arrested and bullied. A year later, when visiting Rome, he refused to make a courtesy call on the Pope.

Pius XI died on February 12, 1939, at the age of eighty two. On March 1, 1939, on the third ballot, Cardinal Pacelli was elected Pope. Obviously intending to continue the work of his predecessor, he took the name Pius XII. He was sixty-three years old. From 1930 to the time of his election, he had always been at the side of Pius XI, and it was generally expected that, in accordance with Pius XI's wishes, he would be succeeded by his Secretary of State. Indeed, Pacelli obtained the necessary majority at the second ballot, but surprised his colleagues by requesting their confirmation in a third ballot before embarking on his nineteen-year pontificate (1939–58).

From the very start of his pontificate he faced the difficulty which Pius XI had so far failed to resolve, namely, was there any possibility of a compromise between totalitarianism and religion? Six months after his election, World War II began on September 1, 1939. From a diplomatic point of view, transactions, however impermanent, may be preferable to dangerous confrontations, and that was the principle to which he and his predecessors had always adhered.

Just as Benedict XV had avoided designating imperial Germany as the aggressor in World War I, when condoling with Belgium, he, too, was careful not to compromise his neutrality by naming the Germany of Hitler. Nevertheless, he later authorized Vatican Radio to censure Nazi oppression of the conquered Poles in much more outspoken terms. His solemn disapproval of Italy's entrance into the war also contrasted with the enthusiasm of many Italian bishops. In fact, it was only too obvious that as long as Fascism was on the winning side, some Italian Catholics would not disavow it.

For the whole year Pius XII retired behind the curtain of his neutrality, and with Europe dominated by the Axis powers, he felt isolated and insecure. But the evil ruthlessness of the Nazi Regime had to be experienced and appreciated to understand the Pope's position. The ability to protect his Catholic peoples against totalitarian abuse had been sadly impaired and, in addition, neither the Axis nor the British would accept him as mediator.

Meanwhile, passionate and occasionally envenomed attacks were made on him for his alleged passivity and reluctance to denounce the wanton genocide. Some of the adverse criticism had been inspired by a sincere conviction that papal action could have achieved the desired results, others by an obvious antireligious or anti-Catholic bias.

On the other hand, as soon as the outbreak of the war swelled the flood of Jewish fugitives, the Church sheltered, fed, and subsidized them on a very extensive scale. According to one Jewish source: "The Catholic Church saved more than four hundred thousand Jews from certain death; it saved more Jewish lives than all other churches, religious institutions, and rescue organizations put together." Many other authorities testified to the Pope's personal interest in these works and his general concern with the sufferings of the Jews.

It can be assumed that he and his advisors were not the last to hear about the gas chambers in Poland, and when these were confirmed, the question frequently asked was why did he not broadcast a flaming indictment of Hitler and his henchmen? There is no doubt that a public condemnation by the Holy See would have caused an immense stir in the world and exonerated the Pope from future charges of indifference. But, as Cheetham reasoned: "If we ask whether it would have brought the massacres to a halt or even slowed them down, we are to confess that the question is unanswerable. We simply cannot judge whether it would have eased or in fact aggravated the plight of the victims."

There were those who found it hard to guess to what extent open papal intervention on behalf of the Jews would have resulted in retaliation against German Catholics by an enraged and paranoiac Fuehrer. However, it was prophetic enough that the outspoken protest in their favour from the Archbishop of Utrecht in the Netherlands was immediately followed by the dispatch of all baptized Catholics of Jewish origin in his diocese to the Polish ovens!

Indeed, a Nazi defendant at Nuremberg was more certain of the outcome. He testified that a direct papal condemnation of Hitler would have driven him to more horrors. According to the July 1997 issue of *Inside the Vatican*, Baron Von Weilzsacker, Germany's Ambassador to the Holy See, and father of the current president of the Republic of Germany, and his assistant Von Hassel, had both advised the Pope against making any public statement. They also said this during the Nuremberg trials. They advised Pius XII to avoid any such action because it would only have worsened the situation, and the Vatican as well would have risked being invaded by the Nazis.

After the war was over, on August 15, 1950, Pius XII proclaimed the dogma of the bodily assumption of the Blessed Virgin. It was the fourth Marian dogma. Pius died on October 9, 1958. Immediately on hearing of his death, Israel's Golda Meir wrote: "When fearful martyrdom came to our people in the decade of the Nazi terror, the voice of the Pope was raised for its victims. The life of our times was enriched by a voice speaking out about the great moral truths above the tumult of daily conflict. We mourn a great servant of peace."

The greatest scientist of the 20th century also paid his tribute, which was published in *Time* magazine on December 23, 1940. It was the declaration of Albert Einstein: "Being a lover of freedom, when the revolution came in Germany I looked to the universities to defend it, knowing that they had always boasted of their devotion to the cause of truth; but no, the universities immediately were silenced. Then I looked to the great editors of the newspapers, whose flaming editorials in days gone by had proclaimed their love of freedom. But they, like the universities, were silenced in a few short weeks. Only the Church stood squarely across the path of Hitler's campaign for suppressing truth. I had never any special interest in the Church before, but now I feel a great affection and admiration because the Church alone has had the courage and persistence to stand for intellectual truth and moral freedom. I am forced thus to confess that what I once despised I now praise unreservedly."

By 1963, five years after his death, a profound change was occurring in Western culture, soon to be spread to the rest of the world. The causes included the discoveries of 20th century science, the rise in materialism, the prodigious acceleration of the communication network, the "pill" and the new sexual freedom, and the decline in traditional religious faith, reflected by the April 8, 1966 front cover of *Time* magazine, which read: "Is God dead?"

Adolph Hitler   Pope Pius XII

188

Chapter 29

The Nuclear Age is Born

Germany was defeated but the war in the Far East was still raging. Enter the atomic bomb. In the book *Final Warning, The Legacy Of Chernobyl*, the authors, Dr. Robert Gale and Thomas Hauser, wrote: "Already there is concern that science has gone too far; that in splitting the atom, man has crossed a threshold that threatens us all." Indeed, nuclear fission and fusion are the most dangerous processes known to man. They have the capacity to turn the earth into desert or make the deserts bloom. It is a power that humanity dare not abuse. Now the fear exists that something is happening which could destroy us all.

In 1905, Albert Einstein published his special theory of relativity. Examining the properties of energy, mass, time, and space, he postulated that mass contained large amounts of latent energy which could, if fundamental building blocks were broken apart, be released. He further postulated that during this process, a certain amount of matter(m) would be converted into energy(e), and that the amount of energy created would equal the amount of mass lost multiplied by the square of the speed of light(c), that is, $E=mc^2$. For example, 1kg (2.2lb) of matter converted completely into energy will be equivalent to the energy released by exploding 22 megatons of TNT. Einstein soon became the most famous Jew in modern times and won the Nobel Prize in Physics in 1921.

In 1919, soon after the end of World War I, an English scientist, Professor Ernest Rutherford, of Manchester University, the 1908 Nobel Laureate in Chemistry, fired alpha particles through hydrogen gas and dislodged their nuclei. He also managed to knock hydrogen nuclei (H-particles) out of the elements boron, fluorine, sodium, aluminum, and nitrogen. He named these H-particles protons. They seemed to be the indivisible building blocks of the nuclei of all elements.

Scientists see the world as being made up of countless particles whose ever-shifting arrangements in space are the reality of all appearances. All that is real are either atoms or some combination of atoms. Atoms are the building blocks of nature. They are unimaginably small, and one hundred million of them placed side-by-side would form a line only one inch long.

Atoms consist primarily of empty space, and their center is composed of protons (electric charge +1) and neutrons (no charge) joined together to form a nucleolus, which carries most of the atom's weight. Electrons are particles which orbit the nucleus of an atom and have an electric charge of –1. But whereas all matter is composed of atoms, not all atoms are alike. Their primary difference is in the number of protons and neutrons that comprise each nucleolus. For example, hydrogen always has one proton and oxygen has eight. Uranium, on the other hand, has ninety-two protons.

Each atom has the same number of orbiting electrons as it has protons. However, atoms of the same element can have different numbers of neutrons. An important example is uranium. One type of uranium atom has 143 neutrons while another has 146. These "isotopes" (as different forms of the same element are called) are known as uranium-235 and uranium-238 (92 protons plus 143 neutrons equal 235, and 92 protons plus 146 neutrons equal 238).

In 1938, Otto Hahn, German radiochemist, with Fritz Straussman determined that when uranium-238 atoms were bombarded by neutrons, their nuclei split apart, releasing energy in accordance with Einstein's theory. Moreover, when these nuclei split, their neutrons shot out at high speed toward nearby atoms, causing these neighbouring atoms to split. Thus, physicists were able to conclude that if enough uranium atoms were gathered together and properly triggered, there would be a chain reaction—the rapid-fire "fissioning" of one atom after another—which would go on until the supply of uranium was exhausted. During this process, enormous amounts of energy would be released. Indeed, properly harnessed, nuclear fission could mean "energy unlimited."

On August 2, 1939, fearful that Hitler's Germany had begun a concerted effort to unlock the secrets of the atom, Albert Einstein wrote to President Franklin D. Roosevelt: "Sir: Some recent work by E. Fermi and L. Szilard, which has been communicated to me in manuscript, leads me to expect that the element uranium may be turned into a new and important source of energy in the immediate future. Certain aspects of the situation seem to call for watchfulness, and, if necessary, quick action on the part of the Administration. I believe, therefore, that it is my duty to bring to your attention the following facts and recommendations:

"In the course of the last four months it has been probable—through the work of Joliot in France as well as Fermi and Szilard in America—that it may become possible to set up a nuclear chain reaction in a large mass of uranium, by which vast amounts of power and large quantities of new radium-like elements would be generated. And now it appears almost certain that this could be achieved in the immediate future.

"This new phenomenon would also lead to the construction of bombs, and it is conceivable, though much less certain, that extremely powerful bombs of a new type may thus be constructed. In view of this situation you may think it desirable to have some permanent contact maintained between the Administration and the group of physicists working on chain reactions in America... I understand that Germany has actually stopped the sale of uranium from Czechoslovakian mines which she has taken over. That she should have taken such early action might perhaps be understood on the grounds that the son of the German Under-Secretary of State is attached to the Kaiser-Wilhelm Institute in Berlin where some of the American work on uranium is now being repeated. Yours very truly, Albert Einstein."

However, apart from $E=mc^2$, this was all that Einstein contributed to the making of the bomb. As he stated later: "My participation in the production of the atomic bomb consisted of one single act. I signed a letter to President Roosevelt."

Thus began the Manhattan Project. Richard Rhodes recorded the complete story of how the bomb was developed in his Pulitzer Prize-winning book *The Making Of*

The Atomic Bomb. Those who worked on the enterprise believed that if Germany manufactured a nuclear weapon before the United States, an unparalleled disaster would follow. Throughout the early 1940s, Roosevelt authorized the secret expenditure of hundreds of millions of dollars to support the programme. The project was kept secret from Congress, and in fact most members of the President's cabinet and Vice-President Truman did not learn of its existence until April 12, 1945, the day Roosevelt died.

Albert Einstein

Robert Oppenheimer

The Enola Gay in a museum

The Hydrogen Bomb

Chapter 30

Trinity

Planning began in March, 1944 for the full-scale test of the atom bomb. According to Richard Rhodes: "Oppenheimer did not doubt that he would be remembered to some degree, and reviled as a man who led the work of bringing to mankind for the first time in its history the means of its own destruction." Sometime between March and October, Oppenheimer proposed a code name for that test. The test and the test site were to be named *Trinity*!

General Leslie Groves, the commanding general of the Corps of Engineers of the Manhattan Project, wrote to Oppenheimer in 1962, enquiring why he chose that name. "Why I chose the name is not clear," replied Oppenheimer, "but I know what thoughts were in my mind. There is a poem of John Donne (1572—1631), *Hymne To God My God, In My Sickness*, written just before his death, which I know and love. From it there is a quotation:

> '*As West and East*
> *In all flat maps—and I am one—are one,*
> *So death doth touch the Resurrection.*'"

I suppose what the poem was saying was that dying, which leads to death, might also lead to resurrection. However, later on in his letter to Groves, Oppenheimer acknowledged that his reply was incomplete. He added: "That still does not make it *Trinity*, but in another, better known devotional poem (Holy Sonnets 14, 11) Donne opens with: '*Batter my heart, three Person'd God...*' Beyond this, I have no clues whatever."

Indeed, whereas Oppenheimer was a devotee of the poetry of John Donne, there is yet another even more famous poem of Donne which I myself consider to be relevant to the karma resulting from the making of the atom bomb. It reads: "No man is an island, entire of itself: every man is a piece of the continent, a part of the main; if a clod be washed away by the sea, Europe is the less, as well as if a promontory were, as well as if a manor of thy friends or of thine own were; any man's death diminishes me, because I am involved in mankind, and therefore never send to know for whom the bell tolls; it tolls for thee." In fact, Hemingway based the title of one of his books on this poem. It was *For Whom The Bells Toll.*

Now, for the testing of *Trinity*, a flat, desolate site with good weather, near enough to Los Alamos to make travel convenient, was needed. An area some sixty miles northwest of Alamogordo, New Mexico, known ominously and prophetically from Spanish time as the Jornada del Muerto (The Journey of Death), was chosen, and a hill named Compañia, twenty miles northwest, was selected as a VIP observatory for the scientists. *Trinity* was to be the greatest physics experiment ever attempted in world history. The year was 1945.

General Leslie Groves decided during the first week in July to fix the test date for July 16. Morning came and evening came. One of observers remarked: "It was an eerie sight to see a number of our highest-ranking scientists seriously rubbing sunburn lotion on their faces and hands in the pitch-blackness of the night, twenty miles away from the expected flash." *Trinity* was fired at 0530 hours just before dawn. "Suddenly there was an enormous flash of light, the brightest light I have ever seen... A new thing has just been born," said Isidor Rabi, the American experimental physicist and Nobel laureate.

Night was turned into day in spite of the very dark glasses the observers were wearing. One other witness of the event, physicist George Kistiakowsky, exclaimed: "I am sure that at the end of the world, in the last millisecond of the earth's existence, the last man will see what we have just seen." Oppenheimer himself later said; "After the blast, we knew the world would not be the same. A few people laughed, a few people cried. Most people were silent. I remember the line from the Hindu scripture; the Bhagavad Gita: 'Now I am become Death, the destroyer of worlds.' I suppose all us thought that, one way or the other."

After the war, he told an audience: "When it went off, in the New Mexico dawn, that first atomic bomb, we thought of Alfred Nobel, and his hope, his vain hope, that dynamite would put an end to wars. We thought of the legend of Prometheus, of that deep sense of guilt in man's new power, that reflects his recognition of evil..."

Indeed, many do recognize it as being evil and it appears that Satan may even have influenced the choice of the site for the test. It was in the desert of New Mexico. In other words, it was in the "New Tenochtitlan." We have already seen that nowhere in world history had Satan so formalized his cult and worship as in the Mexico in the era of the Aztecs. There in Tenochtitlan, now Mexico City, thousands upon thousands of human sacrifices were offered to the pagan sun god.

It is also my opinion that the choice of date, for the occasion of the first fiery atomic explosion, July 16, the feast of *Our Lady of Mount Carmel*, may be linked to the Old Testament account of the great battle on Mount Carmel between the Prophet Elijah and the prophets of the pagan god Baal. It was during the reign of the Jewish King Omri when the Israelites were worshiping foreign gods and idols. It was then that Yahweh told Elijah it was time to call the people to repentance and to single-hearted devotion to him. Elijah called the citizens of Israel to the mountain of Carmel which towered over the plain of Jezreel where they lived.

Once they had gathered, Elijah admonished them saying: "How long will you go limping with a different opinion? If the Lord is God, follow him; but if Baal, then follow him." Then Elijah said to the people: "I alone am left the prophet of the Lord, but Baal's prophets are four hundred and fifty men. Let two bulls be given to us and let them choose one bull for themselves and cut it in pieces and lay it on the wood (of their altar), but put no fire to it. I will prepare the other bull and lay it on the wood (for sacrifice) and put no fire to it. You will call on the name of your god and I will call on the name of the Lord and the god who answers by fire, he is God indeed..."

Then the fire of the Lord fell, and consumed the burnt sacrifice, and the wood, and the stones, and the dust and licked up the water that was in the trench. And when all the people saw it, they fell on their faces and said: "The Lord indeed is God! The Lord indeed is God!" They then seized the prophets of Baal, and Elijah brought them down to the Wadi Kishon and killed them there (1 Kings 18:20 40).

Now, in chapter 6, I referred to Satan's obsession with being "like unto God," and also referred to him as "the ape of God." This is the proud mimic who tries to undo all that God has done. God creates. Satan is the antithesis; he is the destroyer. This jealous instigator of evil has dedicated himself to destroying the world, as voiced, for example, in the monthly message of *Our Lady of Medjugorje*, given on January 25, 1991 to the visionary Maria Pavlovic: "Dear children, Satan is strong and wishes not only to destroy human life, but also nature and the planet on which you live..." Is it a coincidence, therefore, that this satanic weapon was developed and tested in "New" Mexico? The "Old" Mexico of the Aztecs was replaced by the "New" for this Satanic device!

And so, I believe that the great destroyer, Satan, may have inspired the name *Trinity* for the bomb and the bomb site, and chose July 16, the feast of *Our Lady of Mount Carmel*, for the test of this "fireball," in his plan to avenge his defeat in Carmel by "the fire of the Lord" and to ridicule the woman, *Mother of the Word*, whom he hates so much. It was his evil plot against the Trinity and the mother of the second Person of "the three Person'd God."

Chapter 31

The Bells of Nagasaki

I t took two billion dollars, a work force of 100,000, and several years to develop the atomic bomb. Three weeks later, at 2:47 a.m. on August 6, 1945, the *Enola Gay*, named after the given names of the mother of Paul Tibbets, the captain of the B-29, lifted off from an American base on Tinian Island. At 8:15 a.m., the plane's bomb-bay doors opened wide and its cargo fell above Hiroshima. A switch was triggered and forty-three seconds after it had left the *Enola Gay*, the uranium 235 bomb exploded.

On that August 6, Einstein heard on the radio that a chain reaction had given proof of $E=mc^2$ far more spectacularly than he expected. People exposed within a half-mile of the fireball were seared to bundles of smoking black char in a fraction of a second as their internal organs boiled away. In the testimony of the survivors, they described ghastly scenes of people whose skin hung from them "like a kimono" and plunged themselves into the rivers, shrieking in pain.

Now, in June 1997, at a Marian Congress in San Francisco, Dr. Chen-Tzu Theresa Wei, one of the audience, now living in San Jose, California, introduced herself to me. She was born in Hiroshima and graduated from Tokyo's Female Medical School. While she was a student, she returned to Hiroshima for the summer vacation and became a victim of the atomic bomb. Her home was only four or five kilometers away from the epicenter. She is now seventy-two years old and suffers from the long term effects of the fall-out radiation. She related to me a memory which she will never forget. There was a sudden noiseless flash of light, and then she saw "a ball of fire" coming down towards the earth at an angle of about forty five degrees. She lost her sight for over a minute. For two weeks the mushroom cloud lingered over the city and there was no light, electricity, or water for months. But those who were at the epicenter had no memories to relate. They were immediately transformed into carbon. Most of them were followers of the Shinto religion and Buddhism.

Shinto is the indigenous religion of Japan. It is a form of nature-worship with shrines in places of great natural beauty, such as mountain tops or forests where divine spirits are said to be present. Shinto means the "way of the gods." There are not one but many deities. It has no human founder or concept of a divine Creator. It does not have a doctrine of the soul and has no one sacred book but many religious scriptures. Rather than emphasis on sin as disobedience to the deity, there is concern with ritual impurity and purification.

A major tenet of Japan's indigenous cult of Shinto was the Imperial family's direct descent from the sun goddess Amaterasu Omikami, thus establishing the divinity of the emperor. For this reason the emperor had always been the titular head of the cult, with priestly function.

Buddhism was officially introduced into Japan from Korea in 552 AD, a religion which originated in India around 500 BC with the teaching of Siddhartha Gautama, the Indian prince who became Buddha—the Enlightened One. For Buddhists there is no belief in, or worship of, a personal creator God. To reach Nirvana involves the development of morality, meditation, and wisdom. But as John Paul II said in his book *Crossing The Threshold Of Hope*: "It needs to be said right away that the doctrines of salvation in Buddhism and Christianity are opposed. Buddhism is in large measure an 'atheistic' system."

On August 15, 1549, the feast of *the Assumption of the Blessed Virgin Mary*, the Jesuit St. Francis Xavier landed in Kagoshima and the Japanese people heard the Christian Gospel for the first time. Francis left after two years. The Jesuits who followed him attracted many converts from the ranks of aristocrats and commoners, however, evangelization was mainly concentrated in Kyushu, especially in Nagasaki. Great numbers of samurai and tens of thousands of lowly peasants and town people asked for baptism, and by 1582,

Christian converts were estimated at 150,000 when Japan sent its first ambassador to the Vatican.

The much dreaded and powerful warlord Toyotomi Hideyoshi (1534—1598) at first treated the Jesuits with friendship and even his court ladies became Christians, a remarkable achievement. However, he eventually grew apprehensive of this swift increase of Christians and in one of his notorious mood changes, he banned Christianity in 1587. "All Japanese Christians must renounce their religion and all foreign missionaries must leave in twenty days." Although this edict from the shogun was not enforced, nonetheless, the Jesuits went into hiding. They saw it as the beginning of the persecution.

For the next decade Hideyoshi barely tolerated the Christian presence, but in 1597 he took action again. He ordered twenty six Christians to be arrested in Kyoto, the capital city, and marched them through the depths of winter to Nagasaki, a thirty-day journey by foot. There were three Japanese Jesuits, six Franciscans, four of whom were Spanish, one Mexican and one Indian; the other seventeen were Japanese lay people, including a soldier, a physician, and two altar boys. They were dragged from city to city in degrading circumstances, and were to be executed by crucifixion on arrival.

The twenty six were marched to Nishizaka hill, not far from present-day Nagasaki railway station. There twenty six neatly sawn crosses ran from the top of the hill down towards the harbour so that everyone could see the spectacle. The victims were fastened to the crosses by iron rings and straw ropes, and two samurai stood beneath each cross with an unsheathed bamboo lance, waiting to run their weapons up under the rib cages of the Christians. This final act was delayed to heighten the terror of the condemned and the onlookers. The twenty-four year old Mexican, now known as St. Philip of Jesus, was the first martyr. It was sixty-six years after Juan Diego had begun to convert his people!

All of a sudden singing broke out from the line of crosses: "Praise the Lord, ye children of the Lord" (Psalm 113:1), and the murmurings over the hillside ceased. There was silence as the crowd stopped to listen. The Psalm came to end and one of the twenty six began the *Sanctus*, that part of the Latin Mass, sung regularly by all Japanese Christian communities. When the last strains floated across the bay, a Franciscan on another cross began to sing: "Jesus, Mary... Jesus, Mary..." The Christians in the crowd then chanted in unison, four thousand of them. It was becoming a show of Christian strength rather than the blood-curdling spectacle that Hideyoshi had ordered.

A sign was then given and the samurai moved in with their steel-tipped bamboo lances. With deep-throated cries they thrust them into the twenty six. The deadly silence of the crowd suddenly erupted into an angry roar and the samurai hurriedly withdrew. The spectacle of humiliation had gone awry, the honour and the prestige of the Christians rose dramatically, and baptisms rapidly increased. Christians died in Nagasaki, but the Church did not die. She had to go underground, and the Christian message was passed from parents to children. The Nagasaki martyrs were canonized in 1862, and the feast of St. Paul Miki and Companions has since been celebrated on February 6.

Hideoshi died in 1598 and Tokugawa Ieyasu (1543—1618) became the de facto ruler in 1600. Within a few years of the crucifixions, organized persecution commenced again. In 1614, Tokugawa ordered the expulsion of all missionaries and unrepentant Japanese converts, and by 1622, a total of 3,000 believers are estimated to have been martyred. Christianity continued to be suppressed throughout the next century, albeit never fully.

Eventually, in 1865, a group of people at Nagasaki publicly identified themselves as Christians. Soon various communities of "hidden Christians" were discovered in the region. However, Christianity remained banned until the middle of the nineteenth century, when Japan opened its door to the world. At the end of 1944, there were about 1.5 million Christians in all Japan, of whom 444,000 were Catholics and around 1 million Protestants.

On August 9, 1945, at 11:00 a.m., "Fat Man," the name given to the more powerful plutonium bomb, went plummeting down onto a city of two hundred thousand souls of whom more than seventy thousand would immediately die, many without a trace. This time it was in Nagasaki, Japan's first and only Christian city. The bomb exploded over Urakami, the Catholic quarter of the city. The Urakami Cathedral was only five hundred meters from where the bomb detonated. No one could be sure how many perished inside, but several hundred little girls, along with their priests and nuns, were beginning a novena in preparation for the feast of the *Assumption of the Blessed Virgin Mary*, when they were all incinerated.

Six days later, on August 15, 1945, Emperor Hirohito made his historic broadcast, announcing the "unconditional surrender" of Japan. The nation heard the voice of this "god" for the first time. But there was another most historic address later. The emperor, who was revered as a living deity in Japan, a descendent of the sun goddess, the chief divinity of the Shinto pantheon (something that was unique among nations), renounced all claims to divinity!

Dr. Takashi Nagai, Professor of Radiology at the University of Nagasaki, died of "atomic disease" six years after the plutonium bomb incinerated his wife and his home. Born into a medical family of the ancient Shinto faith, he was a Japanese atheist who became a Catholic. Paul Glynn, a Marist, who served over 20 years in Japan, wrote *A Song for Nagasaki*, skillfully weaving Japanese culture and the history of Christianity in Japan into his biography on the life of Dr. Nagai.

He wrote that, after obtaining his medical degree, Takashi was in the Fifth Japanese Medical Corps in 1931 when Japanese armed forces invaded Manchuria. After the conquest of Manchuria, Japan, now ruled by a vicious military clique, resumed its efforts to conquer more Chinese territories. In the summer of 1937, Japan finally seized the opportunity to provoke a full-scale war with China. In November 1937, after their successful invasion of Shanghai, the Japanese launched a massive attack on Nanking. When the city fell on December 13, Japanese soldiers began an orgy of cruelty seldom if ever matched in world history. Tens of thousands of young men were mowed down by machine guns, used for bayonet practice or burned alive. Between 20,000 and 80,000 Chinese women were raped. It is said that so brutal were the Japanese in Nanking that even the Nazis in the city were shocked. By the end of the massacre about 300,000 Chinese had been killed.

In 1937, Takashi joined Japanese forces in Shanghai. He personally treated Chinese prisoners and their wounded with extraordinary kindness. More than once he carried wounded Chinese soldiers on his back to his First Aid station. During the war years, Takashi became a man of prayer. Whenever he came upon a church, he entered and knelt before the Blessed Sacrament, and prayed his Rosary constantly.

Over the few weeks after the bomb fell in Nagasaki, Dr. Nagai heard a number of stories of little groups of junshin girls who were gathered in a field or down by the river. Most were badly injured and many would be dead within days but they kept encouraging each other, singing verses of their hymn: "Mother Mary, I offer myself to you." Indeed, prayer to Mary had been one of the essentials in the spirituality of the hidden Christians of Nagasaki and it became the same for Nagai.

On November 23, 1945, bandaged, limping, burnt, disfigured, and demoralized Catholics gathered beside the shattered cathedral to offer a Requiem Mass for their dead. Nagai had regarded the death of Nagasaki's people as a martyrdom similar to that of the first Japanese Christians in the sixteenth and seventeenth centuries. When his turn came to speak, he rose a little unsteadily, and with a slow bow to the priests and others in the congregation, he began his address to his people: "On the morning of August 9, a meeting of the Supreme Council of War was in session at Imperial Headquarters. Tokyo had to decide whether Japan would surrender or continue to wage war. At that moment the world stood at a parting of the ways. A decision had to be made—peace or further cruel bloodshed and carnage. And just then, at 11:02 a.m., an atom bomb exploded over our suburb. In an instant eight thousand Christians were called to God and in a few hours flames turned to ash this venerable Far Eastern holy place. How happy are the pure lambs who now rest in the bosom of God!

"At midnight that night our cathedral suddenly burst into flames and was consumed. At exactly that same time in the Imperial Palace, His Majesty the Emperor made known his sacred decision to end the war. On August 15, the Imperial rescript which put an end to the fighting was formally promulgated and the whole world saw the light of peace. August 15 is also the great feast of the *Assumption of the Blessed Virgin Mary*. It is significant, I believe, that the Urakami cathedral was dedicated to her. We ask: 'Was this convergence of events—the end of the war and the celebration of her *feast day*—merely coincidental or was it the mysterious Providence of God?'

"I have heard that the atom bomb was destined for another city. Heavy clouds rendered that target impossible and the American crew headed for the secondary target, Nagasaki... Was not Nagasaki the chosen victim, the lamb without blemish, slain as a whole-burnt offering on an altar of sacrificial atonement for the sins of all the nations during World War II?... We are inheritors of Adam's sin, of Cain's sin. He killed his brother. Yes, we have forgotten we are God's children. We (Japanese) have turned to idols and have forgotten love, hating one another, killing one another, joyfully killing one another.

"At last the evil and horrific conflict has come to an end, but mere repentance was not enough for peace... We had to offer a stupendous sacrifice... Cities had been levelled and even that was not enough... Only this *hansai* in Nagasaki sufficed, and at that moment God inspired the emperor to issue the sacred proclamation that ended the war. The Christian flock of Nagasaki was true to the faith through three centuries of persecution. During the recent war it prayed for a lasting peace. Here was the one pure lamb that had to be sacrificed as *hansai* on his altar, so that many millions of lives might be saved... Let us be thankful that Nagasaki was chosen for the whole-burnt sacrifice! Let us be thankful that through this sacrifice peace was granted to the world and religious freedom to Japan..."

As Bonifice Hanley O.F.M. wrote in *The Anthonian* (1986): "Takashi, in his mystical embrace of the crucified Christ, tried to make sense of the atomic horror. At the very moment of the crucifixion he saw the rebirth of resurrection, not only for Nagasaki but for the whole world." This remark reminded me of Oppenheimer's reflection on John Donne's sonnet *Hymne to God My God*:

> "As West and East
> In all flat maps—and I am one—are one,
> So death doth touch the Resurrection."

I also realized that Takashi's "homily" was identical to my own analogy of this fiery sacrifice in Japan to the burnt sacrifice by the fire ball which fell on the altar on Mount Carmel (1 Kings 1:18). At that time it was a victory for Elijah.

Before the bomb fell, the cathedral had two bell towers which housed two large bells. One tower was hurled seven metres away by the bomb. Its bell was cracked beyond repair. When December came, Nagai and a friend decided it might be worthwhile digging for the other bell which was buried under a mountain of rubble. By late morning on Christmas eve, December 24, they could see the top of the bell, and with the help of several young men they were able to lift the bell. It was intact. By the time they had the bell hanging securely on a tripod of cypress logs, it was almost 6:00 p.m. They rang the Angelus.

This "miracle" transformed the winter darkness and to the depressed Christians it seemed that the cathedral had risen from the ashes to announce Christ's birth. That night the title of Dr. Nagai's famous book was born. It was *The Bells of Nagasaki*. Its message would be that not even an atomic bomb can silence the bell of God.

Three years before he died, Nagai wrote: "Atomic energy is a secret that God placed within the universe. Scientists have unlocked this secret, and the human race has now grasped the key to its future destiny. Will this result in a tremendous leap forward for civilization or will it destroy our earth? Is atomic energy a key for survival or for total destruction? I myself believe that the only way to properly use this key is through authentic religion."

Fr. Stefano Gobbi, the founder of the Marian Movement of Priests, and whose authenticity is believed by thousands of priests, nuns, and the faithful, and who, we are told, is a close friend of Pope John Paul II, claims to have received this message while he was conducting a cenacle of prayer with fellow priests and nuns in Nagasaki on October 18, 1996: "Today you are bringing to a close here the journey which you have made through all Japan, where you have been able to see the marvels of love and mercy of my immaculate Heart. And you are bringing it to an end precisely in this city, especially loved by your heavenly Mother.

"In this city the work of evangelization was begun, by Saint Francis Xavier, the great apostle and missionary, who opened the way in this distant continent to the first announcement of the Gospel.

"In this city there were led to their martyrdom twenty-six of my children, heroic witnesses of Christ, to whom they offered their lives on the altar of my Immaculate Heart. You also were here to celebrate Holy Mass in the Shrine raised upon the spot of their terrible execution.

"In this city also lived my son, Saint Maximilian Kolbe, and it is here that he constructed the city of the Immaculata, which still today brings my shining presence to many of my Japanese children, who so love and honor me.

"In this city, there also exploded the atomic bomb, causing tens of thousands of deaths in a few brief instants, a chastisement and terrible sign of what man can do when, distancing himself from God, he becomes incapable of love, of compassion, and of mercy. This is what the whole world could become if it does not welcome my invitation to conversion and return to the Lord. From this place, I renew my anguished appeal to all the nations of the earth."

On Saturday, March 27, 1982, Fr. Hubert Schiffer, a Jesuit priest, at age sixty-seven, died in Frankfurt, Germany. He was 30 years old when he was within the one-mile center of the atomic explosion in Hiroshima, where he was assigned to the parish of the Assumption of the Blessed Virgin Mary. Three other fellow Jesuits, Frs.

Lasalle, Kleinsore, and Cieslik were still alive and well, over 30 years later. It is inexplicable that, of the hundreds of thousands of people within a radius of one mile (1.6km) of the explosion, they were the only survivors, and that none of the priests were affected by the radiation. Moreover, the parish house, which was only eight houses from the center of the explosion, remains standing when all surrounding buildings were completely demolished.

More than two hundred scientists have examined Fr. Schiffer and questioned him, unable to explain how he had survived. The doctors and scientists heard again and again the same response to their many questions: "As missionaries, we were trying to live the message of *Our Lady (of the Rosary) of Fatima*; we therefore prayed the Rosary every day."

Today in the center of the rebuilt city of Hiroshima there is a Marian Memorial Shrine. Its fifteen stained-glass windows depict the fifteen mysteries of the Rosary. Fr. Schiffer's firm belief was that their devotion to the Virgin Mary had protected them, and he gave the hope that even if an atomic war (the possible "annihilation of nations" in the warning of *Our Lady of Fatima*) should come, those who fulfill her messages can expect extraordinary, even miraculous protection from her. This brings to mind the words of the Virgin of Guadalupe to Juan Diego in 1531: "Am I not here, I who am your mother?... Are you not under my shadow and protection?..."

Hiroshima after the explosion of the atomic bomb

A monument to the 26 martyrs of Nagasaki

208

Nagasaki annihilated—The Cross survives

Chapter 32

The Legacy of the Bomb

God's fire which fell from the sky unto the mountain of Carmel sacrificed two bulls, but how many people were a sacrifice to the atomic bomb in Hiroshima? Hiroshima had a population of 400,000. About 100,000 died immediately. There was a similar sacrificial number in Nagasaki three days later.

"We have done the devil's work," exclaimed Robert Oppenheimer, Director of the Manhattan project, soon afterwards. Indeed, Oppenheimer wondered whether the dead of Hiroshima and Nagasaki were not more fortunate than the survivors whose exposure to the bomb would have lifetime effects.

Leo Szilard, the Hungarian emigré theoretical physicist and co-inventor of the nuclear reactor, was one of the scientists who felt a measure of guilt for the development of such a terrible weapon of war: "The development of atomic power," he said, "would provide the nations with a new means of destruction. The atomic bombs at our disposal represent only the first step in this direction, and there is almost no limit to the destructive power which will become available in the course of their further development. Thus, a nation which sets the precedent of using the newly liberated forces of nature for purposes of destruction may have to bear the responsibility of opening the door to an era of devastation on an unimagined scale."

In September, 1950, Albert Einstein, in a letter to his old friend Max Born, one of the first expositors of relativity, wrote: "I have not changed my attitude to the Germans, which, by the way, dates not just from the Nazi period. All human beings are more or less the same from birth. The Germans, however, have a far more dangerous tradition than any of the other so-called civilized nations..." To which Born replied: "...The Americans have demonstrated in Dresden, Hiroshima, and Nagasaki that in sheer speed of extermination, they surpass even the Nazis."

But whereas Einstein considered himself to be a pacifist, twelve years after the war, replying to the Japanese journal *Kaizo* which had reproached him for involvement, however indirectly, in nuclear weapons, he wrote: "While I am a convinced pacifist, there are circumstances in which I believe the use of force is appropriate, namely, in the face of an enemy unconditionally bent on destroying me and my people." Japanese cruelty during the war also did not go unrecorded, and so, the debate still continues as to the justification of using the bomb to end the war.

Britain joined the United States and the Soviet Union in the "nuclear club" in 1955; France in 1960; China in 1964, and India in 1974. South Africa has been able to produce nuclear weapons since 1981, and Israel has also become an undeclared nuclear power. Other places like Libya, Iran, and Iraq have aggressively sought to become nuclear powers themselves. Hans Bethe, a theoretical physicist, who was a member of the scientific team who developed the bomb, said years later: "We thought we could control the genie. It wouldn't go into the bottle. But there were reasonable grounds for thinking we could contain it. I know now that this was an illusion."

There are now more than fifty thousand nuclear war heads in the world—on submarines, in planes, on ships and in missile silos. These weapons have an explosive yield of twenty billion tons of TNT, roughly 1,600,000 times the yield of the bomb that destroyed Hiroshima. We now have missiles capable of being delivered to any spot on the globe with staggering accuracy. We also face the grim reality that Russia could obliterate the United States and vice verse in a matter of hours.

Undoubtedly, the proliferation of nuclear weapons increases the risks of nuclear war and apart from that, an accidental detonation like Chernobyl could possibly occur again. Indeed, Bhopal, Chernobyl, and the Challenger space shuttle demonstrate the limitation of modern technology and the risks of accidents. Each year also increases the odds that a nation with irresponsible leaders or an unstable government will acquire nuclear arms, even if limited, and motives ranging from self-preservation to religious fanaticism, as is possible in today's Middle East politics, could "justify" a nuclear strike.

One nation, supposedly civilized, has already found circumstances that "justified" the use of nuclear weapons against an enemy's civilian population. On that occasion there was no other nuclear power to retaliate. However, a full-scale nuclear war could lead to the extinction of mankind with no one left to tell the tale.

And so, in his encyclical *Peace On Earth*, Pope John XXIII lamented: "We are deeply distressed to see the enormous stocks of armaments that have been, and continue to be, manufactured in the economically developed countries. This policy is involving a vast outlay of intellectual and material resources, with the result that the people of these countries are saddled with a tremendous (financial) burden, and other countries are being deprived of the help they need for their economic and social development.

"The probable cause of this stock-piling of armaments is usually said to be the conviction that under modern conditions peace cannot be assured except on the basis of an equal balance of armaments... While it is difficult to believe that anyone would deliberately assume responsibility for initiating the appalling slaughter and destruction that (atomic) war will bring in its train, there is no denying that war could break out through some unexpected and unprecedented act.

"Hence, justice, right reason, and the realization of man's dignity cry out insistently for a cessation to the arms race... Nuclear weapons must be banned... In the words of Pope Pius XII: 'The calamity of a world war, with the economic and social ruin and the moral excesses and disillusion that accompany it, must not on any account be permitted to engulf the human race for a third time.'"

The final statement from Vatican Council II, which was chaired by Paul VI, had this to add: "Support should be given to the good will of numerous individuals who are making every effort to eliminate the havoc of war; these men, although burdened by the weighty responsibilities of their high office, are motivated by a consciousness of their very grave obligations... In our times this work demands that they put aside *nationalistic* selfishness and ambitions to dominate other nations... For unless animosity and hatred are put aside and firm, honest agreements about world peace are concluded, humanity may, in spite of the wonders of modern science, go from the grave crisis of the present day to that dismal hour, when the only peace it will experience will be the dread peace of death."

Chapter 33

The Aftermath of a Nuclear War

Pope Paul VI once asked: "Are we close to the end?" Hiroshima and Nagasaki are the world's lessons of the ravages of nuclear war, and Chernobyl is the chilling example of how a nuclear accident can occur. In 1983, a Conference on the *Long Term Worldwide Biological Consequences of Nuclear War* was held in Washington, D.C. The report of this conference was the result of a year-long project, involving more than two hundred scientists from many nations. It recorded the best available scientific information on what would happen to the world's life-support system after a nuclear war.

Dr. Carl Sagan, Professor of Astronomy and Space Sciences and the Director of the Laboratory for Planetary Studies at Cornell University, talking about the possibility of a nuclear exchange, said: "It is certainly true that we have gone thirty eight years without a nuclear war. Who knows, we might be able to survive for some longer period of time. But would you want to bet your life on it? I do not guarantee that this is a perfect analogy, but the situation reminds me of a man falling from the top of a high building, saying to an office worker through an open window as he passes by, 'So far, so good.'"

In that nuclear attack of 1945 in Hiroshima and Nagasaki, two relatively small bombs in the range of 10 to 20 kilotons were detonated as airbursts over the city centers. Paul R. Ehrlich of the Department of Biological Sciences at Stanford University put a large scale thermal nuclear war in its perspective. He estimated that if somewhere between 5,000 and 10,000 megatons (a megaton = 1 million tons) of weapons were to detonate mostly in the northern hemisphere, it would be roughly equal to the explosion of one-half to three-quarters of a million Hiroshima-sized atomic bombs. The blasts alone would be expected to cause 750 million deaths. Yet this amounts to only a portion of the current nuclear arsenals of the USA and USSR!

Another study predicted that 1.1 *billion* people would be promptly killed and a like number injured immediately by blast, heat, and radiation. In other words, almost half of the current global population. It would be the greatest catastrophe in human history. The fate of the two to three billion people who were not killed immediately, including those in nations far removed from targets, might in many ways be worse. They would suffer directly from the freezing temperatures, darkness, and midterm fall out, requiring nonexistent medical attention. Indeed, much of humanity's know-how would disappear along with them. Civilization would be set back hundreds of thousands of years.

Dr. Paul J. Crutzen, Director of the Atomospheric Chemistry Division of the Max Planck Institute for Chemistry in Mainz, Federal Republic of Germany, predicted that there would be a production of between 300 and 400 million tons of smoke, 30 percent of which would be strongly light-absorbing elemental carbon. His work indicated that in the area between 30 and 60 degrees latitude in the northern hemisphere where the fires would initially occur, hardly any sunlight would be coming through, and the sunlight at ground level would be less than one-millionth of normal.

This atmospheric soot and dust from the northern hemisphere would soon be transported to the southern hemisphere. Thus, the situation in the southern hemisphere, including the tropical regions, could be as bad as that in the northern hemisphere. Vladimir Aleksandrov, Head of the Climate Research Laboratory at the Computing Center of the USSR Academy of Sciences, estimated that the temperature would fall by tens of degrees to below-freezing levels, even in the summer.

Eight months following the injection of dust and smoke in the atmosphere, the temperature in the United States and the Soviet Union would still be as much as 30°C (54°F) below normal. In Africa it would be as low as 10°C (18°F) below normal and could be less. In fact, the recovery time for solar radiation and temperature rises would be months to a few years, and if the war occurs in the winter, the cold temperatures would be worse. Some 2–3 billion of the world's inhabitants would remain to face the nuclear winter and beyond.

But was it not prophesied by Jesus when he spoke about the last days?: "So when you shall see the abomination of desolation, spoken of by Daniel the prophet, standing where it ought not (let him that readeth understand), then let them that be in Judea flee to the mountains... And pray that your flight be not in the winter. For in those days shall be affliction, such as was not from the beginning of the creation which God created unto this time, neither shall be. And except the Lord had shortened those days, no flesh should be saved..." (Mark 13:14-20).

Food shortages resulting from the inevitable collapse of the agricultural system, the shut down of food transportation and distribution systems, and the incapability of crop plants to survive the climatic changes, could cause hundreds of millions or billions of humans worldwide to starve to death. This would engulf not just those countries directly involved in a nuclear war, but also those nations far removed from the direct conflict and greatly dependent on food exports from North America.

Unfortunately, the consequences of any particular nuclear war scenario are likely to be still more severe than discussed above. We have too incomplete an understanding of the detailed workings of the global ecosystems to evaluate all the interactions, and, therefore, the cumulative effects of the many stresses to which people and ecosystems would be subjected. The question of the survival of the human species is now the issue. As Carl Sagan also stated: "The population of *Homo sapiens* conceivably could be reduced to prehistoric levels or below, and the extinction of the human species cannot be excluded."

And so, it was appropriate that the *Mother of God*, who cares for her children, should choose to give this apocalyptic warning in Japan to Sr. Agnes Sasagawa in the convent of the Institute of the Handmaids of Eucharist on October 13, 1973: "My dear daughter, listen well to what I have to say to you. You will inform your superior. As I told you, if men do not repent and better themselves, the Father will inflict a terrible punishment greater than the Flood, such as one will never have seen before. *Fire will fall from the sky and will wipe out a great part of humanity,* the good as well as the bad, sparing neither priests nor faithful. The survivors will find themselves so desperate that they will envy the dead. The only arms which will remain for you will be the Rosary and the Sign left by my Son. Each day recite the prayers of the Rosary. With the Rosary, pray for the Pope, the bishops, and the priests."

Chapter 34

Nuclear War and the Book of Revelation

T he four horsemen of the apocalypse: famine, pestilence, destruction, and death, symbolize the havoc wreaked upon the earth by the godless. Undoubtedly, the horsemen are galloping at full pace in this, the 20th century. The Book of the Apocalypse (Revelation) records the revelations of Jesus Christ to St. John about what is to happen in the future. It is about the end times, "but as for that day and hour, nobody knows it, neither the angels of heaven nor the Son, no one but the Father only" (Matthew 24:36; Mark 13:32).

Fr. Bernhard Philberth was a physicist of high international repute in Germany and worldwide before he entered the priesthood. His book *Christian Prophecy & Nuclear Power* has been an international best-seller. Like some of us, he, too, believes that the destructive details of a large-scale nuclear war, including the description of all the weapons, their appearance and their effects, have been described quite unambiguously in the Book of Revelation.

Undoubtedly, the Book is extremely difficult to interpret and, indeed, has been subjected to many and varied interpretations by Bible scholars (and non-scholars).

However, especially with respect to chapters 8–9, as Fr. Philberth observed, it is important to remember that St. John lived in a totally nontechnical era some 2,000 years ago when he saw these visions while he was on the island of Patmos.

The only weapons which mankind knew at that time were bows and arrows, spears and swords, and his vehicles were horses and chariots. Accordingly then, the strange machines and weapons of the 20th century which he saw in his visions were unimaginable in his time and could only be described in terms of 1st century images, knowledge, and weaponry. Indeed, it was 1,000 years before gun powder became known in that part of the world, and before the first internal combustion engine, the first airplane, and the first intercontinental missile were invented.

Rev. 8:7 reads: "The first angel blew his trumpet and, with that, hail and fire, mixed with blood were dropped on earth; a third of the earth was burnt up, and a third of all trees, and every blade of grass was burnt."

This could refer to an atomic disaster destroying one third of mankind. "Hail" could also possibly refer to a hail of numerous bombs falling on earth and causing fire, bloodshed, and destruction, reminiscent of the seventh plague in the Book of Exodus: "And the Lord rained down hail upon the land of Egypt... It struck down every man and beast that was in the open throughout the land of Egypt" (Exodus 9:13-34).

In quoting this passage of Scripture in the Old Testament, I am reminded of the prophecy of Jesus in the New Testament: "For at that time there will be great suffering, such as has not been from the beginning of the world until now, no, and never will be. And if those days had not been cut short, no one will be saved; but for the sake of the elect those days will be cut short" (Matthew 24:21-22).

Rev. 8:8-11 reads: "The second angel blew his trumpet, and it was as though a great mountain, all on fire, had been dropped into the sea: a third of the sea turned into blood, a third of all the living things of the sea were killed, and a third of all ships were destroyed. The third angel blew his trumpet, and a huge star fell from the sky, burning like a torch, and it fell on a third of all rivers and springs; this was a star called Wormwood, and a third of all water turned to bitter wormwood, so that many people died from drinking it."

Now, as an intercontinental missile reenters the atmosphere at great speed, glowing with white heat, its descent would resemble a falling star. This trumpeting, therefore, could also be similarly interpreted as atomic missiles falling into the ocean, destroying naval vessels, submarines, and sea life. Of course, a large meteor or comet would have the same effect on falling to earth as an atomic explosion. Indeed, many scientists believe that the extinction of the dinosaurs occurred this way.

The English meaning of Chernobyl is "Wormwood." It refers to a "bitter herb" found in the Ukraine. In 1986, an accidental nuclear explosion occurred in the Chernobyl nuclear power station in the Soviet Ukraine. It was the worst nuclear accident in history. Could it be that the word "Wormwood" in John's revelations was meant to give us a hint of a nuclear disaster to come, accidental or otherwise.

Rev. 8:12 states: "The fourth angel blew his trumpet, and a third of the sun and a third of the moon and a third of stars were blasted, so the light went out of a third of them and for a third of the day there was no illumination, and the same with the night."

This could also signal the post-nuclear darkness which would occur after an all-out atomic exchange. As I mentioned in chapter 33, because of the production of millions of tons of smoke, 30 percent of which would be strong light-absorbing elemental carbon, hardly any sunlight will be coming through and the sunlight at ground level could be less than one-millionth of normal. It is also reminiscent of the ninth plague in the Book of Exodus: "So Moses stretched out his hand toward the sky, and there was dense darkness throughout the land of Egypt for three days. Men could not see one another, nor could they move from where they were for three days..." (Exodus 10:21-23).

Rev. 9:1-10: "And the fifth angel sounded, and I saw a star fall from heaven unto the earth...and he opened the bottomless pit and there arose a smoke out of the pit, as the smoke of a great furnace; and the sun and the air were darkened by reason of the smoke of the pit. And there came out of the smoke locusts upon the earth...and these locusts were like unto horses armoured for battle; they had things that looked like gold crowns on their heads and faces that seemed human, and hair like women's hair, and teeth like lions' teeth. They had body-armour like iron breast-plates, and the noise of their wings sounded like a great charge of horses and chariots into battle. Their tails were like scorpions, and there were stings in their tails..."

Rev. 9:13-18: "Then the sixth angel blew his trumpet...
Now, in my vision this is how I saw the horses and their
riders. The breast plates they wore were fiery red, deep
blue and pale yellow. The horses' heads were like heads of
lions, and out of their mouths came fire and sulphur and
smoke. By these three plagues the smoke and sulphur and
fire which shot out of their mouths a third of mankind was
slain."

In other words, John saw destructive squadrons
attacking humanity from the air like swarms of locusts
attacking a field. The shape of their wings and body, the
stiffness and metallic sheen of their "chitin," and their
movements of flight were likely to be modern fighter planes
in flight, but John sees the metallic body of these planes
and can only compare them to the biblical locusts and the
eighth plague: "Never before had there been such a fierce
swarm of locusts, nor will there ever be... They ate up all
the vegetation in the land and the fruit of whatever trees
the hail had spared... (Exodus 10:1-29).

He sees the water vapour trails of the exhaust vents in
the tail of the planes and compares them to women's hair.
He sees the nose of the planes and the cockpit facade
which look like a face. He sees their teeth like lions' teeth
and, to me, this description fits the design of some fighter
aircraft and missiles, for example, the Flying Tigers, those
American fighter planes of World War II, whose noses were
painted with teeth like those of sharks or lions. The guns
on and under the wings of the planes issued fire, sulphur,
and smoke. He also compares the tails of these strange
locusts to scorpion tails; a good comparison! Finally, he
hears the mighty roar of the engines which he describes as
the noise of locusts' wings in flight and compares it to a
great charge of horses and chariots going into battle.

The Third Secret of Fatima

Now, whereas the first two secrets of Fatima were
revealed to the public in 1927, it was not until 1941 that
Sister Lucia disclosed the existence of the controversial
third secret. She eventually requested it to be revealed to
the Pope at her death or by 1960, whichever came first,
because, as she said: "It would become clearer at that
time." This suggested to me that the contents of the third
secret pertained to the second half of the twentieth
century. In fact, I vividly remember anxiously awaiting the
revelation of the third secret when I was a medical student

in Dublin in 1960. It was not revealed. In fact, four consecutive Popes have so far chosen not to reveal it.

The silence of the Vatican caused much disappointment and confusion in the Catholic world but we did not know at that time that neither Lucia nor the Bishop of Fatima had ever said that the secret would be made public in 1960. All they said was that it was to be opened by the Pope in 1960. Undoubtedly, the present Pope, John Paul II, knows the secret.

An important declaration concerning the third secret is found in an interview with Cardinal Ratzinger, President Prefect of the Congregation for the Doctrine of the Faith, and custodian of the third secret of Fatima apart from Sr. Lucia and the Pope. The journalist Vittorio Messori reported in the August 1984 issue of the *Journal of Jesus* that, referring discreetly to the contents of the third secret, the Cardinal mentioned three important points: The dangers threatening the faith, the importance of the "last times," and the fact that the prophecies contained in the third secret correspond to what Scripture says.

When interviewed about the third secret by the magazine *Jesus*, Cardinal Ratzinger also said: "I have read it. It has not been revealed because according to the judgment of the Popes, it adds nothing different to what a Christian must know about Revelation: a radical call to conversion, the absolute importance of history, the dangers threatening the faith and the life of the Christian, and, therefore, of the world. And then, the importance of the 'novissimi' (the last events at the end of time). If it is not made public, at least for the time being, it is to avoid mistaking religious prophecy with sensationalism. But the contents of this 'third secret' corresponds to what is announced in Holy Scripture."

Finally, to someone who once questioned her on the contents of the third secret, Sr. Lucia, the sole surviving visionary of the apparitions in Fatima, replied: "It is in the Gospel and the Apocalypse (Book of Revelation). Read them." And on another occasion she specified chapters 8–13 of the Book of Revelation. I have attempted to give one possible interpretation of chapters 8–9.

They have teeth like lions' teeth

Tails like scorpions' tails

Fire and brimstone beneath their wings

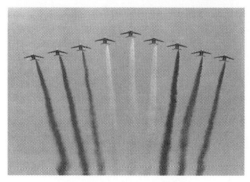

Hair like women's hair

Chapter 35

The Lady of All Nations
1945–1984

The apparitions of the Blessed Virgin in Holland began in the spring of 1945 just before the end of the Second World War and the atomic bombing of Hiroshima and Nagasaki. The visionary was Ida Peerdeman, a humble woman, who at the time was forty years old. She lived with her sisters in Amsterdam. The first apparition was on March 25, 1945, the feast of the Annunciation, in the home of the visionary. Fr. J. Frehe, a Dominican priest, her spiritual director of long-standing, had just arrived on a visit.

Up to the year 1970 inclusive, roughly sixty messages were delivered. The messages of the years 1945–1951 contain a number of prophecies regarding the Church, the world and politics, involving America, Russia, England, China, Formosa (Taiwan), Manchuria, Germany, the Baltics, Israel, and other nations. They make fascinating reading and most of the prophecies have already come to pass.

The visionary also had a number of "Eucharistic Experiences" from 1970 to 1984. Indeed, the Eucharist held a prominent place in the messages of Amsterdam and that tells us why the Virgin chose the city of Amsterdam. A great miracle of the Eucharist had taken place in

Amsterdam in March, 1345, exactly 600 years before the first apparition to Ida.

At her bishop's instigation, the visionary was subjected to a thorough psychological investigation. The report stated: "This person is perfectly normal. There is not a trace of hysterical propensity. On the contrary, she is rather inclined to the opposite, being hardheaded and unimaginative."

As Ida herself was on occasions concerned that she might be the victim of a satanic deception, she begged the Virgin to give her a sign as a proof of the authenticity of the apparitions. It was granted. It was the prophecy of February 19, 1958, predicting that Pope Pius XII would die at the beginning of October, 1958. "The Lady of all Nations, the *Coredemptrix, Mediatrix,* and *Advocate*, will lead him to eternal joy," the Virgin said to her. It was a private message which Ida wrote down, sealed and handed to Fr. Frehe with the understanding that it was not to be opened and read before the beginning of October, 1958. This was observed. Pope Pius XII died quite unexpectedly on October 9, 1958. He had held audiences up to a few days previously.

On Sunday, February 11, 1951, the twenty seventh apparition, the Virgin said: "I am the Lady, Mary, *Mother of all Nations*. You may say: *The Lady of all Nations* or *Mother of all Nations,* who once was Mary. I have come today precisely in order to tell you that I wish to be known as this. Let all the children of men, of all the countries in the world be one!" It was on the date when she first appeared to Bernadette Soubirous in Lourdes in 1858.

It was also on that day that she pleaded that this prayer be said by all: "Lord Jesus Christ, Son of the Father, send down your Spirit over the earth. Let the Holy Spirit live in the hearts of all nations so that they may be preserved from degeneration, disasters and war. May the *Lady of all Nations,* who once was Mary, be our Advocate. Amen." She added: "There is a shortage of priests, but of lay people there is no shortage. Let a great movement among the laity be organized..." She ended her apparition by pointing to a globe and saying: "This time is our time. You, child, are the instrument chosen so that you may pass on these things. Tell them that I wish to be known as the *Lady of all Nations*."

Now, here are but a few abstracts of the many messages which were received over the years: "My sole purpose is to ensure that the will of the Son is obeyed in these times... The spirit of untruth is making such appalling progress that it is necessary to act quickly. The whole world is degenerating, and for this reason the Son sends the *Lady of all Nations*, who once was Mary... Now I stand an oblation before the Cross. For I have suffered with my Son, spiritually and above all, bodily... My Son came into the world as the Redeemer of men and the work of redemption was the Cross, with all its sufferings both of body and spirit."

She then showed herself standing on a globe and in front of the Cross, and said: "The Lady comes to stand in front of it, as the Son's mother, who with Him has accomplished this work of redemption... The Lady, however, really stands here as the *Coredemptrix, Mediatrix,* and *Advocate*. About this much controversy will arise. The Church, Rome, however, should not be afraid to take up the struggle. It can only make the Church more powerful.

"This is what I am saying to the theologians... The new dogma will be the '*dogma of the Coredemptrix*.' Notice, I lay special emphasis on '**Co**.' I have said that it will arouse much controversy. Once again I tell you that the Church, Rome, will carry it through and silence all objections. The Church, Rome, will incur opposition and overcome it. The Church, Rome, will become stronger and mightier in proportion to the resistance she puts up in the struggle. My purpose and my commission to you is none other than to urge the Church, the theologians, to wage this battle. The Father, the Son, and the Holy Spirit wills to send the Lady chosen to bear the Redeemer into this world, as *Coredemptrix, Mediatrix,* and *Advocate*. ...I am not bringing a new doctrine. I am merely restating old themes..." Indeed, as far back as the 4th century AD, St. Augustine had referred to Mary as "the Co-operator in the Redemption" (De Sancta Virginitate, 6 PL 40).

"The following is the explanation of the new dogma. 'As *Coredemptrix, Mediatrix, and Advocate,* I am standing on the globe in front of the Cross of the Redeemer. By the will of the Father, the Redeemer came on earth. To accomplish this, the Father used the Lady. Thus, from the Lady the Redeemer received only—I am stressing the word 'only'—flesh and blood, that is to say, the body. From my Lord and Master the Redeemer received his divinity. In this way the Lady became *Coredemptrix...*

'Now, look hard at my hands. From them emanate rays of grace, redemption and peace. The rays shine upon all peoples, upon all sheep. Among these peoples there are many of good will. To be of good will means to keep the

226

first and great commandment. The first and great commandment is LOVE... This is what the world is lacking: love of God—love of neighbour... I am the *Lady of all Nations*, who once was Mary, means that many people have known Mary just as *Mary*. Now, however, in this era, which is beginning now, I wish to be the *'Lady of all Nations.'* Mankind has been entrusted to the mother... *Coredemptrix* I was already at the Annunciation... This means that the mother became *Coredemptrix* by the *will* of the Father..."'

Never has Miriam or Mary been officially called *Coredemptrix*. Never has she officially been called *Mediatrix*. Never has she officially been called *Advocate*. These three concepts form one whole. This will be the keystone of Marian history. It will become the dogma of the *Coredemptrix, Mediatrix, and Advocate*. The other dogmas had to come first...

"O, you do not know what tremendous forces are threatening this world. I am now not speaking of modern humanism, atheism, modern socialism and communism. There are yet forces of quite a different nature that threaten this world. Nations, do search for the truth. Nations, *unite*... Satan is still the prince of this world. He holds on to everything he can. That then is why the *Lady of all Nations* had to come now, into these times for she is *the Immaculate Conception* and, **as a consequence of this**, she is the *Coredemptrix, Mediatrix, and Advocate*. These three concepts are one. *Is that clearly understood, theologians?*

"Because she is *Coredemptrix*, Mary is also *Mediatrix* and also *Advocate*. Theologians, I ask you: 'do you still have objections against this dogma?' You have only to analyze how well-founded are these words. I ask you to dedicate yourselves to this dogma. Do not be afraid. There will be conflict. The others will attack you. But battle for this dogma. It will be the coronation of your Lady."

The fiftieth apparition was on May 31, 1954. She said: "Once more I am here. The *Coredemptrix, Mediatrix, and Advocate* is now standing before you. I have chosen this day. On this day the Lady will be crowned. Theologians and apostles of the Lord Jesus Christ, listen carefully. On this date the *Lady of all Nations* will receive her official title of *Lady of all Nations*. Note well, these three concepts are one. These three concepts are one whole. I am saying this twice because there are some who would accept only *one* concept..."

I researched the significance of the date, May 31, and discovered that an Office and Mass of *Mary Mediatrix of all Graces*, composed at the initiative of Cardinal Desiré Mercier, and approved by Pope Benedict XV in 1921, was originally celebrated by numerous dioceses and Religious Orders on May 31. On October 11, 1954, Pope Pius XII set that day aside for the observance of the feast of the *Queenship of Mary*, and the feast in honour of Mary's mediation was discontinued by some and transferred by others.

Her prophecy: "On this day the Lady will be crowned," which was told to Ida on May 31, 1954, was therefore fulfilled on October 11. But she also said: "On this date the *Lady of all Nations* will receive her official title of *Lady of all Nations*." It would seem, therefore, that this other prophecy is still to be fulfilled.

But there was yet another event associated with the date, May 31. After the surrender of Napoleon III in 1871, and at the height of the civil unrest which erupted in Paris on March 18, 1871 as a result of this defeat, the religious houses of the Sisters of Charity in Reuilly and Enghien, about fifty miles from the Rue du Bac in Paris, were threatened by the unruly and anticlerical mob known as the Paris Commune. Catherine Labouré, the saint of the Medal of the Immaculate Conception (the Miraculous Medal), was stationed there at that time, and received a message in a dream from the Blessed Virgin telling the Sisters to leave the premises, but Mary prophesied that they will return on May 31.

Catherine then took with her the crown from the statue of the Blessed Virgin in the chapel for safekeeping. In removing it, she promised the *Queen of Heaven* that she would return to crown her again before the month of May had ended. The Paris Commune was suppressed on May 28 and the Sisters began their return journey home, arriving in Paris on May 30. On May 31, 1871, Sr. Catherine carried out the little crowning ceremony which she had promised the Virgin. I found it most significant that 83 years later, Pope Pius XII proclaimed that the feast of the *Queenship of Mary* should be celebrated each year on May 31! This is indeed a special date in the diary of Mary.

But to return to the messages given to Ida Peerdeman, the Virgin also said to her: "My prophecy 'from hence forth all generations shall call me blessed,' will be fulfilled more than ever before, once the dogma has been proclaimed...

228

When the dogma, the last dogma in Marian history, has been proclaimed, the *Lady of all Nations* will give peace, true peace. I repeat, true peace to the world. The nations, however, must say my prayer in union with the Church...

"Science today has made people forget to show gratitude. They no longer recognize their Creator. Nations, be warned, bow down in deep humility before your Creator. Implore his mercy. He is merciful... How thoroughly Satan holds the world in his clutches, only God knows! He now sends to you, to all the nations, his mother, the *Lady of all Nations*. She will vanquish Satan, as has been foretold. She shall place her foot upon Satan's head...

"I said a minute ago that alarming inventions would be made. God permits this. But you, nations, can make sure that it does not result in disaster... To spare you from falling a prey to alarming inventions, nations, the Lady begs you now, today, to ask the Father, the Son and the Holy Spirit to protect his people and restore *unity* among them. *Unity* is what his people must achieve. They must be one, and over them, the *Lady of all Nations*. One community. Nations, I stress these words—One community!"

Eucharistic Experiences

On May 31, 1957, she said to Ida: "Before the Lord Jesus Christ died His bodily death; before the Lord Jesus Christ ascended to the Father...He gave you the great mystery, the great miracle of every day, every hour, every minute. He gave you Himself. No, nations, (she shook her head vehemently as she said this) not merely a remembrance. No, nations, listen to what He said: Not just an idea, but Himself, under the appearance of a little piece of bread, under the appearance of wine. This is how the Lord wants to come among you, day after day. Do accept it. He gives you the foretaste—the foretaste of eternal life."

On July 17, 1958, while at church, preparing for Holy Mass, Ida saw a very bright light. In that light she saw three figures linked with one another in a semicircle. Suddenly the figures spread out towards the center so that all at once a very great sphere of white fire stood before her eyes. Suddenly she recognized the Sacred Host.

It was in the fifty sixth apparition on May 31, 1959, that Ida, after the Lady had disappeared, saw in her stead, a large Host. Then in front of the Host there appeared a chalice. The chalice was of splendid gold. It toppled over and then she saw flowing from this chalice thick streams of blood. Then the scene suddenly changed and all of it became a brilliant, Sacred Host. And a voice rang out: "He who eats and drinks Me, receives everlasting life and the Spirit of Truth."

Pope Paul VI

On May 31, 1963, after Holy Communion, Ida heard a voice saying: "Do not tell anyone before it has happened." The voice ceased for a moment and after a while she heard: "Montini." Pope John XXIII died three days later on June 3, 1963, and Cardinal Giovanni Montini was elected Pope on June 21, 1963. He took the name Paul VI. And so, she prophesied the death of one Pope, Pope Pius XII, and the election of another, Pope Paul VI.

Then, two years later, on May 31, 1965, again during Holy Communion, Ida heard a voice say: "Go to Pope Paul in the name of the *Lady of all Nations* and tell him that this is the last warning before the end of the Council (Vatican Council II). The Church of Rome is in danger of a schism. Warn your priests. Let them put a stop to those false theories about the Eucharist, sacraments, doctrines, priesthood, marriage and family-planning. They are being led astray by the spirit of untruth, Satan, and confused by the ideas of modernism. Divine teaching and laws are valid for all times and applicable to every period." Three months later, on September 3, 1965, Pope Paul VI issued a warning in his Encyclical *Mysterium Fidei* against errors concerning the Blessed Sacrament!

Almost 13 years later, during Holy Mass, on Sunday June 11, 1978, Ida saw lips with a finger across. Then a magnificent radiant figure appeared and said: "Listen. Before two months would have passed Pope Paul VI would enter into eternal life. You should not tell it to anybody, not even your spiritual director, before it has happened. Keep it a secret to yourself." Then the radiant figure slowly disappeared and Ida said: "Dear Lord, thy will be done." And the voice said: "Amen."

Paul VI died on August 6, 1978. Ida was praying that the Holy Spirit would enlighten the minds of the cardinals in the choice of a new Pope and she heard a voice say: "He who comes from afar will be Peter's successor." This was repeated on October 16, 1978. That night, Ida heard over the radio that the Polish Cardinal Wojtila had been elected

Pope in the name of Pope John Paul II. The following year, on May 31, 1979, Ida also heard a voice saying: "The Netherlands will be revived through her whom I have sent. Implore the Spirit of Truth. The Holy Father will proclaim her *Coredemptrix, Mediatrix, and Advocate.*"

Farewell

On May 31, 1981, Ida had her last apparition of the *Lady of all Nations*. At the end of a series of visions, the Lady said to her: "Farewell, till Eternity." Ida felt a terrible emptiness and sadness in her heart and finally on March 25, 1984, the feast of the Annunciation, when it all began in 1945, she saw a light and a voice was heard to say: "The period of the *Lady of all Nations* as *Coredemptix* is drawing near." Then the light slowly disappeared.

On July 17, 1992, I visited the home and private chapel of Ida Peerdeman. She was a sprightly, elderly old lady, very alert and still very evangelical. As she opened the front door to welcome me, she exclaimed: "Did you know that today is the anniversary of the Eucharistic miracle?" I did not. She was referring to July 17, 1958, when she first saw a white dazzling Host. I spent a long time with her and then sat for one hour in the chapel where the painting of the *Lady of all Nations* hung at the side of the altar.

After fifty years of patience, observations, and investigations, and after ensuring that there was no scriptural error in the messages, on May 31, 1996, His Excellency Hendrik Bomers, Bishop of Haarlem, Amsterdam, gave the *Nihil Obstat* approving devotion to the *Lady of all Nations*. The Blessed Mother had promised Miss Peerdeman that she would live to see this approval. The approval now a reality, Ida Peerdeman died on June 17, 1996. She was in her early nineties. Her mission was accomplished and she went home to the Lord. Bishop Bomers chose the day and the month for his approval of the apparitions. It was on May 31!

A painting of the *Lady of all Nations*, as she once appeared to Ida, was entrusted to the German painter Heinrich Repke. It depicts the *Lady of all Nations* standing on top of the globe and in front of the Cross of the Redeemer. She is wearing a white gown with a yellow sash around her waist. "Mark well what this means," she had once said to Ida. "This bespeaks the loin cloth of the Son for I stood as the Lady in front of the Cross of my Son." At the bottom of the painting and all around the globe is seen a flock of sheep, white and black. "This flock of sheep represents the nations of the whole world, who will not find rest until they lie down and quietly look up at the Cross, the center of the world," she explained to Ida.

But incorporated in the messages of Amsterdam was also a call for *unity*. It is the call of *Our Lady of Guadalupe*, who once said: "I am the mother of all who live *united* in this land." Since the declaration of Bishop Bomers in 1996, these important apparitions of the Blessed Virgin in Amsterdam are now being recognized. The fullness of time has come.

232

The Lady of all Nations

Ida's private chapel with a painting of
Our Lady of all Nations

Chapter 36

The Political Prophecies of the Lady

W hen I visited Ida Peerdeman, I was extremely impressed with her account of the apparitions of the Blessed Virgin. I was equally fascinated by the many political prophecies given to her, and so, I researched in great detail these prophecies only to find that many of them have already 'come to pass.' They were given so many years in advance that it is impossible that the visionary, simple and nonacademic as she was, could have invented and surmised these events of history. I will now elaborate on only a few of them as it would take several chapters to document them all. I will record these prophecies as she wrote them in her book *The Lady of all Nations*.

The Korean War

"I see in the Far East, the sun and the moon. The moon is in its half-phase. The red flag waves over China. Here are Mohammedans. Here are all the Orient..." (October 7, 1945)... "'The fighting in Korea is an omen and the beginning of great misery,' the Lady said. Then I see demarcations being marked out. Next I see someone leaning his head on his hand, in deep thought. I take him to be

Stalin: 'I have warned you against that danger,' I suddenly hear besides me" (August 15, 1950)... "'The Eastern nations have been roused by an ideology which does not believe in the Son,' said the Lady. The Lady points to America and moves a disapproving finger to and fro, as she says: 'Do not push your politics too far.'... I see Chinese marching. I see them cross a line" (December 10, 1950).

Indeed, the Eastern nations are predominantly non-Christian, and Communism was also spreading throughout the region. After World War II ended in 1945, the Allied Powers had decided that, after forty years of occupation by the Japanese, Korea would not be immediately ready to undertake the responsibilities of self-government. The country was therefore divided into two spheres of influence on the 38th parallel. Its industrial North was occupied by the Soviet Union and the agricultural South by the United States.

In 1948 and 1949, both the Soviet Union and the United States withdrew their own troops. However, on June 25, 1950, the North Koreans, with the foreknowledge and approval of Stalin, invaded the South at the 38th parallel. President Truman decided at once to send aid to the South Koreans. Eventually, not only were the North Koreans driven out of South Korea, but General Douglas MacArthur, the United States commander, then invaded North Korea.

Just before that, the Chinese Communists, led by Mao Tse-tung, had overthrown the Chiang Kai-shek nationalistic government in a civil war, and in October, 1949, Mao proclaimed the People's Republic of China, which soon converted to a Communist state. "The red flag waved over China." When MacArthur's troops appeared north of the 38th parallel on the Chinese border at the river Yalu, the river frontier of Manchuria, the Chinese reaction was strong and immediate ("I see Chinese marching. I see them cross a line").

On November 4, 1950, 300,000 Chinese "volunteers" attacked the American troops and joined the North Koreans, inflicting a severe defeat on the United States, and recaptured the capital of Seoul. However, they were in turn eventually driven back, and a stalemate ensued. An armistice was signed in July 1953, as a result of which the country was again divided at the 38th parallel, and has remained divided to this day. Estimates suggested that the war was fought at a cost of 3 million casualties in all, civilians included. "Do not push your politics too far," the Lady said of America!

The Vietnam War

As already stated, in August 1950, the *Lady of all Nations* said to Ida that the Korean War was "the beginning of great misery." Indeed, after that war, the Chinese began to supply arms to the Communist guerilla forces in Vietnam. A conference in Geneva agreed to partition Vietnam between a South Vietnamese government and a North. The Communists would eventually come to dominate the North, pending elections which might reunite the country. In fact, the elections never took place. Instead, there opened in the Far East what was to become the fiercest phase of the Asian war against the West since the end of World War II; a war which was begun in 1941, when the Japanese attacked Pearl Harbor.

The Americans backed the South Vietnamese as they backed the South Koreans. However, by 1960, the Vietcong had won control of much of the South. In the end, the United States lost more than 50,000 American lives under the presidencies of John Kennedy and Lyndon Johnson. However, President Richard Nixon began to withdraw American ground forces from Vietnam soon after his inauguration in 1969, and a new policy of normal and direct relations with China came to a climax with the state visit of Nixon to China in February, 1972. It was the first visit by an American president to mainland Asia.

China Invites Trinidad On A State Visit

Now, in the early 1960s, Peking's interest turned increasingly towards the underdeveloped nations, and the second head of government to be invited to China following President Nixon's visit was Dr. Eric Eustace Williams, the Prime Minister of Trinidad and Tobago, a senior and respected politician of the Third World. Although I was not in politics, Dr. Williams invited me to join his small entourage to China, particularly as he was also going to visit universities in China and elsewhere.

On November 5, 1974, Dr. Williams requested me to accompany him at the political talks to be held in the Great Hall of the People with the entire Chinese Cabinet. At that time the tension between Russia and China was extremely high. Premier Chou En-lai was ill in hospital, and the Vice Premier Li Xian Nian chaired the meeting.

During a long two-hour discourse on world politics, he made several remarks which I will never forget, including:

236

"Some time ago, in the middle of the night, my generals rang me, saying: 'Vice Premier, Chinese reconnoitering forces have discovered 1 million Russian troops on Chinese border!' I asked them: 'Why do you wake me up in the middle of the night to tell me that?' They repeated: 'But, Vice Premier, Chinese reconnoitering forces discovered 1 million Russian troops on Chinese border. What do we do?' I repeated to them: 'Why do you wake me up in the middle of the night to tell me that? 1 million Russian troops on Chinese border are also reconnoitering forces. Too small to invade China. Go back to sleep!'" Then he continued: "Mr. Prime Minister, Russia wants to be big brother to China. China does not mind being little brother to Russia. But, Mr. Prime Minister, Russia also wants to be father to China. China does not want to be little son to Russia!"

The stark realism of the statistics and the philosophy of these remarks struck a note in me. China has over 1 billion people. Russia has about 300 million, and the United States about 270 million people. China also has the largest army in the world and the greatest number of reserves. I then recalled J. M. Roberts' remark in his book *The Penguin History Of The World*: "She (China) was in the 1960s stronger than ever before. Her leaders even talked as if they were unmoved by the possibilities of nuclear war; Chinese would survive in greater numbers than the peoples of other countries."

"Father to China," the Vice Premier criticized. This also correlated with Stewart C. Easton's viewpoint. He said in his book *World Since 1918*: "The Chinese have never in their history been willing to take second place to any foreign rulers, and the similarity of Communist ideologies made little difference to this tradition... There were considerable differences between Soviet (Stalinist) and Chinese Communists, even though both claimed to be the rightful heirs of Marx and Lenin... A marriage of convenience was thus a natural outcome for as long as the Soviet Union could remain the senior partner!"

Formosa (Taiwan)

Ida also wrote about the following vision: "Next I see the outline of an island. It seems to be Formosa (Taiwan). A smaller island lies further down. Now I hear the words: 'America be forewarned'" (August 15, 1950).

When the Communists, led by Mao Tse-tung, overthrew the Kuomintang (KMT) regime in 1949, driving Chiang Kai-chek and his followers over to the island of Formosa (Taiwan), where they set up a government, it was backed by vast contributions from the United States, who protects it and regards it as the government of the Republic China. The US government was so deeply committed to the support of the KMT regime that its president announced in 1975 that the United States would protect not merely the island itself, but the offshore islands of Quemoy and Matsu within sight of the mainland, and which were thought essential to its defense. However, China considers Taiwan and its neighbouring islands to be part of mainland China, and this is an ever-present source of tension. If China decides to invade Taiwan and the neighboring islands, and America decides to come to their defense, then a major war could be precipitated. "America, be forewarned," the Lady advised.

United States—Russia Cold War

Here are some of the Virgin's prophecies concerning post-World War II Europe, as recorded in Ida's book: "Europe must be on her guard. Warn the peoples of Europe... The East against the West... Be on your guard, Europe" (February 7, 1946)... "Now, a great conflict is coming. America, Russia... It is drawing near" (February 14, 1950)... "Germany must start to restore its unity. Let a beginning be made by everyone in his own home. The children must be reunited with their father and mother. Let them kneel down together again, and say the Rosary" (November 16, 1950)... "The Lady shows Ida a heavy line across Germany. She adds: 'Europe is divided into two'" (December 10, 1950).

Indeed, at the end of World War II, world history was dominated by a prolonged and bitter Soviet-American antagonism. The result was a world seemingly divided into two camps, one led by the USSR, and the other by the United States. Hungary, Romania, Bulgaria, and Poland became satellites of Russia. Czechoslovakia followed in 1948. Berlin was divided into two: a German Democratic Republic under Russian control was set up in the East, and the Federal Republic emerged from the three Western zones of occupation.

The Western powers then signed a treaty setting up a new alliance, the North Atlantic Treaty Organization (NATO) in April, 1949. It was the first Cold War creation to

238

transcend Europe. The United States and Canada were
members, as well as most Western European states (only
Sweden, Switzerland, and Spain did not join). It was
explicitly a defensive alliance, which provided for the
defence of any member attacked. The foundation of NATO
suggested that as well as two Europes, there might also be
two worlds. An "iron curtain" divided Europe. It was "the
East against the West," as prophesied by the *Lady of all
Nations.*

The Berlin Wall

In August 1961, after some two years of drawn-out
diplomacy, the East Germans suddenly erected a wall to
cut off the Soviet sector of Berlin from the Western. They
felt driven to do this because of a huge increase in the
outflow of refugees as the atmosphere of hostility over
Berlin had deepened. It was not until 1989 that the wall
was pulled down and the two Germanys were united.

Israel

"'And Israel would rise again.' The Lady said this after
showing me the Exodus from Egypt and the image of Cain
and Abel" (April 21, 1945)... "Now I see a round dome. It
seems to be situated in Jerusalem and I hear: 'In and
around Jerusalem heavy battles would be waged.' All at
once I see Cairo clearly and the sight fills me with a
strange sensation. I see various Eastern tribes—Persians,
Arabs, and so on" (December 26, 1947).

This prophecy came to pass three years later. After the
end of World War II, there was the Jewish decision to
establish a national state in Palestine by force. Its catalysts
had been the Nazi persecution of the Jews by the Third
Reich in Germany. The issue was dramatized as soon as
the war was over by a World Zionist Congress' demand that
a million Jews should be admitted to Palestine at once. In
the end the British took the matter to the United Nations,
which recommended partition. However, this was a
nonstarter for the Arabs. Fighting between the two
communities grew fiercer and the British decided to
withdraw without much ado. On the day that they did so,
May 14, 1948, the state of Israel was proclaimed.
The Arab nations at once levelled an attack upon them
but were badly defeated. In 1949, the Israeli government

moved to Jerusalem, a Jewish national capital again for the first time since 2,000 years, with the exception of a few months in 135 AD. There are few moments in the 20th century so soaked in religious history as the establishment of Israel. The announced policy of the new state was the "ingathering of the exiles," in other words, unlimited immigration of Jews who could at once become Israeli citizens. This is of important religious significance as it fulfills one of the prophecies of the Bible, the return of the Jews to their homeland. It is said to be one of the omens of the last days.

Something On The Moon

"Then I see all of a sudden two lines, each with an arrow at the end. And on one it said: 'Russia' and on the other 'America.' Then I see the Lady before me and the moon. I say: 'There is something getting on that moon.'" (February 7, 1946).

Eleven years later, on October 4, 1957, the USSR launched the first satellite Sputnik, which had a big impact on history. The Soviet Union roared ahead in the space race, a frantic competition between the USSR and the US, having as much to do with propaganda as with science. By 1958, the lagging US had created the National Aeronautics and Space Administration (NASA), but in 1961, the Soviets put Yuri Gagarin in orbit—the first man in outer space. On September 13, 1959, Luna 2 (USSR) crashed on the moon, the first man-made object to land there. This is what Ida saw in 1946, thirteen years previously! Ten years later, on July 20, 1969, the eagle had landed. American astronaut Neil Armstrong placed his foot firmly on the moon at exactly 10:56 a.m. eastern. After a brief pause, the first man on the moon spoke the first words on lunar soil: "That is one small step for man, one giant leap for mankind."

Germ Warfare

Ida also described in detail a horrid vision she was shown by the Virgin: "Now I see something like a cigar or a torpedo flying pass me so rapidly that I can scarcely discern it. Its colour seems to be that of aluminum. All of a sudden I see it burst open. I feel with my hand and experience a number of indefinable sensations. The first is a total loss of sensation. I live and yet I do not live! Then I see faces before me, swollen faces, covered with dreadful ulcers, as it were, a kind of leprosy. Then tiny little black

240

things are floating around me. I cannot distinguish them with my eyes, and it is as if I were made to look at them through something (a microscope), and now I see slides of extraordinary brilliance, and upon them those little things enlarge. I do not know how I am to interpret this. 'Bacilli?' I asked. Then the Lady says: 'It is hellish!'

"I then feel my face swelling and it is swollen when I touch it, all bloated and quite stiff. I can no longer move. Then I hear the Lady again, saying: 'Just think! This is what they are preparing!' And then very softly: 'These Russians, but the others as well' Finally the Lady says: 'Nations be warned. It is diabolical—and that is what they are in the process of inventing.'" (December 26, 1947).

This vision was seen in 1947, and, therefore, after World War II. In 1992, there was worldwide fear that germ warfare would have been used in the Persian Gulf War, and the United Nation forces and the Israelis were supplied with gas masks. Now, according to *Time* magazine of November 24, 1997, an article with the caption *A disaster is just waiting to happen if Iraq unleashes its poisons and germs*, stated: "Germ weapons are small, cheap, easy to hide, simple to dispense and horribly effective. They may be the threat of the near future... This is the poor man's atom bomb. A gram of anthrax culture contains a trillion spores, theoretically enough for 100 million fatal doses... Saddam has produced anthrax in large amounts along with botulinum, a poison that kills by paralyzing the victim. Mustard gas was used by Iraq against Iranian soldiers and Kurdish civilians during the Iran-Iraq war. Exposure caused severe eye and lung damage as well serious skin blistering. It is lethal in large dosage. VX gas is an extremely toxic agent which attacks the nervous system. One tiny drop of the liquid form of VX absorbed through the skin causes convulsions and seizures, killing victims quickly."

There are unconfirmed reports that the Russians assisted Iraq in their germ warfare buildup. In December 1997, the United States government decided that all U.S. military forces are to receive anthrax vaccinations in anticipation of possible germ warfare. The cost to the government would be 300 million dollars. The threat is obviously being taken seriously.

The Fall of Communism

Ida also wrote: "I see the sickle and hammer, but the hammer breaks away from the sickle, and they both drop into a whirlpool" (December 26, 1947)... "In Russia a great upheaval would take place..." (December 31, 1951).

Russia became a Communist state in October, 1917, and, to the surprise of the world, the Communist Party suddenly collapsed in 1992 during the Mikhail Gorbachev and Boris Yeltsin era. It was on August 22. It was the feast of the Queenship of Mary. Whether this is the "great upheaval" about which the Blessed Virgin also referred or another one is still to come, I am unable to say.

The War In Yugoslavia

She also foresaw the conflict in Yugoslavia: "Then suddenly I see the Balkans. There is a war. 'They are fighting again,' the Lady says. 'My child, there will be a fierce struggle. We have not seen the end of this struggle yet... I warn for the Baltic'" (August 27, 1977).

"They are fighting again," she said. My own emphasis is on "again," because the history of Yugoslavia and the Baltics is one of a series of wars which began centuries ago. Suddenly in 1992, war once more in Yugoslavia was the lead story in all the newspapers of the world. It was a fierce war of "religious and ethnic cleansing." It was a war among Catholics, Orthodox and Moslems. It was in this Yugoslavia, in a little village called Medjugorje in Bosnia-Hercegovina, that the Blessed Virgin is said to be appearing every day since 1981 as the Queen of Peace.

World War III?

But the prophecies which were most disturbing were made on August 29, 1945 and June 9, 1946, after the end of World War II in Europe. Ida wrote: "I see the Lady standing before me... Then she refers to a new, yet strange war in the distant future, which will cause terrible havoc..." (August 29, 1945) "...Then the Lady says: 'I predict another great catastrophe for the world.' This she says very sadly and she kept shaking her head: 'If people would only listen—but they will not!' ...Then the Lady points to the east. I see a great number of stars in the air 'That is where it is coming from,' she says" (June 9, 1945).

And so, it is going to be "a strange war," which will cause "terrible havoc." In other words, it will be a different kind of war from that of World War II, and it will start in the east. If this is indeed so, it does not surprise me because I also see it in terms of Mary's battle with "Satan and his seed," and his mimicry.

The Aztecs taught that the legendary Quetzalcoatl returned from the east to reclaim his land from Moctezuma (see chapter 8). Likewise, the Virgin came at dawn from the east when she appeared on Tepeyac hill to Juan Diego in 1531 to convert the Aztecs to Christianity, and also when she appeared to the children in Fatima. She was the "Morning Star." But wasn't the birth of her Son also announced by a star in the east (Matthew 2:1-2)? And so, the mimic of God, Satan, would want to strike back from the east (Middle or otherwise)! I am referring to a possible nuclear attack and the annihilation of many nations, as prophesied in Fatima "if people do not convert." I will speculate no further.

A man lands on the moon

Mao Tse-tung under the red flag of China

244

Mao with Ho Chi Minh.
Solidarity with North Vietnam

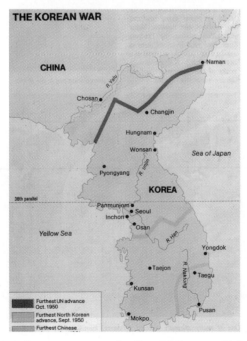

UN forces approach the 38th parallel

245

1972
President Richard Nixon meets Premier Chou En-lai

1974
The author meets Chairman Mao Tse-tung

1992
The fall of Communism in Russia

Chapter 37

Comets and Meteors

On March 20, 1953, among the many prophecies which she made in Amsterdam, the *Lady of all Nations* also said to Ida: "There are meteors. Watch out for them. There will be calamities; there will be cataclysms..."

Now, in addition to the sun, moon, and the planets, the universe includes a vast number of relatively tiny bodies known as comets and meteors. It is estimated that there are about 100 thousand million of them, created at the same time as the sun and the planets, some 4.6 billion years ago.

Edmund Halley (1656–1742) was the first astronomer to state that comets are members of the solar system, travelling in long orbits, firmly under the control of the sun. He closely studied the appearance and the orbit of the comet of 1682, noting that they were similar to those of records of the comets seen in 1531, and seventy six years later, in 1607. Could they be the same comet? He thought so, and predicted that it would return seventy six years later in 1758. It did. However, as far as I know, Comet Halley is the only vigorously active comet with an orbit well enough known to permit detailed scientific planning years in advance.

Ever since early history, men, rightly or wrongly, have seen comets as signs of ill-omen, death of princes, fall of kingdoms, disasters, and changes of fortune. For example, in 1066, the Normans witnessed a bright comet, later discovered to be the same comet of 1682. Since it must, they thought, presage the fall of *some* kingdom, it encouraged the invasion of England by Duke William of Normandy, known as William the Conqueror. He defeated King Harold at Hastings and became King of England!

William Shakespeare (1564–1616) also voiced the ominous interpretation of comets when he penned from the lips of Calphurnia, Caesar's wife: "When beggars die there are no comets seen; the heavens themselves blaze forth the death of princes" (Julius Caesar, II, ii, 30).

Gottfried Kirch, the German astronomer who discovered the great comet of 1680, was also convinced of the supernatural nature of comets: "I have read through many books on comets, heathen and Christian, religious and secular, Lutheran and Catholic, and they all declare comets to be signs of God's wrath... There are some that oppose these beliefs but they are not very important!"

Four and a half centuries later, the Aztec Emperor Moctezuma II (1466–1520) was anxiously dreading the arrival of the legendary white-bearded god, Quetzalcoatl, who was prophesied to return to Mexico and reclaim his empire which he lost when he was vanquished by the evil Aztec god, Huitzilopochtli.

Ten years before the arrival of the white-bearded Cortez in Vera Cruz, a dazzling comet appeared. The Aztec soothsayers were incapable of interpreting this phenomenon and Moctezuma condemned them to death by starvation. Nezahualpilli, ruler of Texcoco, then forecasted calamities which were to destroy the kingdom, and Moctezuma took it as a sure omen that Quetzalcoatl was on his way. The leader of the greatest empire in the Western Hemisphere suddenly became indecisive because of a comet and a prophecy!

Indeed, it may well be said that the conquest of the Aztecs several years later was in a significant measure due to a fatalistic dread of comets. Years after the Spanish conquest, there was another comet in 1531. In retrospect, it supposedly heralded the "death" of a pagan culture and the conversion of the Aztecs to Christianity. It was in the year that the Blessed Virgin Mary appeared in Mexico to Juan Diego!

Meanwhile, across the Atlantic, the Protestant Reformation (1517–1650) was on its way. Moctezuma and

Martin Luther (1483–1546) shared a common sentiment about comets, and in one of his sermons, Luther preached: "The heathen writes that the comet may arrive from natural causes, but God creates not one that does not foretoken a sure calamity." An unusual statement to make from a pulpit!

Now, in 1826, a comet was independently discovered by Wilhelm von Beila and Jean Gambart. The latter made the disquieting prediction that his comet would strike the earth on its next return, around October 29, 1832. The comet appeared on schedule, but it did not impact the earth. However, it caused near panic to earthlings in 1832. It was around the time of the revolutions in Paris, which were the sparks to a series of revolutions in Europe.

Its reappearance in 1846 was extremely spectacular. As astronomers peered through their telescopes in amazement, it was discovered that there was not one, but two comets on almost identical trajectories, each with its own tail. The comet had split in two since its earlier appearance in 1832. Coincidentally, 1846 was also the year the Blessed Virgin appeared in La Salette with tidings of woe, warning the world of calamities to come if men did not convert.

But what really are comets? They are merely snow balls in orbit filled with small mineral grains and complex organic matter. They are made mostly of ice and dirt (dirty snowballs), carbon monoxide ice, carbon dioxide ice, ammonia ice, methane ice, and ices of other complex chemicals. There are millions of them roaming about the sun. When passing close to the sun, a comet's tail, extending away from it for distances of several hundred *million* kilometers, can be seen even in the daytime.

Fortunately, the earth's gravity is insufficient to drag passing comets to us. But every now and then, by chance, a comet would make a close pass by the earth. It is only a matter of time, but sooner or later a large comet may indeed strike the earth, with consequences that we can be quite sure will be catastrophic. It is clear, therefore, that the ancient global fear of comets is not without some foundation.

There was a great comet in the year 1910. It had a tail 50 million miles long and it seemed that the earth was about to brush against its tail. It was Halley's comet again. The idea of the earth flying through a cloud of cyanide generated great apprehension. Camille Flamarion, the prominent French astronomer, raised the possibility that "cyanogen gas would impregnate the atmosphere and possibly snuff out all life on the planet" (Indeed, it was hydrogen cyanide, Zyklon B, which was used in the Nazi gas chambers). There was worldwide comet frenzy. There were parties. People were making merry before the world ended of cyanogen poisoning. Entrepreneurs hawked in numerable gas masks. But in 1910 the comet passed. No one was asphyxiated.

Meteors and Meteorites

Comets do not streak across the sky, meteors do. A meteor is an object that, as it falls through the earth's atmosphere, produces a trail of light. It looks something like a magnesium flare. The brightest meteors are called fireballs, and the brightest fireball can outshine the moon or even the sun. By definition, a meteor does not strike the ground. If one that looks like a meteor falls as a rock newly fallen from the sky, it is not a meteor, but a meteorite. Meteorites come from meteors. They are pieces of other worlds. Like comets, they are believed by some to be portents of impending evil. However, meteors are much more common than comets.

Every year about 1,500 meteorites are so big that they do not burn up in the atmosphere but strike the surface of the earth. Really large meteorites are estimated to strike the earth about once every 10,000 years, and when they do, they sink deep into the crust and then explode with the force of an atom bomb. Indeed, some of the many impact craters on the moon are made by meteorites, but most are made by comets. The sun and the planets also have their share of cometary impacts, but the sun, being made of gas, does not retain impact craters.

There is a crater 1.2 kilometers in diameter in Arizona. It was probably produced about fifteen thousand years ago when a lump of iron twenty five meters wide impacted the earth at a speed of fifteen kilometers per second. The energy released was roughly equivalent to that of a four-megaton nuclear explosion. It is a meteorite crater.

On June 30, 1908, something fell out of the sky in Siberia and, at an altitude of eight kilometers, exploded and devastated 850 square miles of Siberian forest. No impact crater was ever found but the blast was more powerful than that of the highest yield nuclear weapon in current arsenals. It had the force of 1,000 Hiroshima bombs. This explosion in Tunguska was caused by an asteroid exploding in the air. The Soviet Academy of Sciences eventually conducted a thorough survey several years later, apparently reluctant to travel to a site so swampy and remote. The explosion, the Academy reported, was caused by a comet, probably several kilometers in diameter and weighing a million tons, about a millionth of the weight of most comets. Earth was lucky! However, there is still debate as to whether the asteroid was a comet or a meteorite.

Comets striking Jupiter are not exceptionally rare events. Indeed, the world was transfixed when, on March 25, 1993, the *feast of the Annunciation*, a small band of comet and asteroid hunters was amazed to find some twenty small, bright objects that no one had ever seen before, all orbiting Jupiter. They were first discovered by Eugene Shoemaker and David Levy. It soon became clear that each of them was about to crash into Jupiter one by one, each behind the other.

The first explosion occurred on July 16, 1994. It was on *the feast of Our Lady of Mount Carmel*. Coincidence? The impacts ended on July 22. The size of the cometary fragments is estimated to have been a few hundred meters to perhaps a kilometer across, plummeting into Jupiter at sixty kilometers a second. Every impact left a dark blemish about the size of our earth. But Jupiter, like Saturn, Uranus, and Neptune, is made mostly of gas. They have no solid surface on which to form a lasting record of a comet crater.

Such catastrophes have occurred throughout the whole history of the earth. Sixty-five million years ago, a comet came out of space, hit the earth, and extinguished much of the life on this planet. But how can such a cometary impact kill hundred-ton dinosaurs as well as our plant life halfway around the world? The answer lies in the probability that for months or even years afterwards, the earth would have been darkened and cooled, a sort of nuclear winter which could not sustain life.

None of the near earth objects (NEOs) are known to have orbits that would impact the earth in the next few centuries but tomorrow one might be discovered that will. There might be a comet with our name on it. There is also the remote possibility of a long-period comet soaring out of the Kuiper Belt on a beeline for the earth with only a few months' notice to us. In that case, a cosmic doomsday clock may be ticking away even now.

Indeed, it does seem strange that a purely accidental event could possibly destroy the earth. However, in 1850, Thomas Dick philosophized: "Believing that every object and every event in the universe is arranged and directed by an omnipotent Contriver, we must admit that when the Almighty formed the wondrous plan of creation, 'foreseeing the end and the beginning,' he arranged the periods and the velocities of comets in such a manner that, although occasionally crossing the planetary orbits, they should not pass these orbits at a time when the planets were in their immediate vicinity. And should such an event ever occur, we may rest assured that it is in perfect accordance with the plan and the will of the Creator, and that it is on the whole, subservient to the happiness and order of the intelligent universe, and the ends intended by the divine government." An interesting "theology"!

Halley's comet

A crater in Arizona formed 50,000 years ago by a meteorite

A mysterious asteriod hits Siberia

The Last Time Earth Got Hit

Nine decades ago a mysterious fireball slammed into our planet. But only now are we learning its true identity

The Tunguska forest is wiped out

A depiction of the comets hitting Jupiter (*Time* Magazine)

Chapter 38

Rosa Mystica
1947—1966

I t was in 1531 that the *Mother of God* appeared
to Juan Diego in Tepeyac hill in Mexico and performed
"the miracle of the roses" as proof to Bishop Zumarraga
of her presence. Roses never grew on that rocky terrain,
and certainly not in December. Moreover, when, in their
surprise, the bishop's attendants tried to pick and take
some of them from his tilma, they could not do so because
they became, as one author put it, "not roses that they
touched, but as if they were painted or embroidered."
Indeed, they were "mystical roses" from the hands of the
Mystical Rose herself.

The Litany of Loreto lists many of her titles, but there
is a flower amongst them; the *Mystical Rose*. Truly, the
rose is the queen of all the flowers, and there is something
in the heavenly arrangement of its petals and its colouring,
there is something in its scent and symmetry, in the
modesty of its green leaves, which makes it very special. It
is the flower which captures the heart at nearly every stage
of its growth, even when a bud. While it grows, its petals
gradually unfold as a token, as it were, of the blossoming
of the lover's love for his loved one.

Mary, the most beautiful of God's creation, is indeed "the Incarnate Rose," especially chosen for God's garden. She is the "rose of Sharon and the lily of the valleys" (Song 2:1). There is no rose comparable to her and she has made Paradise ever so much more beautiful.

But if you call her a rose, white is the colour of her purity; gold, the tint of her royalty; red, the hue of her suffering. The rose grows out from a stem of thorns and in the heart of this flower, the red of the Cross of her son was forming. Indeed, without thorns a rose is not a rose, and without the thorn of great suffering, Mary could not have become the *Mystical Rose* of God's Paradise.

Now, there are reports of Marian apparitions in Northern Italy, in Montichiari, in the diocese of Brescia, where, significantly, as we shall see later, Pope Paul VI (1963–1978) was born in 1898. Montichiari is a small town, whose name means in English "Bright Mountains." Interestingly, Pope John Paul II in his homily in Jasna Gora, Poland, on June 6, 1979, said: "Our Lady of the Bright Mountain, Mother of the Church! Once more I consecrate myself to you 'in your maternal slavery of love': *Totus Tuus*! I am all yours!"

The apparitions began in 1947, just after the end of World War II, when Paul VI was Monsignor Giovanni Montini and not yet Pope. It was two years after Mary's first apparition to Ida Peerdeman in Amsterdam. Many bishops and priests have expressed their belief in the genuineness of the apparitions. Monsignor Abate Rossi, who was for twenty two years the parish priest of Montichiari, once declared: "I am convinced that the apparitions are genuine... When one is twenty-two years a parish priest in the same place, one has a lot of experiences. One sees and hears a lot. First, I ordered the statue of the Madonna to be carved and later I put it in the church of Montichiari and I experienced many great graces and conversions."

There is also evidence that Pope Paul VI believed in the authenticity of the apparitions. In fact, on one occasion he called on the Church to invoke Mary as *Rosa Mystica*. And so, on May 30, 1997, I visited Montichiari-Fontanelle, researching the history of the apparitions.

Pierina Gilli (1911–1991) worked as a nurse in the hospital there and it was in a room in the hospital in May of 1947 that the Blessed Virgin first appeared to her. It was in the month of May that she also first appeared in Fatima in 1917. She was dressed in mauve and her heart was pierced by three swords. Very sad she was, and her eyes were filled with tears which fell to the floor. All she said to Pierina was: "Prayer, sacrifice, penance."

The Virgin explained the meaning of the three swords to Pierina. The first sword means the loss of vocation in priests. The second sword refers to priests, monks, and nuns who live in mortal sin. The third sword denotes priests and monks who commit the treason of Judas. While giving up their vocation, they often lose their faith also, and become enemies of the Church.

In fact, I discovered that her beloved Pope Paul VI had also said words to that effect: "There are forces within the Church, and priests in religion are numerous among them, who are doing far more damage to it than its bitterest enemies outside. Many priests and religious are giving the Church the 'Judas kiss.' Satan himself has made his way into the temple of God!"

I was curious about her being dressed in mauve, a colour of mourning. Then I discovered the relevance of this and its association with the 13th of the month. It is in the Book of Esther, named after the great Old Testament Jewish queen who put on garments of mourning for three days when she heard of the plot to exterminate all the Jews living in the Persian empire. It was planned for the 13th of the month. After the three days, Esther then took off her mourning attire, pleaded with King Ahaseurus and saved her people. In short, she came to Montichiari as the mournful Esther of the New Testament in an attempt to save her consecrated ones and the people dedicated to God.

In the following month, on June 13, the Virgin appeared again in the hospital early one Sunday morning. This time she was dressed in white and instead of three swords, there were three roses: a white, a red, and a golden yellow one. She also explained the significance of the roses. The white rose means the spirit of prayer; the red rose, the spirit of sacrifice, and the golden yellow rose refers to the spirit of penance and conversion.

She said: "I am the *Mother of Jesus* and the *Mother of all of you*" (In other words, *Mother of Mankind, Mother of all Nations*). She paused for a while and then continued: "Our Lord sends me to bring a new Marian devotion for all male and female institutes, religious orders, and secular priests I wish the 13th of each month to be celebrated as the feast day of Mary. On this day I shall send to these religious institutions, members of orders, and secular priests, who have honoured me in this way, a superabundance of graces and great sanctity. I wish the

13th of July of each year to be celebrated in honour of the *Rosa Mystica*, the Mystical Rose."

Several other apparitions occurred within the chapel of the hospital and in the parish church, but the sixth apparition, a very special one, occurred on the eve of the feast of *the Immaculate Conception*. It was on December 7, 1947. This time the Virgin wore a white cloak. This was held on the right side by a boy and on the left side by a girl, both of whom were also dressed in white. She said to Pierina: "Tomorrow I shall show you my immaculate heart of which mankind knows so little." She then paused for a while before she added: "In Fatima I spread the devotion to my immaculate heart. Here in Montichiari, I wish the devotion of the *Rosa Mystica*, together with the veneration of my immaculate heart, to increase in the religious institutions and the monastic communities, in order that these souls dedicated to God may receive more graces from my motherly heart."

Pierina was then told that the two children at her side were Jacinta and Francisco, the two young visionaries of Fatima, who had since died in 1918. Indeed, her apparitions at Montichiari were a continuation of her Fatima requests, except that they were primarily given for the clergy, although not excluding "people dedicated to God."

On the following day, December 8, 1947, about a thousand people had gathered in the overcrowded parish church for the great feast of Mary. This time she appeared to Pierina and said, smiling and full of radiance: "*I am the Immaculate Conception*" (the first time she said this was in Lourdes in 1858). Then she added: "*I am Mary of grace, that is, 'full of grace*,' mother of my divine Son Jesus Christ. I come here to Montichiari because it is my wish to be venerated as the *Rosa Mystica*. I wish to be celebrated each year on December 8, at noon, the 'hour of grace' for the whole world."

It was the counterpart of her Son's "hour of mercy," three o'clock, as was told by Jesus to Sr. M. Faustina Kowalska of Cracow, Poland, recently proclaimed "Blessed" by Pope John Paul II. The Virgin also lamented: "Look at this heart which loves men so much, and which is showered with insults by so many..." This, too, was a similar lamentation to that of her Son, "the Divine Mercy," when He said to Sr. Faustina: "My heart drinks only of the ingratitude and forgetfulness of souls living in the world... Ingratitude in return for so many graces is my heart's constant food. In return for my blessings, I get ingratitude."

Saint Sophronius, Patriarch of Jerusalem, asserts that the reason for which the Archangel Gabriel calls her full of grace, ("Hail, full of grace!") was because only limited grace was given to others, but it was given to Mary in all its plenitude... It follows that divine grace did not come into Mary by drops as in other saints, "but like rain on the fleece," as it was foretold by David. But to be full of grace, she had to be *the Immaculate Conception!*

A resumption of apparitions in Northern Italy then occurred after the end of Vatican II in 1966, this time in the town of Fontanelle, which is only about four kilometres away from Montichiari. The first apparition in Fontanelle was on the Sunday after Easter, April 17, 1966. Notably, it is the same day that Jesus, speaking to Sr. Faustina, requested to be celebrated as Divine Mercy Sunday!

In Fontanelle there is a well and an old stone staircase which leads down to it. That Sunday, Pierina was walking up and down the pathway above the well, praying the Rosary, when the Virgin appeared to her. Wrapped in her arm hung a white Rosary. She said: "My divine Son is all love and He sent me here to bestow upon this well healing power." The Virgin then bowed down and touched the water of the well at two places with her hands and then added: "I wish that the sick and all my children can come here to this miraculous well." When Pierina asked her what should the spring be called, she answered: "the Spring of Grace."

It was during the fifth apparition in Fontanelle that were seen in large letters of bright orange-red light around the Virgin: *Fiat della Creazione*, which means *Fiat of the Creation*. A bit deeper and below was another writing in shining red: *Fiat della Redenzione*, meaning *Fiat of the Redemption*. And still a bit deeper in shining blue, *Maria della Corredenzione*, which means *Mary, Coredemptrix*. The Virgin herself did not speak but smiled, and it was an angelic voice from nowhere which was heard to say: "Mary's fiat which she spoke to the angel made her *Mother of God* and *Mother of Mankind*. It may be compared with the fiat of the creation because by her fiat she *received all graces from God the Father*." And so, as I said before, she was "*full of grace!*" This correct translation is of major theological significance.

The Rosa Mystica statue

One of the many weeping statues of the Rosa Mystica

262

Nuns in the monastery of St. Clare in Salamanca, Spain

A rainbow appears on a photograph of the Fountain of Grace

Chapter 39

Pope Paul VI and Vatican II
1962—1963

The Second Vatican Council was opened by Pope John XXIII on October 11, 1962, at that time the feast of the Divine Maternity of the Blessed Virgin Mary. Pope John died on June 3, 1963 and was succeeded by Pope Paul VI on June 21. He continued the Second Vatican Council. Considered by some to have been indecisive, he certainly proved them wrong during Vatican Council II.

Paul VI saw "collegiality" as one of the great issues facing Vatican II. He foresaw that some were trying to use the term to undercut the Magesterium. Vatican I (1870) had defined the role of the Pope and promulgated the doctrine of infallibility and there were many bishops who were out to challenge Papal authority, including many of the so-called European liberals. However, Paul, although liberal and moderate in most matters, was never liberal in his concept of the Papacy. To him, the primacy of Peter was an article of faith, and never to be compromised, never to yield to expediency or fashionable theological theories.

This stand was expressed when he addressed the faithful of Milan in 1962: "It is important to understand the position of the Pope in relation to an ecumenical council. The Pope alone, it must be remembered, has supreme, full power of jurisdiction over the whole Church. This is an 'episodical', that is, a pastoral power given directly by Christ and not by the Church, and it is his alone... The Pope's power is that of a 'vicar' in respect to Christ, but it is his alone, supremely and universally, in respect to the Church."

According to Robert Moynihan, writing in the March 1966 issue of *Inside the Vatican*, Paul VI tended to abide by the will of the majority, but was well aware, in the words of John XXIII, that "in spiritual matters quantitative judgments do not apply." In other words, Paul knew that majority votes were no guarantee of truth. As he himself was to learn painfully, the Holy Spirit frequently speaks through a single, often lonely and isolated individual, and the emotional swings of large gatherings, accidental events, and the ever present tidal pull of the *Zeitgeist* (the spirit of the times) had to be guarded against. One practical way to be on guard was by listening to the still, small voice within. Indeed, he operated according to his own self-definition: "I am neither liberal nor conservative. I am the Pope."

Inside The Vatican staff writers, in the April 1996 issue, stated that the battle over how to define Mary's relationship to the Church was also one of the central battles of Vatican II. Whereas the Council fully reaffirmed essential Catholic teachings on Mary, that reaffirmation was cautious and controversial. There was an attempt in the Council to speak little of Mary, to downplay her role, to isolate discussion of her in one chapter of a document rather than giving her an entire document of her own.

The forces opposed to traditional Marian piety and those defending it hardly concealed their battle flags at the Council. But there were some surprises in store. The determination of conservatives and moderates, and the intervention of Paul VI, saw that the final document would contain almost all that the traditionalists insisted on.

On the other hand, liberals spoke and expressed concern about how the statement on Mary would affect ecumenism. Those remarks led Bishop Luigi Carli of Segni, Italy, to complain that the ecumenical obsessions of some bishops were making it impossible to speak of traditional Catholic doctrines concerning Our Lady. Very quickly it became apparent that discussions on Mary might bring disharmony in the Council.

Two Marian titles were predominantly in dispute; *Mediatrix of all Graces* and *Mother of the Church*. There were those who were particularly disturbed by the title of Mary as *Mediatrix of all Graces*. The liberals thought that anything which presented a problem to Protestants must be omitted, and that the phrase *Mediatrix of all Graces* must go. On the other hand, they were slightly less opposed to the more restrictive *"Mediatrix."* This was particularly the view of German and Austrian bishops. Indeed, the position endorsed by this group became pretty much the position of liberals during the Council.

In the end, more than two thousand one hundred voted. Those favouring a document on Mary as part of a larger document on the Church won by seventeen votes only! Even Martin Luther was invoked on behalf of Mary by Archbishop Giuseppe Gawlina, director of the Polish Hospice in Rome, who, referring to *"Mediatrix,"* quoted the words of the reformer: "What can please her (Mary) more than if you come in this way through her to God... Mary does not wish that you come to her, but that *through her* you should come to God." However, they rejected the controversial "of all graces."

The Blessed Virgin appeared to St. Catherine Labouré in 1830 and showed her an image of herself with rays emanating from rings on her fingers: "These rays," she said, "symbolize the graces I shed upon those who asked for them." Catherine was canonized by Pope Pius XII on July 27, 1947. One may well ask what credence did those bishops really give to St. Catherine Labouré's visions and testimony, which have been approved by the Church, and what sort of duplicity are we witnessing in the Church by some of its bishops?

The *Mother of the Church* they also rejected. But while the inclusion of '*Mediatrix*' disturbed liberals and Protestants, the rejection of '*Mother of the Church*' stunned traditionalists. *Mother of the Church* had been debated for nearly two years. For traditional bishops, if the Church began with her, with Jesus in her womb, she deserved this title. Indeed, in his opening address to the second session (1963), Paul VI had asked the Council for a "loving acknowledgment of the place, privileged above all, which the *Mother of God* occupies in the Church... After Christ," he said, "her place in the Church is the most exalted, and also the one closest to us, and so we honour her with the title '*Mother of the Church*' to her glory and to our benefit."

266

When the Theological Commission finally rejected it, perhaps the major reason was that it might be offensive to Protestants. However, what the Theological Commission denied Mary, her title *Mother of the Church*, Paul would grant by decree. Yes, he was Paul, but he was also Peter!

On November 21, 1964, Paul acted decisively, correcting both Commission and Council by formally bestowing the title *Mother of the Church* upon Mary on his own authority as successor of Peter. He announced to the crowd: "Very many Council Fathers have made this wish their own, hoping for an explicit declaration during the Council of the role as Mother which the Virgin exercises over the Christian people. To achieve this aim, we have considered it opportune to consecrate, at this public meeting itself, a title in honour of the Virgin, which has been suggested by various parts of the Catholic world. Therefore, for the glory of the Virgin Mary and for our own consolation, we proclaim the Most Holy Mary as *Mother of the Church*, that is to say, of all the People of God... And we wish from now on that the Virgin should be still more honoured and invoked by the entire people by this most dear title."

According to Brother R. M. Wiltgren, S.D.V.: "The standing ovation which greeted this announcement signified the warm assent of most of the Council Fathers. The Pope was interrupted seven times by applause in his address, and the applause increased in intensity as the address continued." And so, the one thing the Council's liberals sought to avoid, giving primacy of place to Mary, was in the final analysis given to her anyway.

Pope Paul VI, that great lover of Mary, died on August 6, 1978, as prophesied in Amsterdam by the *Lady of all Nations* on June 11, 1978: "Before two months will have passed, Pope Paul VI will enter eternal life," she said to Ida.

Pope John Paul II, in the tradition of Paul, wrote in *Redemptor Hominis, 22*: "Since Paul VI proclaimed the Mother of Christ 'Mother of the Church,' and that title has been known far and wide, may it be permitted to his unworthy successor to turn to Mary as *Mother of the Church* at the close of these reflections which it was opportune to make at the beginning of his papal service."

And in his book *Crossing the Threshold of Hope*, he added: "Each one of us must realize that we are not dealing simply with emotional needs, with sentimental tendencies, but with the objective reality of the *Mother of God*, Mary, the new Eve, beginning with the Annunciation, through the night of birth in Bethlehem, the Cross on Golgotha, until the Pentecostal Cenacle: Mother of Christ the Redeemer and *Mother of the Church.*"

The Secret of Paul VI, written by Jean Guitton, records these significant words of Paul VI in 1977, one year before his death: "There is great uneasiness at this time in the world and in the Church, and that which is in question is the faith. It so happens now that I repeat to myself the obscure phrase of Jesus in the Gospel of St. Luke: 'When the Son of Man returns, will he still find faith on the earth?' I sometimes read the Gospel passage of the End Times and I attest that, at this time, some signs of this end are emerging. Are we close to the end? This we will never know. We must always hold ourselves in readiness, but everything could last a very long time yet. What strikes me, when I think of the Catholic world, is that within Catholicism there seems sometimes to predominate a non-Catholic way of thinking, and it can happen that this non-Catholic thought within Catholicism will tomorrow become the stronger. But it will never represent the thought of the Church. It is necessary that a small flock subsist, no matter how small it might be."

After the Second Vatican Council, Paul VI also remarked that the smoke of Satan was seeping into the Church of God through cracks in the wall, and on October 13, 1977, he said: "The tail of the devil is functioning in the disintegration of the Catholic world. The darkness of Satan has entered throughout the Catholic Church even to its summit. Apostasy, the loss of the faith, is spreading throughout the world and into the highest levels within the Church."

On the occasion of the millennium of Poland's conversion to Christianity, the Polish episcopate in 1966 solemnly consecrated Poland to Mary, *Mother of the Church.* Pope Paul VI was denied participation in the celebrations at Jasna Gora by Communist authorities. However, in 1979, the first Polish Pope, John Paul II, began his pilgrimage to Jasna Gora, saying: "Mary's will is being fulfilled. I am here..."

Pope John XXIII

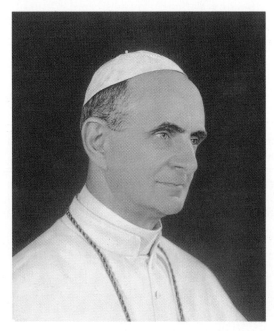

Pope Paul VI

Pope Paul VI—Karol Wojtyla to his right

Chapter 40

Akita and Medjugorje
1973

The message of the Blessed Virgin when she appeared in Akita, Japan, is linked to the message of Fatima and the miracle of the sun seen there. Now, when the *Lady of the Rosary* appeared in Fatima, she wore no crown on her head, but there was a bright golden star on the hem of her dress. And so, just as the great Old Testament Jewish Queen Esther pleaded with King Ahaseurus and saved her people from annihilation in Persia on the 13th of the month, a day selected by lot, so did this Queen of the New Testament, Mary, come to Fatima on the 13th of the month to prevent many nations from being annihilated. She came to Fatima therefore, *in the spirit of Queen Esther*. Esther means—Star! It was on the hem of her dress.

The sun is our nearest star and is about 93 million miles away from Earth. It has a diameter of close to a million miles while Earth's diameter is only 8,000 miles. But, we fail to recognize that the miracle of the sun in Fatima in 1917 when, to the alarm of the people, this gigantic sun came hurtling down to Earth, was of major apocalyptic significance. The rays of the sun are so bright that they easily damage the retina of the eye and can cause blindness when looked at continuously for a minute or so. However, during the miracle of the sun in Fatima, the 70,000 people gathered there were able to look at the sun for minutes without hurting their eyes in the slightest way. Indeed, many of us have also had the same privilege on occasions in Medjugorje.

Now, deep in the core of the sun there is an immense quantity of hydrogen which is highly compressed at a temperature of about 15 million degrees centigrade. In this process some of the hydrogen is converted into helium in this great nuclear furnace, and a tremendous amount of nuclear energy is released. It is this energy which warms the earth, illuminates the sky, and sustains life.

It is estimated that every second 600 million tons of hydrogen are changed to helium in this manner. The sun is already thousands of millions of years old, but has used up only about 5 per cent of its hydrogen, therefore, the amount of light and heat from the sun is not expected to alter significantly for several thousands of millions of years!

In fact, the principle and idea of a hydrogen bomb is to produce an extremely rapid conversion of hydrogen into helium, that is, to do exactly what the sun does, but to do it rapidly. The sun, in other words, is nothing but an enormous hydrogen bomb which just keeps on exploding! The possible implication and connotation of that Fatima miracle should now assume greater apocalyptic significance.

To the great relief of the 70,000 witnesses in Fatima, the sun was seen to retreat to its celestial abode at the command of the *Queen of the Universe*, and they all breathed a sigh of relief as they thanked God. The Queen had saved them, as it were, from a nuclear annihilation. It was in October, 1917. It was on the 13th of the month. In a symbolic way, therefore, it was Esther saving her people from annihilation. The question is, will she be enabled to save us, in this the "century of wars," from a man-made nuclear annihilation, or are we going to spurn her messages and her call for conversion, prayer, and penance?

Akita

Fifty six years later, in 1973, she chose a little village in Japan called Akita to weep from one of her images, which also bled from its right hand. The phenomenon was declared to be supernatural by Bishop John Ito in 1984. I have visited this shrine on three occasions. Of immense significance is the fact that the image of *Our Lady of Akita*, which wept 101 times between 1973 and 1981, is a faithful replica of the painting of *Our Lady of all Nations*, the representation of the *Coredemptrix, Mediatrix, and Advocate*.

On August 3, 1973, Sr. Agnes Sasagawa, a nun of the Order of the Handmaids of the Eucharist, heard a voice of indescribable beauty coming from the wooden statue in the chapel: "My daughter, my novice, listen to what I have to say to you. It is very important. You will convey it to your superior. Many men in this world offend the Lord... In order that the world might know His anger, the heavenly Father is preparing a great chastisement on all mankind. With my Son I have intervened so many times to appease the wrath of the Father. I have prevented the onset of calamities by offering Him the sufferings of the Son on the Cross, His precious blood, and the beloved souls who console Him and form a cohort of victim souls..."

Then in October 1973, Sr. Agnes heard the beautiful voice speaking from the statue once more: "The work of the devil will infiltrate even into the Church in such a way that one will see cardinals opposing cardinals, bishops against other bishops. The priests who venerate me will be scorned and opposed by their confreres, churches and altars will be sacked. The Church will be full of those who accept compromises and the devil will press many priests and consecrated souls to leave the service of the Lord. The demon would be especially implacable against souls consecrated to God. The thought of the loss of so many souls is the cause of my sadness. If sins increase in number and gravity, there will be no longer any pardon for them."

She continued, "As I told you, if people do not repent and better themselves, the Father will inflict a terrible punishment on all humanity. It will be a punishment greater than the Flood, such as one will never have seen before. Fire will fall from the sky and will wipe out a great part of humanity, the good as well as the bad, sparing neither priests nor faithful. The survivors will find themselves so desolate that they will envy the dead. The only arms which will remain for you will be the Rosary and the Sign left by my Son. Each day recite the prayers of the Rosary. With the Rosary pray for the Pope, the bishops and the priests."

She made these remarks on October 13, 1973, the anniversary of the miracle of the sun in Fatima. The statue wept for the last time on September 15, 1981. It was the feast of *Our Lady of Sorrows*. Why Japan? Japan, of course, had already experienced the abomination of desolation from the atomic bomb in 1945 when in Hiroshima and Nagasaki about 1,000,000 people were annihilated in a second, and the survivors envied the dead.

Medjugorje

Eight years later, she first appeared in Medjugorje on the feast of John the Baptist, June 24, 1981. John prepared the way for the First Coming. Was she telling us, therefore, that she is preparing us for the Second Coming? Is this why she said in Medjugorje?: "I came to Lourdes in the morningtime, to Fatima at noon, and to Medjugorje in the eveningtime." In fact, this was figuratively and also literally true. She appeared to Bernadette in Lourdes at 6 o'clock in the morning, to the children in Fatima just after noon and to the visionaries of Medjugorje at 5:40 in the evening. The symbolism is quite clear. We are in the eveningtime. I am simply attempting to interpret the signs of the times. Let us, however, remember that she also said in Medjugorje that prayer can prevent war and even change the laws of nature. But are we all listening to her?

But why did she choose Yugoslavia of all countries to appear as the *Queen of Peace*, significantly, the very last of her titles in the Litany of Loreto? In my view, it is because it was an event in Sarajevo, the capital of Bosnia-Hercegovina, which was the spark that ignited World War I in 1914, the first of the great world wars. It was the assassination of Archduke Franz Ferdinand and his wife Sophia of the Austria-Hungary empire by a Serbian nationalist, Gravilo Princip. Medjugorje, like Sarajevo, is in Bosnia-Hercegovina! This war led to World War II and who knows what else to come!

In short, the *Queen of Peace* came in 1981 to Yugoslavia to warn us of the possibility of another greater war, which is being instigated by her adversary, the prince of war, that great destroyer of peace and harmony, Satan. Medjugorje did, but the rest of Yugoslavia did not listen to her messages. War came to Yugoslavia. Hundreds of churches and thousands of homes were destroyed in the midst of atrocities of unspeakable dimension.

But Medjugorje is still untouched. It is the city of Mary, and Satan had no access to this garden, east of Eden. In fact, I have always professed that if Medjugorje and its church were destroyed during the war, then the *Queen of Peace* is not appearing there at all. However, I have always believed that she is appearing there, and so, I never felt insecure when visiting Medjugorje, even during the height of the war.

The same sequence of events happened in Africa. She appeared in Kibeho in Rwanda as the *Mother of the Word* from 1981 to 1988. Her pleas were not heeded. Rwanda and Zaire have since experienced their own apocalypse, and are still doing so to this day.

The wooden statue of Our Lady of Akita

Our Lady of Akita weeps

Viska, Ivan and Marija of Medjugorje

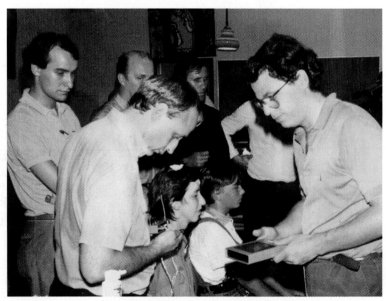

Italian and French scientists investigate the
visionaries during an apparition

Author with Marija Pavlovic and his daughter Maria

Our Lady of Medjugorje
The Shekinah appears in front of His "ark"
(Courtesy Janie Garza)

Chapter 41

The Tears of a Mother

Whereas December 8 (and not December 9 as in Juan Diego's time) is celebrated as the feast of *the Immaculate Conception*, not only in Mexico but throughout the Catholic Church, December 12 is the feast of *Our Lady of Guadalupe*, a great feast day in Mexico. It was the date of the miracle of the tilma in 1531.

I arrived in Mexico City on December 8, 1996, in time for the week's celebration, and attended the High Mass beginning at 11:30 a.m. on the morning of December 12. As I approached the Basilica of *Our Lady of Guadalupe*, emblazoned in huge gold letters above the main entrance, were the historic words: "Am I not here, I who am your Mother?"

The large esplanade outside the basilica, called the Plaza of the Americas, was overcrowded with thousands of people and Aztec dance groups in traditional colourful Indian costumes. Many of them were there since midnight, swirling and dancing in rhythmic unison to the beat of the Aztec drums as they celebrated the feast of the new Mother Tonantzin, *Our Lady of Guadalupe*. Inside the basilica the Archbishop of Mexico City and 73 priests were concelebrating the sacrifice of the Mass. On a huge wall behind the altar hung the glass-protected tilma of Juan Diego, around which was draped a large Mexican flag.

There were two magnificent choirs, one adult and the other a boys' choir, some thirty feet apart, yet in synchronous harmony with each other. About seventeen thousand people packed the huge circular basilica from wall to wall, and while the choirs were singing the *Agnus Dei*, the *Kyrie Eleison*, and other hymns throughout the solemn High Mass, the sound of the Aztec drums in the huge plaza outside were reverberating inside the basilica. It was not a distraction. It was the exciting admixture of the musical expressions of the two different eras, the old Mexico and the new, now *"one in their love" (unus in suis amore)* for the Virgin.

One in their love! It was what she spoke about in her first message to Juan Diego: "...I am your merciful Mother, the Mother of all who lived *united* in this land, and of all mankind." And so, she is calling for the day when all will be one. It is the prayer of her Son on Maundy Thursday: *"Holy Father, keep through your own name those whom you have given me, that they may be one, as we are one"* (John 17:11).

At the Offertory, about a dozen chosen members of the congregation brought to the altar large baskets containing hundreds of red roses, which were received by the Archbishop himself. The late Bishop Zumurraga would have known that it was not the first time in the history of Mexico that a bishop received a bouquet of roses! These gifts of flowers were "offerings" of thanksgiving as taught by Quetzalcoatl. Towards the end of the Mass the Archbishop distributed the hundreds of roses first to the concelebrants and the choir, and then he joyfully threw the rest into the air for the congregation.

Now, there was standing room only during that glorious and emotional two-hour service, and as I stood there among the "New Aztecs," in "New Spain," for the first time I fully appreciated Peter's exclamation of joy and appreciation at the transfiguration of Jesus on Mount Tabor: "Lord, it is good for us to be here" (Mark 9:5).

But the spiritual ecstasy was not to end in the basilica. At 4:00 p.m. that same day, two friends of mine took me on a forty-minute drive to see another of the miracles which humiliates science. During the previous week, a statue of *Our Lady of Guadalupe* began to weep blood in the humble home of Mrs. Maria Cortez. As I entered the narrow lane off the street to Maria's little house, the name plate of the street was seen on the wall. It was Quetzalcoatl Street! They were the tears of the *Mother of*

280

Sorrows. It was "Rachel weeping for her children" (Matthew 2:18).

Now, there have been a number of weepings of sacred images over the years in both the Eastern and Roman Churches, but never in the history of our world have there been so many weepings and apparitions of Mary as in the second half of this 20th century. The first recorded weeping of the Virgin occurred in La Salette nearly a century and a half ago in 1846. These were ordinary tears, but today many of her weepings are tears of blood. The significance is quite clear. Scientists have investigated many of these "miracles" and have found the tears to be human tears. They have also found no explanation for these phenomena other than the ability of God to alter the laws of science and nature as He wills.

One miraculous weeping occurred in an Orthodox church, which serves the Albanian community in Chicago. It was reported in the *Washington Post* of December 18, 1986. The event happened in St. Nicholas Church which was built in 1961 on the northwest side of Chicago. The parish priest was Father Phillip Kuofos and he had held the post for two years. St. Nicholas is very popular in the Eastern Church and his feast is celebrated with great solemnity. On December 5, the eve of his feast, Fr. Kuofos was saying vespers during which both he and the people in the congregation noticed something strange on the icon of the Virgin and Child in front of the iconostasis. It seemed to be moisture, and on looking closely, they could see a trail of it from each of the eyes of the Virgin.

On the following day, Fr. Dali, who had built the church, joined Fr. Kuofus to celebrate Mass on the feast day, during which occasion the icon wept copiously. "How we got through the liturgy, I will never know. Both of us were leading each other through it. At one point Fr. Dali leaned over me, and said: 'I am going to cry.' It was very emotional for us," said Fr. Kuofos in an interview. Not long afterwards, long queues began to file past the icon, and the television and newspaper men joined in to spread the word further as the moisture continued to ooze from the painting daily.

I read about this weeping in Chicago in the 1987 Epiphany issue of the *MIRecord,* a bulletin of the Medjugorje Information Service of Sussex, England and I immediately became curious. Coincidentally, about one month later, I was invited to a medical conference in Chicago and accepted the invitation, mainly because I also saw this as an opportunity to visit the Church of St. Nicholas. Soon after arriving in Chicago on May 7, 1987, I telephoned Fr. Kuofos to be told that happily, the icon, which had stopped weeping for the past month, had resumed weeping the day before.

I immediately took a taxi and eventually found this small church in the northwestern area of Chicago. There, in front of the iconostasis, I saw the icon of the Theotokos (Mother of God) with light tears slowly oozing down from her eyes. I stayed for one hour in the front pew of the church observing this wondrous phenomenon. The following day I returned to the church and witnessed the weeping again. I then had a long conversation with Fr. Kuofos who was convinced that the phenomenon was a sign of the apocalyptic times in which we are now living.

In 1993, I visited the home (now chapel) of Mrs. Odette Loudonadje in Turmero, about two hours by car from Caracas, Venezuala, where an icon of *Our Lady of Perpetual Succour* has been oozing copious amounts of oil since January 27, 1986. Once more, I was witness to a weeping.

Then, on February 11, 1996, the Thursday before the Mardi Gras, a statue of *the Immaculate Conception (Our Lady of Lourdes)* wept tears of blood in the Convent of the Corpus Christi Carmelite Sisters in Diego Martin, Trinidad. I was called to witness and investigate the phenomenon. I also tested a minute sampling of the clotted blood at the Government Forensic Sciences Laboratory. It was human blood. The image wept tears of blood for a second time the following year, on Thursday, February 13, 1997. It was on the Thursday after the Mardi Gras. A third weeping (more copiously each successive time) took place one week later on February 20, 1997, once more on a Thursday.

I believe that I do understand the significance of this weeping. It was in Lourdes in 1858 that Mary identified herself as *the Immaculate Conception,* and her first apparition there was on February 11, the Thursday before the Mardi Gras in France. It is a time of great revelry and debauchery. Her last apparition to Bernadette Soubirous in Lourdes was on July 16, 1858. It was the feast of *Our Lady of Mount Carmel.* It was, therefore, not surprising to me that heaven in its wisdom chose an image of *the Immaculate Conception* (Our Lady of Lourdes) to weep tears of blood in Trinidad around the time of the Mardi Gras in a convent dedicated to *Our Lady of Mount Carmel.* It is also little known that she did also weep during her apparitions in Lourdes.

I was to witness yet another weeping. On May 7, 1995, an icon of the Mother of God was discovered weeping myrrh by one of the monks in a small chapel at Christ of the Hills Monastery in New Sarov, Blanco, Texas. The monks' first step was to discern if the manifestation was authentic and to immediately notify their ecclesiastical superiors of the event. All attested to the miracle's authenticity. The icon wept continuously from May until October, 1985 and continues to weep intermittently even to this day. The monks follow the ancient Russian Typicon and are part of the Russian Orthodox Church.

On July 12, 1996, Mrs. Janie Garza of Austin, Texas, took me on a pilgrimage to the monastery. I witnessed the icon oozing myrrh, a sweetly smelling perfumed oil, a sample of which, soaked in a small ball of cotton, was given to me by one of the monks. And so, once more I can testify to its authenticity.

Fr. Stefano Gobbi claims to have received these inner locutions from the Blessed Virgin: "The reason for my tears, for a mother's tears, is my children who, in great numbers, live unmindful of God, immersed in the pleasures of the flesh, and are hastening irreparably to their perdition. For many of these, my tears have fallen in the midst of indifference and have fallen in vain.

"Above all, the cause of my weeping is the priests—those beloved sons, the apple of my eye, these consecrated sons of mine. Do you see how they no longer love me? How they no longer want me? Do you see how they no longer listen to the words of my Son? How they frequently betray Him? How Jesus present in the Eucharist is ignored by many, left alone in the tabernacle; often sacrilegiously by them, with wanton negligence?

"I want to help this poor humanity return to its Lord, along the road of conversion and of repentance, and so I am giving it evident signs of my motherly affliction and my sorrowful anxiety. This is why I am causing *tears and blood* to flow down from some of my images.

"How can a child not be moved before its mother who is weeping? How can you, my beloved children, not be moved before your heavenly mother who is weeping *tears of blood*? And yet, these very grave signs, which I am giving you today, are neither accepted nor given credence, but on the contrary are openly opposed and rejected. Thus the extreme action that I am undertaking to lead you to salvation is being obstructed by you.

"So then, my poor children, I am no longer given the possibility of holding back the hand of the justice of God who, by His terrible chastisement, will purify this humanity which cannot be helped because of its obstinate refusal to accept all these extraordinary interventions of your heavenly mother.

"At least you, my beloved ones, remain with me beneath the Cross, together with your brother John, to give comfort and consolation to your sorrowful mother, pierced once again by the sword of such a vast rejection, and unite your sorrow with mine, to implore once again the miracle of Divine Mercy upon the world."

The old Basilica and the new Basilica

Thousands of modern day Aztecs outside the Basilica

Television Azteca recording the Mass

The image of Our Lady of Guadalupe draped with
the Mexican flag

286

Statue of Our Lady of Guadalupe weeps blood

The family of Maria Cortez

The icon of the Theotokos weeping

A statue of Rosa Mystica weeping blood

A statue of Our Lady of Lourdes weeps blood in Trinidad one week apart—note change in facial expressions.

Chapter 42

Our Lady of Hope

All the apparitions of Mary are linked in a mosaic and are meant to be studied and researched, whereupon a panoramic plethora of revelations and motherly pleadings will be unfolded.

She first appeared in Medjugorje on the feast of John the Baptist, who prepared the way for the First Coming of her Son, and many interpret her choice of that date as signifying that she is appearing on earth in these times to prepare us for the Second Coming.

As St. Louis Marie Grignion de Montfort (1673–1716) wrote in his classic book *True Devotion to Mary*: "It was through Mary that the salvation of the world began, and it is through Mary that it must be consummated. Mary hardly appeared at all in the First Coming of Jesus Christ, in order that men, as yet but little instructed and enlightened on the Person of her Son, should not remove themselves from Him by attaching too strongly, and too grossly to her... But in the Second Coming of Jesus Christ, Mary has to be made known and revealed by the Holy Spirit in order that, through her, Jesus Christ may be known, loved and served. The reason which moved the Holy Spirit to hide His spouse during her life, and to reveal her but very little since the preaching of the Gospel subsists no longer. God, then, wishes to reveal and make known Mary, the masterpiece of His hands, in these latter times. Being the way by which Jesus came to us the first time, she will also be the way by which He would come the second time, though not in the same manner."

We are witnessing in this 20th century, "in these latter times," a rapid evolution of events, particularly in the last fifty years or so—an upsurge of wars, murders, violence, materialism, hedonism, drug addiction, pornography, family disintegration, same-sex marriages, same-sex couples legally adopting children, and environmental contamination as never before in known history. We live in a century where rock stars and male and female sex symbols are presented as role models and idols to be emulated, and the earthly prince and princess receive greater veneration than the Prince of Peace and His heavenly Queen. Indeed, it is said that in one of the Holy Virgin's apparitions, she lamented that the sins of today are worse than at the time of Noah.

As for faith, the *Lady of all Nations* said to Ida Peerdeman on March 28, 1951: "My child, do you realize what times you are living in? Never in its history has the world experienced a time like the present one—such a decline of faith." In fact, this was only an echo of her Son's lament: "But when the Son of Man comes will he find any faith on the earth?" (Luke 18:8). Not so, however, with Mary. She was the Woman of Faith. By her faith, she responded to God's invitation to her and began her pilgrimage of faith, a pilgrimage which took her uphill to Calvary. At the foot of the Cross she stood, still with faith, including the moment when her Son requested the disciple to take care of her.

Now, man was entrusted by God to cultivate and take care of the earth (Genesis 2:15), but, on the contrary, he has fared badly as a caretaker and has polluted the earth, and also cared little about his brother. In past centuries, the primary causes of an untimely death were famine and plagues. However, in the 20th century man-made deaths have surpassed natural disasters. Ten million people died in World War I and 50 million people in World War II. Since then, we have endured over a hundred national conflicts and civil wars, claiming 10 to 20 million lives, yet, as awesome as these numbers are, a more frightening specter looms.

Nuclear weapons were given birth in 1945, and we now have missiles capable of delivering them to any spot on the globe. We face the grim reality that Russia could annihilate the United States in a matter of hours, and vice versa, and we remain dependent for peace upon weapons of war! This is because we have lost the sense of God, the sense of love, and we have been unfaithful to the first and second commandments given to Moses on Mt. Sinai.

Indeed, on April 8, 1966, *Time* Magazine had on its front cover the caption "Is God dead?" The inside article continued: "Is God dead? These three words represent a summons to reflect on the meaning of existence. No longer is the question the taunting jest of skeptics for whom unbelief is the test of wisdom. Even within Christianity, now confidently renewing itself in spirit as well as form, a small band of radical theologians has seriously argued that the Churches must accept the fact of God's death, and get along without him."

But God is very much alive and well. He is only "sick" of our ingratitude. However, as the *Lady of all Nations* said in Amsterdam: "The nations of the world will not find rest until they lie down and look up at the Cross, the center of the world." It is the proclamation of Solomon in Psalm 72: "All kings will bow down before him; all nations will serve him" (Psalm 72:11).

His mother is appearing all over the world as a concerned mother and her mission is solely to bring her children back to God. She is never here for her own aggrandizement, for she is the handmaid of the Lord, who has looked upon His servant in her lowliness (Luke 1:48).

On April 14, 1982, she told Mirjana, one of the visionaries in Medjugorje: "You must know that Satan exists. One day he asked to test the Church for a certain period with the intention of destroying her. God gave him leave to try the Church for one century. Satan then chose the 20th century..." This correlates perfectly with the remarkable mystical experience of Pope Leo XIII in 1884. It is well known that after saying Mass he heard a mysterious conversation between Christ and Satan. Satan asked for 100 years of greater freedom. It was granted but with the provision that there would be a greater power loosed against him (I wonder whether that "greater power" was not the Woman of Genesis 3:15!). It was then that the Pontiff composed the famous prayer to St. Michael and ordered that it be said at the end of every low Mass throughout the Church for protection against Satan.

Thirty two years later, according to the Portuguese visionaries of the approved apparitions in Fatima, the Archangel Michael appeared to the children three times in 1916 before the Blessed Virgin appeared on May 13, 1917.

Was this linked in part to Pope Leo's vision and prayer to St. Michael? World War I soon came to an end after her apparitions there.

There are many who see the rapidly progressive calamities of this century as representing signs of the end times, as predicted in the Gospels. Notably, in his book *Crossing The Threshold Of Faith*, Pope John Paul II wrote: "And thus we come to May 13, 1981, when I was wounded by gunshots fired in St. Peter's Square. At first, I did not pay attention to the fact that the assassination attempt had occurred on the exact anniversary of the day Mary appeared to the three children of Fatima in Portugal and spoke to them the words that now, at the end of this century, seem to be close to their fulfillment."

As far back as the 15th century, the Aztecs, like the ancient Mayas, were convinced that the end of the world would come in the year 2000 *y pico* (and a little), and as Graham Hancock said in his book *Fingerprints of the Gods*: "When human beings from around the globe, and from many different cultures, share a powerful and overwhelming intuition that a cataclysm is approaching, we are within our rights to ignore them. And when the voices of our distant ancestors, descending to us through myths and sacred architecture, speak to us of the physical obliteration of a great civilization in remote antiquity (and tell us that our own civilization is in jeopardy), we are entitled, if we wish, to stop our ears.

"So it was," he continued, "the Bible says, in the antediluvian world: 'For in those days, before the Flood, people were eating, drinking, taking wives, taking husbands, right up to the moment that Noah went into the Ark, and they suspected nothing till the floods came and swept all away.' In the same manner it has been prophesied that the next global destruction will fall upon us suddenly 'at an hour we do not suspect, like lightning striking in the east and flashing far into the west... The sun will be darkened, the moon will lose its brightness, the stars will fall from the sky and the power of heaven will be shaken... Then of two men in the fields, one is taken, one left, and of two women at the millstone grinding, one is taken, one left...' What has happened before can happen again. What has been done before can be done again. And perhaps there is, indeed, nothing new under the sun..."

Indeed, in the Second Letter of Peter, he prophesied: "We must be careful to remember that during the last days there are bound to be people who would be scornful, the kind who always please themselves whatever they do, and they would make fun of the promise and ask, 'Well, where is this coming? Everything goes on as it has since the Fathers died, as it has since it began at the creation.' They are choosing to forget that there were heavens at the beginning, and that the earth was formed by the word of God out of water and between the waters, so that the world of that time was destroyed by being flooded by water. But by the same word, the present sky and earth are destined for fire, and are only being reserved until Judgment day so that all sinners may be destroyed... The Day of the Lord will come like a thief, and then with a roar the sky will vanish, the elements will catch fire and fall apart, the earth and all that it contains will be burnt up" (2 Peter 3: 3-7). This is also the message of *Our Lady of Akita*, given in Japan on October 13, 1973!

She is appearing to us almost daily, in fact, daily, preparing and warning us to convert before it is too late, but we are still not listening to her. What more must she do? She has also said in Medjugorje that prayer can prevent wars and even change the natural laws of nature. In short, it is within our power to save the world from disaster even at this late stage. The decision is completely up to us—but many believe that time is short. And so, her repeated calls are always: "Pray, pray, pray. Continue to pray. Make sacrifices. Convert yourself."

Four centuries ago, on December 9, 1531, she appeared on Tepeyac hill in Mexico to Juan Diego and identified herself: "Know for certain, my dearest and youngest son, that I am the perfect and perpetual Virgin Mary, mother of the true God, through whom everything lives, the Lord of all things, who is Master of creation and of heaven and earth. I ardently desire a temple to be built here for me where I will show and offer all my love, my compassion, my help and my protection to the people. I am your merciful mother, the mother of all who live united in this land, and of all mankind, of all those who love me, of those who cry to me, of those who seek me, of those who have confidence in me. Here I will hear their weeping and their sorrow, and will remedy and alleviate their sufferings, their necessities and their misfortunes... Listen, do not be afraid or troubled with grief. Do not fear any illness or vexation, anxiety or pain. Am I not here, I who am your mother? Are you not under my shadow and protection? Am I not the cause of your joy? Are you not in the fold of my mantle? In the crossing of my arms? Is there anything else you need?"

"Are you not under my shadow and protection?" she asked. Indeed, there have been many instances of her protection. Constantinople had fallen in 1453, and the whole of the East was under Moslem rule when the Virgin appeared in Guadalupe in 1531. In the year 1571, a huge Turkish armada set sail to capture the Eternal City and a vastly outnumbered combined Christian fleet of Spain, Venice, and the Papacy assembled in defiance at Lepanto near Greece.

It was a spectacle that no survivor of that great sea battle would ever forget. Two great galleys, one flying the pennant of the crucified Christ, the other, a huge flag with verses from the Koran, were rowing directly at each other, gathering speed all the time as the galley masters whipped their slaves to even greater efforts. In La Real, the Spanish flagship, Don John of Austria drew his sword and braced himself for the inevitable head-on clash as Ali Pasha, the Turkish commander, ordered his men on the Sultana to prepare to board. The Cross was meeting the Crescent in what many at that time believed to be the last great encounter between galley fleets. The date was October 7, 1571.

Now, a year before, in 1570, Archbishop Montufor, the successor of Bishop Zumarraga, had a small reproduction of the holy image of *Our Lady of Guadalupe* made, touched it to the original tilma and sent it to King Phillip II of Spain. It was then given by the king to Admiral Giovanni Doria and it was in the Admiral's cabin during that great naval battle of Lepanto. He is said to have prayed for Mary's intercession to save his fleet from what looked like certain destruction.

From the human point of view, the outcome was inevitable. The Pope of the day, Pope Pius V, called upon every Catholic in Europe to evoke the aid of the Mother of God under her title *Help of Christians*, and to storm heaven unceasingly with Rosaries. The faithful responded and the battle got under way. At a critical moment when it seemed that the Christian forces would lose, insignificant as they were, a tremendous wind came up and blew the Turkish navy into total disarray. It would be many days afterwards before word reached Rome of the outcome of the struggle. The Turks lost 230 galleys; the Christians, 16.

Forthwith, Pope Pius V proclaimed that day of the victory, October 7, a new feast day in honour of *Our Lady of Victories*. The following year it was renamed the feast of

Our Lady of the Rosary. And so, the title *Mary, Help of Christians* became linked to *Our Lady of Victories* and then to *Our Lady of the Rosary,* a trinity of titles referring to the same event and the same woman.

In 1844, the Virgin Mary appeared to Don Bosco and requested him to build a church under the title *Mary, Help of Christians,* providing him with precise instructions down to the last detail of its construction. This great Basilica of *Mary, Help of Christians,* in Turin, Italy, was consecrated in 1868. I visited Turin on August 11, 1993, and with the help of one of the Salesian priests there, I toured the great basilica. Poised on top of the large cupola of the church is a beautiful golden statue of *Mary, Help of Christians,* and on the facade of the basilica are two lateral cupolas, on each of which stands an angel holding a banner.

Don Bosco, subsequent to having received a vision, had one banner inscribed with the date 1571 (the date of the battle of Lepanto), and the second banner with the incomplete date, 19--. This is said to indicate that in the latter part of this twentieth century, *Mary, Help of Christians* will again be called upon to rescue the Church from a seemingly all-powerful enemy. If this is so, it certainly will not be novel.

In the great Battle of Britain in World War II, Hitler had hoped to crush England. The Germans threw in the bulk of their planes, but were severely mauled by the numerically inferior British Air Force. Two days were particularly important in the decisive victory of Britain. They were August 15 and September 15, 1940. The victories on those days gave birth to Winston Churchill's famous speech: "Never in the field of human conflict was so much owed by so many to so few." The prayers of Britain were heard. August 15 was the feast of the *Assumption of the Blessed Virgin Mary* and September 15 was the feast of *Our Lady of Sorrows!*

After the Japanese attack on Pearl Harbor during World War II, the United States entered the war on December 8, 1941, the feast of the *Immaculate Conception.* It was the turning point of the war. Italy surrendered to the Allies on September 8, 1943, the feast of the *Nativity of the Blessed Virgin Mary.* World War II ended on August 15, 1945 with the unconditional surrender of Japan. It was the feast of the *Assumption of the Blessed Virgin Mary.* Six years later, on September 8, 1951, Japan also signed a formal pact in San Francisco pertaining to its surrender. It was called the Second World War Peace Treaty. Once more, it was on a feast day—the feast of the *Nativity of the Blessed Virgin Mary*.

The signing in Washington of the Intermediate Range Nuclear Forces Treaty (INF) by Mikhail Gorbachev and Ronald Reagan, abolishing medium range missiles in Europe, took place on December 8, 1987, the feast of the *Immaculate Conception*. Is it also a coincidence that the Communist Party died in Russia on August 22, 1991 after Gorbachev survived the aborted coup by the diehard Communists? It was on the feast of the *Queenship of Mary*!

She is the *Queen of Peace* and, according to the Fatima chronicles, the peace of the world has been entrusted to her by her Son. When she first appeared in Fatima, she was wearing what has been termed her most powerful spiritual weapon—a Rosary, and later she revealed: "*I am the Lady of the Rosary*." But her first apparition there was on May 13, 1917. At that time it was the feast of *Our Lady of the Blessed Sacrament (Our Lady of the Eucharist)*. She was, therefore, calling us to the adoration of her Son in the Eucharist. It is the dream of St. John Bosco in 1862, namely, that devotion to the Eucharist and to *Mary, Help of Christians* will bring about a great victory in the near future.

It was on a Thursday night, the eve of "the hour of the Redemption," that Jesus instituted the Eucharist and longingly requested: "Do this in memory of me" (Luke 22:20). The Virgin of Guadalupe once said to Juan Diego: "I am the mother of all who live *united* in this land," and she, too, is longing for the day when all will be one (*ut unum sint*)—one community; one Church. It will be the long-awaited answer to her Son's prayer before he went to the Garden of Gethsemane: "Father, may they all be one, as we are one" (John 17:21). Then all will celebrate a common Eucharist "in memory" of Him. And the heavens will all sing: "Thanks for the memory!"

But I cannot end this discourse without quoting once more one of the greatest lovers and "slaves" of Mary, St. Louis Marie Grignion de Montfort (1673–1716). His *True Devotion To Mary* is considered to be one of the greatest books on the Blessed Virgin Mary ever written. He wrote: "We ought to understand that first and celebrated prediction and curse of God pronounced in the terrestrial paradise against the serpent: "I will put enmity between you and the woman and your seed and her seed; she would crush your head, and you will lie in wait for her heel" (Genesis 3:15)... But the power of Mary over the devils will especially shine forth in the latter times, when Satan will lay his snares against her heel: that is to say, her humble slaves and her poor children, whom she will raise up to make war against him. They shall be little and poor in the world's esteem, and abased before all like the heel trodden underfoot, and persecuted as the heel by the other members of the body. But in return for this they shall be rich in the grace of God, which Mary shall distribute to them abundantly.

"They shall be great and exalted before God in sanctity, superior to all other creatures by their lively zeal, and so well-sustained with God's assistance that, with the humility of their heel, in union with Mary, they shall crush the head of the devil and cause Jesus Christ to triumph.

"In a word, God wishes that His holy mother should be at present more known, more loved, more honoured than she has ever been... Then they will see clearly, as far as faith allows, that beautiful Star of the Sea. They will arrive happily in harbour, following its guidance, in spite of the tempests and pirates. They will know the grandeurs of that Queen, and will consecrate themselves entirely to her service as subjects and slaves of love. They will experience her sweetness and her maternal goodness, and they will love her tenderly like well-beloved children. They will know the mercies of which she is full, and the need they have of her help; and they will have recourse to her in all things, as to their dear *Advocate* and *Mediatrix* with Jesus Christ. They will know what is the surest, the easiest, the shortest and most perfect means of going to Jesus Christ; and they will give themselves to Mary, body and soul without reserve, that they may thus belong entirely to Jesus Christ.

"But who shall those servants, slaves and children of Mary be? They shall be the ministers of the Lord who, like a burning fire, shall kindle the fire of divine love everywhere... They shall be the true apostles of the latter times, to whom the Lord of Hosts shall give the word and the might to work marvels and to carry off with glory the spoils of His enemies... They shall carry on their shoulders the bloody standard of the Cross, the Crucifix in their right hand and the Rosary in their left, and the sacred names of Jesus *and* Mary in their hearts."

This was predicted in the 18th century and was all based on Genesis 3:15. In short, it was the woman *and* her seed who will crush Satan *and* his seed. It is Jesus *and*

His helpmate Mary. It is the second Adam *and* the second Eve. It is *Redeemer and* the *Coredemptrix*. And so, anyone who leaves the "woman" out of that battle is only preaching half Genesis 3:15, half the Gospel, half the truth.

Her Son has sent her as the second Esther to save her children from annihilation, but few are listening to her. It is late in the day, but still not too late to respond to her call. Let us not forget that when, in 1870, the people of Pontmain prayed to her for protection from the Prussian forces which were only a few miles away from their little town, she appeared there and said: "God will answer you in a short while. My Son will respond to your prayers." The next day Pontmain was miraculously saved from invasion and all its menfolk returned home safely. To this day she is known there as *Our Lady of Hope*. And so, like Columbus and his crew did, we should pray: "Hail holy Queen, Mother of mercy, hail our life, our sweetness and our hope."

The dream of Don Bosco

Our Lady of Guadalupe

Our Lady of the Blessed Sacrament (Eucharist)

Pope John Paul II

Bibliography

1.   Able, Dr. Robert Peter, *Final Warning—The Legacy of Chernobyl*, Waener Brooks, Inc., New York, 1988.

2.   Asimov, Isaac, *Guide To Earth And Space*, Ballantine Books, New York, 1991.

3.   Auclair, Raoul, *The Lady Of All Peoples*, Les Press Lithographiques, Inc., Quebec, 1978.

4.   Boone, Elizabeth Hill, *The Aztec Templo Mayor*, Dunbarton Oaks, Washington, 1987.

5.   Breunig, Charles, *The Age of Revolution and Reaction, 1789–1850*, W.W. Norton & Co., New York, 1977.

6.   Bunson, Margaret R., *John Paul II's Book Of Mary*, Our Sunday Visitor, Inc., Indiana, 1996.

7.   Buscaglia, Leo, *Love*, Ballantine Books, New York, 1972.

8.   Carrol, Joan, *Miraculous Images Of Our Lady*, Tan Books and Publishers, Inc., Illinois, 1993.

9.   Carroll, Warren H., *1917: Red Banner, White Mantle*, Christendom Publication, Virginia, 1981.

10.   Churchill, Sir Winston, *Great War Speeches*, Transworld Publishers, London, 1963.

11.   Clark, Ronald W., *Eubsteub: The Life And Times*, Avon Books, New York, 1984.

12.   Clarke, Fr. Hugh, *Message Of Love—Reflections on the Life of St. Therese*, Carmelite Press, Kent, 1976.

13.   Coe, Michael T., Breaking The Maya Code, Penguin Books Ltd., Middlesex, 1992.

14.   Cowie, Leonard W., and Wolfson, Robert, *Years of Nationalism—European History 1850–1890*, Hodder & Stoughton, Kent, 1992.

15.   Cronin, Denis J., *The Love of Christ as made known at Paray le Monial*, St. Richard's Press Lt., West Sussex, 1983.

16.   Cruz, Joan Carroll, *The Incorruptible*, Tan Books and Publishers Inc., Illinois, 1977.

17.   Dawn, Peter, *St. Margaret Mary Alacoque*, Catholic Truth Society, London, 1979.

18.   De Narchi, John, *Fatima From the Beginning*, Missoes Consolata, Fatima, 1983.

19.   De Montfort, St. Louis, *True Devotion To The Blessed Virgin*, Montfort Publications, New York, 1987.

20. Dennis, Mary Alice, *Melanie And The Story of Our Lady of La Salette*, Tan Books and Publishers, Inc., Illinois, 1995.

21. Derum, James Patrick, *Apostle In A Top Hat*, Fidelity Publishing Co., Michigan, 1960.

22. Diaz, Bernal, *The Conquest of New Spain*, Penguin Books, London, 1963.

23. Dirvin, Fr. Joseph I., *Saint Catherine Labouré of the Miraculous Medal*, Tan Books and Publishers, Inc., Illinois, 1958.

24. *Divine Mercy In My Soul—The Diary of the Servant of God, Sister M. Faustina Kowalska*, Marian Press, Massachusetts, 1987.

25. Duffner, Rev., Father, *Sorrowful and Immaculate Heart of Mary*, World Apostolate of Fatima, Washington, New Jersey.

26. Easton, Stewart C., *World Since 1918*, Barnes & Noble, Inc., 1966.

27. Ehrlich, Paul R., and Sagan, Carl, *The Cold and The Dark*, W.W. Norton & Co., New York, 1984.

28. Eudes, St. John, *The Admirable Heart of Mary*, P. Kennedy & Son, New York, 1948.

29. Eymard, St. Peter Julian, *The Real Presence*, Emmanuel Publications, Ohio, 1938.

30. Garcia and Valdes, *Aztec Calender*, Grupo Cultural Especializado, Mexico, 1995.

31. Garraty, John A., and Gay, Peter, *The Colombia History Of The World*, Harper & Row Publishers, Inc., New York, 1988.

32. Gary, Peter, *The Irish Famine*, Thames and Hudson Ltd., London, 1995.

33. Gobbi, Fr. Stefano, *To The Preists, Our Lady's Beloved Sons*, 16th English Edition, U.S.A., 1995.

34. Gouin, Fr. Paul, *Sister Mary of the Cross*, The 101 Foundation, New Jersey, 1981.

35. Gruzinski, Serge, *The Aztecs—Rise And Fall Of An Empire*, Thames and Hudson, London, 1992.

36. Guadalupe, Miguel, *The Seven Veils Of Our Lady Of Guadalupe*, Our Lady of Guadalupe Helpers, Kirkland, WA, U.S.A., 1995.

37. Habkey, Boniface, *The Saintly Samurai*, The Anthonian, New Jersey, 1986.

38. Haffert, John, M., *The Meaning Of Akita*,
The 101 Foundation, Inc., Asbury, 1989.

39. Hancock, Graham, *Fingerprints of the Gods*,
Crown Trade Paperbacks, New York, 1995.

40. Hayden, Doris and Vilasenor, Louis Francisco,
The Great Temple And The Aztec Gods,
Minutiae Mexican, Mexico, 1995.

41. Herbert, Albert Joseph, *Signs, Wonders And
Response*, 1988.

42. Herbert, Albert Joseph, *The Tears of Mary and
Fatima*, 1984.

43. His Holiness Pope John Paul II,
Crossing The Threshold Of Hope,
Alfred A. Knops, New York, 1994.

44. Hockey, Thomas, *The Comet Hale-Bopp Book*,
ATL Press Inc., 1996.

45. Holton, Gerald, *Einstein, History, and Other Passions*,
Anderson-Wesley Publishing Company, Woodbury,
New York, 1995.

46. Horcasitas, Fernando, *The Aztecs Then and Now*,
Minutiae Mexicana, Mexico, 1992.

47. Hughes, Philip, *A Popular History of the Catholic
Church*, Macmillan Company, New York, 1947.

48. Illescas, Dr. Juan, Rojas, P.B.R.O., Mario, and Salazar,
Mons., Enrique, *La Virgen ade Guadalupe Y Las
Estrellas*, Litho Seleccioned de Color, Mexico, 1995.

49. Johnston, Francis, *The Wonder of Guadalupe*,
Augustine Publishing Company, Devon, 1981.

50. Johnston, Francis, *When Millions Saw Mary*,
Augustine Publishing Co., Chulmleigh, Devib, 1980.

51. Johnston, Francis, *Fatima: The Great Sign*, AMI Press,
Washington, N.J., 1980.

52. Jones, Peter, *The 1848 Revolutions*, Logman Inc.,
New York, 1991.

53. Kibbe, Pauline R., *A Guide to Mexican History*,
Minutiae Mexicana, Mexico, 1991.

54. Kondor, Fr. Louis, *Fatima In Lucia's Own Words*,
Postulation Centre, Fatima, 1976.

55. Kraljevic, Svetozar, *The Apparitions of Our Lady at
Medjugorje*, Franciscan Press, Chicago, 1984.

56. Kunzli, Josef, *The Message of the Lady Of all Nations*,
Miriam-Verlag, Jestetten/Germany, 1987.

57.	Ladame, Jean, *St. Margaret Mary And The Visitation In Paray*, Paray le Monial, 1977.

58.	Larkin, Francis, *Enthronement of the Sacred Heart*, St. Paul Editions, Boston, 1978.

59.	Laurentin, René, and Ljudevit, Repcic, *Is The Virgin Mary Appearing At Medjugorje?*, The Word Among Us Press, Washington, D.C., 1984.

60.	Laurentin, René and Joyeux, Henri, *Scientific and Medical Studies on the Apparition at Medjugorje*, Veritas, Dublin, 1987.

61.	Laurentin, René, *The Apparition at Pontmain*, 1987.

62.	Laux, Fr. John, *Church History*, Tan Books and Publishers, Inc., Illinois, 1989.

63.	Ligouri, Alphonsus, *The Glories of Mary*, Tan Books and Publishers, Illinois, 1977.

64.	Malaty, Tadros, *St. Mary in the Orthodox Concept*, Palaprint, Australia, 1978.

65.	Margenau, Henry and Barghese, Roy Abraham, *Cosmos, Bios, Theos*, Open Court Publishing Co., Illinois, 1992.

66.	Martel, Gordon, *The Origins of the First World War*, Essex, 1996.

67.	Martini, Teri, *Christopher Colombus*, Paulist Press, New Jersey, 1992.

68.	Maury, Jean-Pierre, Newton, *Understanding the Cosmos*, Thames and Hudson, London, 1992.

69.	Meagher, James L., *How Christ Said The First Mass*, Tan Books and Publishers, Inc., Illinois, 1984.

70.	Miravalle, Dr. Mark I., *Mary—Co-Redemptrix, Mediatrix, Advocate*, Queenship Publishing Co., Santa Barbara, 1997.

71.	Miravalle, Dr. Mark I., *Mary—Co-Redemptrix, Mediatrix, Advocate Theological Foundations— Towards a Papal Definition?*, Queenship Publishing Co., Santa Barbara, 1995.

72.	Miravalle, Dr. Mark I., *Mary Co-Redemptrix, Mediatrix, Advocate*, Queenship Publishing Co., Santa Barbara, 1993.

73.	Moctezuma, Eduardo Matos, *The Great Temple of the Aztecs*, Thames and Hudson, Ltd., London, 1988.

74.	Odell, Cathrine M., *Those Who Saw Her*, Our Sunday Visitor Publishing Division, Indiana, 1986.

75. Palairet, Michael, *The Life of the Blessed Virgin Mary: From The Visions of Anne Catherine Emmerich*, Tan Books and Publishers, Inc., Illinois, 1970.

76. Papali, Rev. Cyril, *Mother of God, Mary in Scripture and Tradition*, Augustine Publishing Co., Devon, 1987.

77. Pelletier, Joseph A., *The Immaculate Heart Of Mary*, Assumption Publications, Worcester, 1976.

78. Pelletier, Joseph A., *The Queen Of Peace Visits Medjugorje*, An Assumption Publication, Worcester, MA, U.S.A., 1985.

79. Pennington, Basil M., *Mary Today*, Doubleday and Company, Inc., N.Y., 1987.

80. Persey, John, *Hiroshima*, Vintage Press, New York, 1985.

81. Philberth, Bernhard, *Christian Prophecy & Nuclear Power*, Christian Catholic Bookshop, Melbourne, 1994.

82. Pirlo, Fr. Paolo O., *My First History of the Church*, Catholic Publications, Manila, 1996.

83. Price, Roger, *A Concise History of France*, Cambridge University Press, Cambridge, 1993.

84. Rhodes, Richards, *Dark Sun The Making Of The Hydrogen Bomb*, Touchstone, New York, 1995.

85. Roberts, J.N., *The Penguin History Of The World*, Penguin Books, Helicon Publishing, Ltd., 1992.

86. Rumble, the Rev. Dr. Leslie and Carty, Rev. Charles Mortimer, *Radio Replies*, Tan Books and Publishers, Inc., Illinois, 1979.

87. Sagan, Carl, *Cosmos*, Ballantine Books, New York, 1980.

88. Sagan, Carl and Druyan, Ann, *Comet*, Ballantine Books, New York, 1997.

89. Sandhurst, B.G., *We Saw Her*, Longmans, Green and Co. Ltd., Bristol, 1953.

90. Schram, Stuart, *Mao Tse-tung*, Great Britain, 1975.

91. Schreck, Alan, *The Compact History of the Catholic Church*, Servant Books, Michigan, 1987.

92. Scott, Fr. John N., *Without Thorns, It's Not A Rose*, Our Sunday Visitor, Inc., Indiana, 1988.

93. Seal, Marcia Castro, *Archaeological Mexico*, Monclem Edicionas, Mexico, 1995.

94. Sharkey, Don and Derbergh, *Joseph and Our Lady Of Beauraing*, Abby Press, Indiana, 1973.

95. Sodi, Denetrio, *The Mayas*, Panarama Editorial, Mexico, 1996.

96. Speckbacher, Franz, *Novena to the Rosa Mystica, Mediatrix*, Verlag, Austria, 1986.

97. The Editors of Time, *Great Events Of The Twentieth Century*, Time Books, New York, 1997.

98. The Sisters of the Visitation, *The Biography of St. Margaret Mary Alacoque*, Tan Books and Publishers, Inc., Illinois, 1986.

99. Thomas, Fr. B.C., *A Compact History Of The Popes*, St. Paul Publications, Bombay, 1994.

100. Townsend, Richard S., *The Aztecs*, Thames and Hudson Ltd., London, 1992.

101. Verheylezoon, Fr. Louis, *Devotion to the Sacred Heart*, Tan Books and Publishers, Inc., Illinois, 1978.

102. Weigl, A.M., *Maria Rosa Mystica*, Druckerei, Burger, Essen, 1975.

103. Wirt, Sherwood, *The Confession of Augustine*, Lion Publishing, Herts, 1971.

104. Woodham-Smith, Cecil, *The Great Hunger Ireland 1854–1859*, Penguin Books, Ltd., London, 1962.

105. Yasuda, Teiji, *Akita: The Tears and Message of Mary*, 101 Foundation, Inc., New Jersey, 1992.

106. Zaki, Pearl, *Our Lord's Mother Visits Egypt*, Dar El Alam El Arabia, 1977.